"Julia Hollenbery guides us to cc .... selves and recognize the abundant joy that always resides there."

– **David R. Hamilton, Ph.D.,** scientist and author of
I Heart Me: The Science of Self-Love

"Hollenbery's recipes for pleasure introduce readers to the Universe of Deliciousness that awaits them just around the corner, within their own bodies. Read and enjoy."

– **Sarah Peyton**, neuroscientist and author of
Your Resonant Self and *Your Resonant Self Workbook*

"Julia Hollenbery has taken the journey and now shares it in her own inimitable style. I had a teacher once who told me that learning through pleasure was the highest form of learning. As Julia shares in her own poetic and soul-deep style, she didn't begin there. She arrived there after a long journey. In *The Healing Power of Pleasure,* she shares the fruit of her work. As anyone who has taken the journey knows, fruit is the result of years of digging and composting. The more real the journey, the sweeter the medicine. Go on, take a sweet apple from this Tree of Knowledge."

– **Ya'Acov Darling Khan**, shaman, cofounder of Movement Medicine,
and author of *Jaguar in the Body, Butterfly in the Heart*

"In this thoughtful exploration of our emotional, logical, creative, and sensual selves, Julia Paulette Hollenbery's innate gentle wisdom, knowledge, and understanding shines through on every page. A book to keep on your shelf and return to whenever you need more insight and guidance into greater awareness and understanding of the unique delights of the lived experience that are on offer to you."

– **Judy Piatkus**, publishing entrepreneur
and author of *Ahead of Her Time*

"This book is a doorway to an inner world, allowing us to enter a new adventure while still very much being fully in the body and in the creative magical mystery of life."

— **Steve Nobel**, spiritual coach, founder of Soul Matrix Healing, and author of *The Enlightenment of Work* and *Freeing The Spirit*

"A helpful handbook toward a new birthing in our hearts, encouraging us to savour the delights to be found within a lifetime in the material world. It also serves as an introduction to discovering the deeper and less visible dimensions of life within the rapidly changing context for our lives today. This is a journey of our time."

— **Janice Dolley**, author of *Awakening to a New Reality* and coauthor of *The Quest*

"Julia has created a meaningful and moving exploration of joy and pleasure at a time when the world needs the uplift of this wisdom. A courageous and stimulating book."

— **Malcolm Stern**, psychotherapist, cofounder of Alternatives, and author of *Slay Your Dragons with Compassion*

"Julia's call to inhabit our bodies fully, to become aware of and attend to the delight inherent in every moment, speaks to the deepest sense of ourselves. She shows us a way of being in the world that is nothing short of revolutionary."

— **Alison Jones**, publisher and host of *The Extraordinary Business Book Club*

"Very personal, individual, and readable in its fluency, this book is filled with information and ideas gathered from readings, observations, thoughts, experiences, and imagination, richly and wisely put together."

— **Maggie McKenzie**, director of the Spectrum Centre for Humanistic Psychotherapy

"*The Healing Power of Pleasure* connects us to Divine Life through the portal of interconnectedness, bringing us into relationship with our bodies and senses and pointing the way to how we reclaim our darkness as well as our light. It honours life as profoundly relational and shows us how to access the innate sensuality of the place where body and soul meet. This is a glorious celebration of a book and also an important book for our times, as living through this relational lens naturally gives us respect for Earth, for each other, and for the oneness of all life—human and nonhuman, visible and invisible. It points toward a way of being for both men and women that includes a deep honouring of the feminine principle, which is the missing element in our culture and has the potential to lead us deeper into the new story we so urgently need."

— **Justine Huxley, Ph.D.,** director of St. Ethelburga's Centre for Reconciliation and Peace and editor of *Generation Y, Spirituality and Social Change*

"This book is a much-needed remedy! I heartily recommend this powerful, lovely, fun, interesting, magical, comprehensive, and practical guide to doing intimacy and life well. Enjoy the inspiring real spirituality, interesting grounded science, and practical well-being exercises for your personal and our planetary happiness. We all need this embodied warm wisdom."

— **Jamie Catto**, musician, filmmaker, and author of *Insanely Gifted*

The Healing Power of Pleasure

Seven Medicines for Rediscovering the Innate **Joy of Being**

JULIA PAULETTE
HOLLENBERY

FINDHORN PRESS

Findhorn Press
One Park Street
Rochester, Vermont 05767
www.findhornpress.com

Text stock is SFI certified

Findhorn Press is a division of Inner Traditions International

Disclaimer

The information in this book is given in good faith and is neither intended to diagnose any physical or mental condition nor to serve as a substitute for informed medical advice or care. Please contact your health professional for medical advice and treatment. Neither author nor publisher can be held liable by any person for any loss or damage whatsoever which may arise from the use of this book or any of the information therein.

Cataloging-in-Publication data for this title is available from the Library of Congress

ISBN 978-1-64411-326-4 (print)
ISBN 978-1-64411-327-1 (ebook)

Printed and bound in the United States by Lake Book Manufacturing, Inc.
The text stock is SFI certified. The Sustainable Forestry Initiative® program promotes sustainable forest management.

10 9 8 7 6 5 4 3 2 1

Edited by Jacqui Lewis
Illustrations by Julia Paulette Hollenbery
Text design and layout by Richard Crookes
This book was typeset in Adobe Garamond Pro

To send correspondence to the author of this book, mail a first-class letter to the author c/o Inner Traditions • Bear & Company, One Park Street, Rochester, VT 05767, USA and we will forward the communication, or contact the author directly at **www.universeofdeliciousness.com**

With thanks to all my teachers –
family and friends, formal and informal, flora and fauna –
that informed my growth from silenced shut
to dynamically expressive.

Especially to my mother Susan who with passion modelled
making the world a better place.

And with great thanks to divine destiny
that has protected and guided me.

.

Contents

Foreword

I had my first sexual relationship aged 15, and it felt to me like pleasure was sacred, part of the fabric of creation. When my parents heard about it, a torrent of judgement and shame came my way, and I felt quite traumatized. How could something I experienced as so beautiful be so wrong? But my parents were Methodists, and my dad was a lay preacher, and the idea of self-denial and self-martyrdom seemed to come naturally to them. If it felt good and pleasurable, don't trust it! "Give me pain and suffering any day," seemed to be their unspoken mantra. "Give me something to feel guilty about, and the less pleasure I have, the less I have to feel guilty about!" I felt broken-hearted and learned to numb out many of my feelings for a long time.

It has been a gradual and ongoing journey to regain my trust in pleasure, and to understand that joy and pleasure are holy, and are available to us in each moment. To fully allow myself to enjoy life rather than deny my own pleasure. Joy and pleasure are sacred and healing, the sign of a loving creator. It seems that somehow many of us have been misled and misinformed. My wounds went very deep, the healing I've needed, profound. And thankfully Julia has identified the medicine we need. We can heal our relationship with ourselves and our wounded and neglected parts, and we can learn to connect with each other in beautiful and trusting ways.

I certainly could have done with Julia's book and her guidance when I was 15. She could have guided me away from my impending fear and shame, and lead me into trusting my feelings more, and knowing that they were nothing for me to be afraid of, or disapproved of. Julia teaches us that we can be our own best friend and develop a truly healthy love for ourselves. If there is a God or Goddess, they know and welcome pleasure, joy, and delight. There is often such a gap between the potential of how we could experience ourselves and how we actually do experience ourselves. Julia has done a beautiful and skilled job of creating a map of the territory of coming home to the essence of who you are, when, like me, you have been away from home. She is leading the way back to the joy of your existence, being comfortable in your own skin and simply increasing your capacities to delight in the simple joys of being alive. I honour Julia's courage and bravery to offer leadership in this area.

In the *Book of Joy* the Dalai Lama and Archbishop Desmond Tutu agree that "*The greatest joy lies in doing good for others.*" Julia's joy is helping you come home to your joy and delight. Her gift is that it is her passion, but she is also a very competent and capable guide.

Thank you, Julia, for your insight, love and courage, and for leading the way. Whether you are recovering your lost delight in pleasure, or simply expanding your capacity for greater joy and pleasure, read this book and become happier and more open to pleasure you were born for. Leading with joy and pleasure will help nudge us one step nearer to creating Heaven on Earth.

Nick Williams, leadership guide and author of eighteen books,
including *The Work We Were Born To Do*
Finchley, North London, March 2021

Welcome

Welcome

There is an abundance of pleasure possible for us all, a great deal more than we currently live. It is freely available to everyone without discrimination or expense. It is constantly accessible in each moment and with every interaction . . .

The Universe of Deliciousness is a reality hidden in plain sight. It is an essential state of pleasure, satisfaction and connection that has been experienced and described by many throughout history. Ancient Indian poet-saints referred to "this body of bliss". Tukaram Maharaj, a sixteenth-century poet-saint from southern India, wrote in "Anandatse Dohe": "In the great flood of bliss, waves are surging and they too are nothing but bliss, for bliss is the nature of every particle of this body of bliss." Ancient Tibetans chanted the word "Mahāsukha" to invoke the great bliss: *Om Amrita Bindu, Java, Maha Sukha, Swaha,* meaning, "the sacred sound of creation with the nectar sweetness of being, within the human container of nerves, creates the great bliss, so be it."

I am inviting you to make a journey without moving, from the surface of life to the depths, where delicious, satisfying pleasure awaits. We will travel by way of paying attention to ourselves and to others, and by choosing awareness of our perception and experiences, exploring our physical body with all of its sensations, feelings, imaginations and knowings, and opening ourselves up to the multi-dimensional richness . . .

This is an adventure that may change your life, allowing you to enter into a dynamic stillness of full-bodied being. It is about sexuality and healing, sustainability and the Earth, love, creativity and mystery. It shows how pleasure is nourishment, transforming us from an existence as competing individuals to collaboration as a cooperative community.

Life itself wants to evolve through us. We, just like the rest of the natural world, yearn to be fully alive, full of passion and pleasure, humility and sensuality, purpose, dynamism and peace.

Life is uncertain. We do need the nourishment of the Universe of Deliciousness – so we can feel our fears and pains, our despairs and failures – and can then create something new and beautiful. When our hearts break, instead of violence can we be curious? Despite disaster, can we also find delight? Can we co-create together with Life, each of us a sensual intelligence within the multi-dimensional sensual intelligence of Life?

The global requirement now is compassion, consideration and cooperation. For this to easily happen, we each need to be sustained by a subtle experience of pleasurable abundance.

This book is a guide to a new way of being, rooted in body and relational heart, exploring how to follow the spontaneous insight of our instinctual intelligence. It begins with where we find ourselves, in a MESS, and goes on to explore the possibility of MAGIC, which we can rediscover through the MEDICINE: seven simple steps that will allow us to enter the Universe of Deliciousness.

FROM ME TO YOU

The pages you are reading were born from my discovery of the pleasure of sharing my pleasure with others . . . I naturally perceive life through my bodily sensations and feelings rather than my head. I "translate upwards", turning my direct felt experience into words, ideas and actions. Through my body, I perceive things about people and objects, a connection I call "knowing-without-knowing".

As a child my real home was out in the garden. There I could be in contact with it all. I loved the huge willow tree and the fragrant pine trees, the golden wheat fields at the bottom of the garden stretching all the way up to the horizon. I loved the dark earth and the big blue sky, the small insects and colourful flowers, and my freedom to exist in the invisible and imaginal spiritual world. I was living in the Mystery, the huge boundless whole.

One day, I danced and changed the weather. It was probably spring, and in England that means changeable rain and sunshine. But nonetheless, I danced and the sun came out. And I danced again and the rain fell. I did this several times, and nobody could tell me it wasn't true. It was for me the most vibrant and satisfying experience.

My challenge was being in the ordinary material world. I was alone with all my deeply felt connectivity. I didn't see other people living or talking about the things that I was experiencing, so I thought I was wrong and had to hide my truth . . . I was unable to communicate my experiences with those around me. As a result, my childhood was full of hyper-alertness and tension when I pretended to be something other than what I was, trying to fit in. But I didn't lose touch with my essential innocence.

A teenage breakdown was followed by young adulthood breakdowns . . . and then several intense decades exploring a great variety of therapies, healing and spirituality. I was determined to realize the bigness that I felt inside.

Over many years I trained professionally as a bodyworker, therapist and facilitator. Over decades of working with hundreds of people, in individual sessions and group workshops, I have become a highly skilled and experienced practitioner. I bring people back to their essence.

My unique capacity is to really see people in a way they have probably never been seen before, profoundly with acceptance and love. I guide people to inner confidence so they can create satisfying relationships, meaningful work and a passionate life.

At last, I am truly able to embody my soul, in this body in this lifetime. This book is the articulation of my lifelong inner "knowing". It is a kind of reverse engineering of the way I live, in order to share with others the bounty of this unusual and hard-won way of life.

There is something my heart knows that it wants to share. This isn't acquired knowledge. It is that we all have the potential for an infinitely pleasurable, wise and precious life. I am delighted to share with you this sacred entry into the Universe of Deliciousness, to restore your soul to the pleasure it is made for.

I hope you enjoy your experiences.

Julia xxx

Part 1

Mess

WHERE WE FIND OURSELVES

*"I fear the day that technology
will surpass our human interaction.
The world will have a generation of idiots."*[1]
Albert Einstein, Nobel physicist

*"In times of turmoil, the danger lies not in the turmoil,
but in facing it with yesterday's logic."*[2]
Peter Drucker, businessman and educator

*"In the desire to avoid what is almost unbearable,
we sell the divine gift of consciousness
for the safety of unconsciousness."*[3]
Llewellyn Vaughan-Lee, Sufi mystic

When, as adults, we believe our pleasure is dependent not on ourselves but on other people and things, we can come to feel that we have given away our power. We become resentful of others, whoever they are, although actually it was we who made the unconscious choice to rely on them. This misunderstanding lies at the root of the frustrating fundamental mess we are all in.

As babies and small children, we may have learnt that love, nourishment and pleasure came to us from outside. However, as we grow up, we need to realize that pleasure arises within us; it lies in our experience, whatever the external stimulus may be – a person, food, touch, song, fragrance or a picture.

In this book, I will guide you home, restoring your innate capacity for vibrant pleasure. I will show you how pleasure is your fuel – whether it is expressed through appetite, desire, libido, vitality, aliveness, energy or presence.

Messy Modernity

Humans are sensitive beings, far more so than is generally acknowledged. We have a great capacity for creativity, happiness and ease. But being sensitive is often demanding and sometimes really hard work. Squashing our sensitivity can make life seem easier, quicker and simpler, but it also makes us weaker and less happy, able to achieve less than our fully pleasurable powerful potential.

Unfortunately, unhappiness drives the economy. Companies sell stuff to unhappy people who think they need to buy expensive solutions. Consumerism is fed by suppressed desire, as our naturally happy organic selves do not need to buy more new products. If we could allow our sensitive selves to savour more, we would be more satisfied and crave less. Recovering our sense of everyday pleasure may help us to save the planet. We need to learn to trust again in our own direct bodily experience, our natural instinct, our wise knowing.

Let's have a look at some of the issues of messy modernity we find ourselves in. What kind of mess is bothering you?

Feeling Unseen

When we feel we are not really seen by others, we may develop strategies to try to get the attention we need.

The feeling of being unseen can start young: many young children are now given devices to keep them quiet in their prams. In the future, they may be driven to act in strange and dramatic ways, to do anything or everything to get attention. As the African proverb says, the child who is not embraced by the village will burn it down to feel its warmth.

Babies and children are not generally regarded with respect or seen as small people in touch with their own feelings and intelligence. They are often treated by adults with suspicion and irritation for disturbing them. They get trained out of their inherent enthusiasm, natural wildness and innate kindness, and their unbridled, out-of-the-box creativity is replaced with obedience and learning of facts. Constantly telling them they are "good" in some way only encourages them to think authority lies outside rather than inside themselves.

Until we feel truly, deeply soul-witnessed, we will be hungry for someone to provide a reflection for us and in this way our relationships become a focus for our projected feelings. We want our favourite people to meet our needs . . . but when they disappoint us, we treat them as psychological triggers and love can turn to hate, delight to pain.

STRESS

Almost everyone in the modern world is stressed and traumatized; our nervous systems are constantly switched on while we rush around, trying to do many things at once, all as quickly as possible.

When we have had an overwhelmingly busy, full-on day, we are left suffering from mild trauma. In fact, anything experienced as "overwhelming" causes us trauma. It can be caused by an obvious and shocking big event, such as an accident, or by a relatively small and quick event, like, when we are a baby, being temporarily unable to move because we are strapped in a chair.

It is possible to be traumatized and not know it. Our society's norm is to live in survival mode, out of sync with our bodies, oversensitive to possible hurt to ourselves and therefore unintentionally insensitive to others. To try to avoid feeling bad about ourselves, we often blame other people for our own suffering, causing them to feel stressed and who then want to blame other people in turn . . . We create an escalating spiral of charged feelings, oblivious to the effects of our feelings and behaviour on other people and the world around us.

It is not just our behaviours and words that trigger each other, but also our personal chemical atmospheres. On a very basic level, adrenalin, the stress hormone, could be said to be contagious. When adrenalin is released from one person's body into the air, it can trigger a reaction in those of us with a traumatic past. Unless we collectively treat our trauma, our stresses will escalate, causing fear and attack.

We all need a basic level of relaxation in order to feel safe and experience our pleasure.

MASCULINIZATION OF LIFE

Our cultural story emphasizes the importance of thinking, visibility and usefulness over kindness.

The typical modern attitude is that efficiency, productivity and competition are our human normal. We tend to think in binary terms: either/or, win/lose, superior/inferior; "I" can only win if "you" lose. This view is that of a masculine perspective made dominant. Meanwhile, the counterpart that offers balance – a nuanced, inclusive and receptive feminine view – has been disrespected and forgotten. Somehow men and women have become opponents, rather than opposite equals in partnership.

Through history, the female capacity to create and sustain life has been dismissed as negative. Women were thought of as just being possessions and even, in some cases, labelled "witches". During the Inquisition in the fifteenth to eighteenth century, nine million women were killed; that's a third of the population. Even now, in the twenty-first century, 137 women are killed globally each day by a family member, 200 million girls are genitally mutilated, while 15 million adolescent girls experience forced sex.[4]

Modern medicine prevents many unnecessary deaths, but its rise eroded the influence of local female herbal healers and replaced their natural plants and their expertise with centralized expensive chemical duplications. For good health we need access to both scientific and intuitive approaches, so that, for example, a birthing woman is safe yet she is able to use her body's instinctual power in this natural process.

We usually think of human conception as male sperm competing for and then penetrating the female egg, whereas in reality, says Bonnie Bainbridge Cohen, contemporary American researcher, 400 million sperm race towards the egg, but it is actually the egg that does the choosing, opening up to receive just one of those sperm.[5]

In another area of sex, pornography epitomizes masculinization, with the emphasis on anonymity, action and physicality. It lacks the feminine counterpart, the inclusion of relational receptive sensuality. It is sensation without soul.

The conventional, masculinized view of society is lopsided. It tells only half the story. It ignores the power of the feminine. It elevates thinking, ideas and remote spirituality-in-the-sky, mocking the sacredness of body and Earth. We need to have and enjoy having a good balance in our lives of both masculine and feminine principles.

The Inhumanity of Technology

Technology is now present in every aspect of our lives. Mobile phones promise entertainment and ease, but are really portable promotion platforms. We are addicted to the fast flashing images and the illusion of social connection. We now trust devices more than ourselves to solve simple problems. We have become so reliant on technology that most of us can no longer sense the direction of the wind, navigate by the stars, let alone read a map. We've forgotten our natural instinct, intuition and erotic impulse.

As social media has rapidly increased, so has unhappiness. According to a recent survey, 18 per cent of young people aged sixteen to twenty-five in the UK don't think life is worth living.[6] More than a quarter disagree that their life has a sense of purpose. For every 10,000 teenagers, five will commit suicide.[7]

Inauthenticity

Modernity and social media increase the pressure for us to be somehow "perfect" airbrushed happy people, without ever allowing ourselves quite naturally to feel we're sometimes in a bit of an emotional mess. We tend to think we must hide our raw feelings; that the messy truth of ourselves is unacceptable. Yet when we ignore what we are really experiencing, to try to fit in, we often feel unseen and on our own.

There is no emotion, however uncomfortable or awkward, that we should not allow ourselves to feel. It is human to feel both happy and sad, confident and shy, excited and tired. Our pleasure begins with our honesty and intimacy.

Loneliness

Socially we often present ourselves to other people in the way that we think they want us to be. While we might be liked for our personality, if we haven't shared what we really think, we can be left feeling alone, even at a party. Today, even in company, we tend to stare down at our devices, increasingly isolated, rather than looking up and relating in person with other real people.

Even when in relationship, we can feel alone. Relationships can disappoint us despite there being mutual attraction, love and best intentions.

We can vacillate between feeling lost as we merge with the other and feeling isolated in opposition against them. Although sex is visible everywhere, the attitude towards it is often selfish and superficial. Bodies are criticized while hearts are not seen. Fantasy can be exciting, but outfits, positions and props without a soul connection are unsatisfying. In many instances, our human potential for erotic sensuality remains disappointingly unlived.

FRAGMENTED SELVES

The modern perspective on life is often divisive, emphasizing analysis, cause or effect, compare and contrast.

There is a sacred sexiness to life. Everything exists in dynamic relationship with everything else. But when we think this vibrant wholeness has to be divided up into good or bad, sky or Earth, pleasure or pain, we can become stuck in the endless busyness of doing the dividing, of analysing, categorizing and labelling. Our relationship with the raw sensory data of life is lost.

Alongside this analytical approach, we are continually distracted by non-stop noise and light, channels, bleeps, updates, adverts and radiation. Torn between several devices, constantly scrolling or surfing, we rarely pause to focus, learn and enjoy.

Without realizing it, we are often split inside into several personas. These represent parts of ourselves that were hurt and separated and parts that compromised, in order to please and belong to our family, school or culture. We are unknowingly divided between what others call good and bad, and the sense of our own heart. We have often disowned our naturally good and healthy pleasure, settling instead for artificial treats as rewards.

The Three Levels of Mess

Some of the experiences I've just mentioned will resonate with you more than others. The messiness of modernity is more than any of our individual personal stories. With this in mind, let's take a look at the three main levels of mess in all our lives:

INDIVIDUAL MESS

Most of us, most of the time, are doing the very best we can. We hope that if we work hard enough and do all the "right" things, we will earn a better future either in a few years' time or in a life after death.

In the meantime, we live with a gnawing sense of lack, a secret hole inside we don't want to feel. We keep blaming other people for our own unhappiness – our boss or colleagues, partners or children – and looking outside of ourselves for something to satisfy us. But however much we consume and however busy we are, we can't seem to reach that elusive delicious fulfilment.

We believe our sense of identity comes from our thoughts. We've forgotten there is another way.

COLLECTIVE MESS

As we've seen, although there is more technology in our lives today, there is also more human loneliness and stress. There are areas of tremendous abundance, but also great division between those with money and those without.

We think we need to be so-called perfect and constantly strive to improve ourselves, our homes, our cars, etc. We criticize our body as being not good enough and suppress its healthy, valuable hearty appetite. Instead, we hunger for more artificial social media "likes", approval from authority and for the sweet taste of sugar.

After all our striving, if we don't get the sweet reward that we expect and feel entitled to, we are frustrated, sometimes violently so. But we do not really want to sell our sensual souls in order to belong.

GLOBAL MESS

Disrespect and neglect of our own feeling bodies are reflected in our disrespect and neglect of the feeling body of the Earth. We have tried to control wild nature and our naturally wild selves.

In our human self-importance, we have turned everything natural into something to be bought and sold. I believe this unkind and unsensual approach has directly led to the world being in a state of critical climate change, biodiversity loss and food insecurity. Human activities have caused 1.0 °C of global warming.[8] Some 83 per cent of mammals and 50 per cent of plants are extinct[9], a third of fertile food-growing land is lost[10] and over fifty million people displaced by conflict.[11]

It is likely there will be big practical and social changes in the near future; how might we best respond?

We are the planet's custodians and consciousness; can we bring gentle loving enjoyment to our care?

BUT PLEASURE IS MESSY

When we see animals and children playing and enjoying themselves, we often smile in response, recognizing pleasure as natural, healthy and valuable. Pleasure is an essential dynamic in human existence.

Yet the body and its potential pleasure are all too often considered somehow dirty, bad or base – messy. It is often thought that pleasure needs to be controlled, that we must protect ourselves from it.

Why do we fear pleasure? Just what might it lead us to? Being out of our head and out of control, connecting with our authentic vulnerability, creative power and self-authority – living free. What might we do? Paradise lies in our experience of the variety of respectful relationships within the unity of living. Pleasure is connected with the sacred creation of life, rejuvenation, inspiration and nourishment. It can be trusted as a physical principle to guide us in everyday life, freely available to wisely enjoy.

One thing is for sure: whenever spontaneous pleasure is repressed, it becomes stagnant and manifests as disease, abuse or manipulation. Surely natural messiness is preferable to this?

MESS IS WHERE WE ALL BEGIN

There are many types of painful personal mess: absence, accident and abuse are only a few. The good news is that messy difficulty can be fuel for a personal journey towards wholeness and light. Mess is the inchoate mud out of which the glorious lotus flower grows. Mess can be motivation and empower us towards finding healing and order.

We have to begin where we are; we have to see and accept our messy reality before we can begin to make positive healing changes. Acknowledgment is the start, kindness to self, before we can tidy up and deep-clean.

We each have our own unique personal mess. Mine began at birth. In the darkness of my mother's womb, my twin brother died and I did not want to leave him. The birthing contractions had begun to convulse from my belly through my body, but I stiffened my legs to stop the process. I did not want to be born.

Stuck in the birth canal, I was pulled out by hard metal pressing my head, twisting my soft temples. Shocked out of my little body, flooded with fear, alone in time and space, I was not sure I would survive. I could feel my mother's fear too; she was young, her husband had not yet arrived at the hospital, and she was afraid. During my birth, I tried to help her so I would survive.

I was, without knowing it, brain damaged, my nervous system set on hyper-alert. I began life traumatized. Consequently, as a child I always felt unsafe. I had what felt like invisible "flaps" all over my body, which were constantly raised, on alert, like the flaps on an aeroplane wing, or as if every hair on my body were standing on end, like the fur of a terrified cat. I couldn't close the flaps. I was always open. Raw. Petrified. No one knew what I was feeling and I didn't know how to explain . . . I was lost in plain sight. Pretending to be normal.

I've mentioned earlier how, as a young adult, I went through a few breakdowns, each of which removed a layer of falseness. It was a painful but purifying process, deeply healing, sifting the false from the true, bringing my mystical perception into physical form. I passionately wanted to live the real me.

Life is never going to be airbrushed perfection. It is always in motion and a bit messy. We are responsible for clearing up our own mess, inside and out. Left untended, mess gets worse. Mess can be the impetus to do what is needed. It's the primordial chaos from which creativity emerges.

We have to begin where we are, because there is nowhere else we can be. Sometimes what looks like a horrible mess – not at all what we want to be happening – is, without us realizing it, just right . . . The truth is that pleasure is hidden inherent in everything. When we commit to seeing, feeling, painting, dancing, writing and singing our mess, then magic and medicine do take place.

The great opportunity before us now is to transform our individual mess into collective healing, for sustainable global peace.

Amongst the Mess

Occasionally, just occasionally
There is a moment
Rich in satisfaction and meaning
That stands out in its visual brightness and bodily felt clarity
Relaxation
And subsequent vivid memory.

We know that there we were –
That moment illuminated on a busy train
Something tiny happened that shifted it into real
Which is another word for impactful or alive or yes, damn it, yes!

This is what I want more of –
Before again falling asleep to habit and compulsion
Convention and so-called correct and appropriate,
According to the rules we were bequeathed.
Half-asleep in life, sleepwalking really
What a waste of precious life.

What does this chapter stir up for you?

How might we be able to live differently, with more pleasure and connection? How can we move from this mess into the magnificent Universe of Deliciousness? . . . Perhaps the first shift is to open up, enough to see that magic might still exist.

All is not lost, just forgotten, covered in layers of dust. It is the task for us, individually and generationally, to uncover what is awaiting us all just below the messy surface. We are the ones we've been waiting for, our own guides to remembering the magical truth – the amazing, deep, beautiful, harmonious, pleasurable potential of life.

Part 2

Magic

THE BEAUTY THAT IS POSSIBLE

*"The world is full of magic things,
patiently waiting for our senses to grow sharper."*[12]
W. B. Yeats, poet

*"If the doors of perception were cleansed everything
would appear to man as it is, infinite."*[13]
William Blake, artist and writer

*"The universe only pretends to be made of matter.
Secretly it is made of love."*[14]
Daniel Pinchbeck, author and journalist

When we look out at the world from a predominately rational viewpoint, we see only what we can see. That which can be touched, measured and named. Door. Table. Chair. Tree. Cat. If we can touch it, taste it, smell it, hear it, then it exists. If not, nonsense. This is the world of black and white, yes or no, in or out, now or never. Here, of course, the rules of Newtonian physics apply. Everything has a cause and an effect. If we drop an object, it will fall. If someone crosses a road in front of a car, they may get knocked over.

There is nothing wrong with this world view. It is the truth. However, it is not the only truth, nor the only reality.

We trust quantifiable data without realizing numbers and facts can be used to illustrate anything. Statistics are not proof of truth. Margaret Heffernan, author of *Beyond Measure*, says what really matters can't be measured.[15] There is a great deal more going on than immediately meets the eye, hand or calculator. Just like there is more pleasure possible than we usually experience in our lives, in this diminished version of reality.

Children know what we have forgotten – that we are all magical, abiding within a universe of magic. It is all play within this universe of infinite possibility. Life is fluid, until it becomes solidified into one fixed option.

All that we explored in MESS is what sent MAGIC underground . . .

Let us slowly go then, you and I, from the concrete jungle of mess into the ocean of magic.

Unmagical Modernity

In modernity, magic has often been dismissed, ridiculed and banished as suspect, woo-woo nonsense. It can seem that only those people who are foolish, young and crazy deal in such things. The image of magic is now mostly cartoon-like, of witches in black hats and wizards with wands. Meanwhile, we like to think of ourselves as sensible, rational, capable adults. Almost all of us have learnt from infancy and, over the course of our lives have been continuing, to shut out magic, to live in a "normal" yet impoverished view of reality.

Some babies and children have eyes filled with sparkle and depth, while others sadly already have shutters covering them. As children, many of us may have had a vivid "magical" experience. For some, perhaps it took the form of a ghostly visit at the end of the bed, or for others a conversation with a wise grandpa or funky grandma, a book we loved, an encounter with a favourite tree, a moment in a church or by a stream . . . the precious experience of living magic . . .

But perhaps when we shared these experiences with adults we were dismissed. They might have said, "Don't talk nonsense" or "There is no such thing as . . . " or "Stop being silly!" Maybe they gave us a stern look or generated a disapproving atmosphere. We learnt to shut down our sense of the miraculous, to adapt to fit in. We learnt that accessing magic might be fun but that it is unwelcome.

As Peter Pan told Wendy, "The moment you doubt whether you can fly, you cease for ever to be able to do it."[16]

As we grow older, we often become less open. We close ourselves down in order to be accepted and safe. We adopt an identity that fits in with our family, school and culture. The reason most people become "old" is not because of the physical age of their body, but because they have become static in themselves, limited and rigid.

Let's face it, just surviving in this world is often hard enough when we are busy and under pressure; when we have to quickly sort out what is immediately in front of us. We haven't got the time to indulge in fancy notions of magic! We must be practical, we must be tensed, ready and alert!

Our natural magical ability has been taken over by technology. We are enchanted by images on brightly flashing screens. Adverts use the magic of ritual. They induce a little trance and utilize our need for resolution by offering us mini-stories with a beginning, middle and end: the shocking disaster of a dirty spot on a shirt is magically transformed by this powder into a sparkling white shirt and a happy life! We have become passive consumers of magical thinking. If this, then that.

We are scared of the darkness and the unknown. We are addicted to upbeat niceness, newness and happiness; we love sparkle, constant music and frequent sales. But this is a sanitized half-reality.

Modern films, TV and stories tend to feed this world view by showing us a flat formula of good against evil. The solution to this conflict is presented as external action. The magic of human transformation is frequently absent: characters do not have an inner emotional life and there are no deeply resonant symbols and signposts.

We mistakenly think that because we can touch physical reality, that is all there is. We arrogantly assume that because we can name, label and categorize stuff, it is we who are in control of it. We are left with a two-dimensional impression of life: what you can see is all we can get!

Culture has devalued, discredited and monetized the idea of magic. Nature and the divine have been banished, leaving humans apparently alone and powerful. Of course we think that our decisions and actions are the cause of our failures or successes, and can see no further. But we are being cheated of our birthright! When we shut out magic, we are also shutting out life itself. We lose something intrinsic to our well-being: our capacity to experience the multi-dimensionality of existence.

We are not just practical modern all-powerful machines. We are a blend of survival body, emotional heart, logical mind, creative soul and sensual life force.

CHALLENGING ASSUMPTIONS

We usually assume that what we think is reality. But to a large extent, our perception depends on the attitude of us, the viewer. Do we realize that our experience is often only a small part of what is really there? Science shows us repeatedly that reality is so much more than we can see and touch.

Let's look at some examples.

Physics

We do not see the full spectrum of light available; we only see the humanly visible light portion of the full light spectrum. Nor do we hear the full sound spectrum.

What appears to be solid matter is 99.9 per cent space at a subatomic level.[17] An atom's central nucleus is 100,000 times smaller than the atom itself: if the nucleus were the size of a peanut, the atom would be a football stadium in relation to it. Apparent solidity is created by the non-stop movement of a trio of quarks within that space. When we touch something, our electromagnetic force pushes against the object's electromagnetic force.

Botany

We don't notice 80 per cent of reality, which is formed of tiny microorganisms like bacteria, virus and fungi.

Trees communicate via fungal root networks, exchanging nutrients and sugars, to collectively manage resources available for the whole forest tree community.[18] Plants can also communicate via "voices" of vibrations.[19]

Astronomy

The observable universe is 92 billion light years in diameter (each light year is nearly six million miles) but the ENTIRE universe is at least 250 times bigger than the observable universe!

When planets orbit in space, they draw beautiful patterns according to the harmonic mathematics of music. The planet of Venus draws a five-petalled flower every eight years,[20] in a geometric sequence that reflects the structure of plants. Jupiter's two largest moons draw a perfect four-fold flower.

Neurology

The brain is a complex electrical circuit, forming only 2 per cent of our body weight but using 20 per cent of our energy. It contains eighty-six billion nerve cells, and each nerve connects with up to 10,000 other nerves. Research[21] says that babies' brains shut out about 90 per cent of reality, otherwise their nervous system would be overloaded and they would literally go mad. Everything we see, hear, touch, taste, smell or feel is an interpretation. Everything has been turned into an electrical impulse in the nervous system before being converted into conclusive data. Electrical currents pass along each nerve as a flow of sodium- or potassium-charged ions. At the end of the nerve, the electrical current is communicated chemically to the next nerve cell.

We "see" reconstructions of the real world. The neocortex creates an image of reality. It turns the visual image upside down before turning it the right way round. Consciousness is the subjective interpretation of data based on our past experiences.[22] The brain is always seeking patterns. It is constantly interpreting data from the external world, such as the sound of someone's voice, according to our previous experiences and conclusions. Our subjective experience is largely based on assumptions and is not always totally accurate.

What else don't we know that we don't know?

THE INVISIBLE WORLD

So now we have opened up our thinking, we can return to what we already know. We do have contact with magic as adults, we just call it something else. It shows up as creativity, flow, intuition and synchronicity. We glimpse it in response to images, symbols and archetypes; to nature and elements; to spirits, angels and energy; heroes, heroines and monsters; and God or gods.

Beyond this tangible, immediate reality is a deeper reality. It is the magical and mysterious, invisible and imaginal world. It is no less real than the material world. Just a different kind of real. Indeed, it is the unseen reality that shapes material reality. It informs and moves us.

In the imaginal world, things are not seen with physical eyes, but known by the inner eye of spiritual vision and by the inner heart. Here anything is possible. It is an inner plane of existence that is vital and energized, full of love and wisdom. It is a realm of infinite possibility. Here, the impossible is possible. As Richard Rudd, author of *The Gene Keys*, notes, "Throughout history men have flown, ascended and dematerialized right before people's eyes."[23]

The imaginal world is not a made-up fantasy; it has a constant subtle existence and is always accessible. My young daughter tells me that when she is bored at school she goes on a shamanic journey. "Does the upper world and your spirit guide always appear the same way for you?" she asked me. "For me it does!" Yes, she was engaging her imagination, but she was not "making things up". She was tuning in.

As J. K. Rowling had wise Dumbledore say in *Harry Potter and the Deathly Hallows*, "Of course it is happening inside your head, Harry, but why on earth should that mean that it is not real?"[24]

To activate magic, we need to break free from the limiting beliefs imposed on us by parents, schools and society. We need to access the boundless consciousness that can bend the laws of matter by recognizing that we too are magical.

RECOGNIZE THAT YOU ARE MAGICAL TOO

We are all natural magicians. We can conjure up visions from the realms of the invisible inside our own minds. When we meditate or go on a spiritual journey we often "see" visual images. Images are the key to thought: early historical languages were pictorial, based on drawn images and spoken descriptions. We are wired to think visually, in pictures rather than words and ideas. Imagery is the universal language of soul. However, it might need to be decoded to be fully understood. Our magical capacity to receive images and actively imagine is our superpower! If we don't use this ability consciously, the danger is that it will be utilized by others for their goals, rather than for our individual and collective benefit.

Vision is both physical and emotional. We see images because photoreceptors in our eyes are sensitive to wavelengths of light falling on them from outside. And at the same time, our internal visual imagery has an effect on the way we see the external landscape. If we focus on fears they can turn into a difficult reality, and similarly when we focus on positive imagery we can decrease anxiety.[25] The parameters of our internal perception actually shape our external world. Our fixed idea about someone can limit how free they feel to show up. Studies show how the attitude of teachers towards children affects their behaviour and learning results.[26]

Our internal attitude can block or free our vision of what is happening. I have a sensible friend who once saw a fairy when she was in an unusually happy mood. Surprised to see it, she doubted her own perception, remembering the idea that fairies don't exist . . . and then she couldn't see the fairy any longer.

We are wise to use this powerful capacity with awareness. When we acknowledge only what we see and touch, we are in contact with only a small part of the immensity of reality. To be fully alive and in touch with the magnificent magical potential of existence, we need to be able to access and live in both worlds: the spiritual invisible imaginal world and the material temporal tangible world. We need insight and emails, sensitivity and wages, subtlety and spaghetti.

The two worlds are not really separate; they are nested within each other, entwined together, coexisting all of the time. The sacred is not above, below, future or past, but is right here, right now.

MAGIC AS PERCEPTION

Magic is healthy, natural and positive. It is about being in contact with something bigger than just small "me". It is a pleasurable experience of the rich and varied dimensions, aspects and multiple layers of existence. Accessing magic is opening ourselves up to a higher-resolution life. We perceive life in units of perception, a bit like the boxes on squared paper. Most people usually only notice the bigger squares – the large, loud, obvious things. But in addition to the big squares, there are also many smaller squares, each containing much more information than we are usually aware of.

When people start to relax, they begin to notice everything in greater detail – more vivid colours, wider range of sound and the depth of silence. David Eagleman, author of *Incognito: The Secret Lives of the Brain*, says that there is a looming chasm between what your brain knows and what your mind is capable of accessing.[27]

As we open our perception, we discover that a higher-resolution life is possible. This is the key to increasing our experience of pleasure and satisfaction. Life is not just black and white; it is all of the colours, tones and textures in between. We access magic when we can accept both the happy, light and bright parts of life and the sometimes difficult, dark and frightening parts.

Fear, anger, frustration and hatred are inevitable, integral parts of life. Although it can be very challenging to really feel down and into the darkness, doing so can bring healing. In these situations, it is helpful to have the support of a practitioner as we descend below mental thought, into body. Feeling both the up and the down makes us whole, radiant people, in contact with the magical. Within the darkness is light. Within the pain is pleasure. Within doubt is truth. Within the ordinary is the magical.

Life is not simple, it is amazingly complex. We live within an ocean of information. Accessing magic means embracing all details. Mythologist Joseph Campbell said that the psychotic drowns in the same waters in which the mystic swims with delight.[28]

In different cultures and traditions, healing and spiritual work is about strengthening the nervous system. In this way, people learn to "tolerate" the impact of increased perception and sensory data coming into them from the world, with the accompanying increased flow of bioelectrical information within their body. Our capacity for pleasure depends on the capacity of our nervous system to allow these data waves to flood us. In order to enjoy having more access to sensual information, we need to be grounded, take care of our basic needs and make sure that we are not overwhelmed. We need to access magic with intention and attention.

MAGIC AS INTENTION

Magic is accessible right here and now in our everyday life. It is a creative exchange of energy. Hidden inside everything is a subtle substance, a creative potential.[29] Everything has a vitality, force and inner life of its own. Even a cardboard box, ceramic plant pot, metal lamp or concrete wall. Everything contains Life.

This is why we can access magic when we begin to treat all matter with respect. Simply take a moment to pause without any agenda, gently touch the table or chair, just because . . . and enjoy it . . . Soul awaits our interaction, dedication and receptivity, to come alive. When we honour someone or something, then they can reveal to us their inherent gifts.

For this reason, nothing is finished until it is received. A painting, song, poem, casserole or perfume is only really complete when seen, heard, read, tasted or smelled. In the receiving, an enlivening alchemy occurs.

We access magic when we bring together our inner and outer worlds of attention and action. Traditional rituals for the health of crops, community and individuals combine an outer activity, such as dancing, drumming, singing, walking, lovemaking, etc., with the inner action of attention. We do something smaller but similar when we bless our food or sing while walking. Awareness of our physical action quietens our mind, inducing a subtle trance, opening us to magical possibility.

As children, we were taught to stop, look and listen at the kerb before crossing a road. That ritual activated perception and kept us safe. Why not bring that attention to all our activities? Stop, look and listen right now: what do you notice? What if you do that at work, at supper with the family, in the supermarket, gym or car? Does something change? Can you sense the magic?

To access magic, it's helpful to allow ourselves quiet space without the distraction of constantly beeping flashing devices, and to unplug ourselves from radiation. We can calm down and explore the complexities of our experience.

Beyond the Ordinary

There are no answers
There is no objective meaning
No right and wrong
No up or down, left or right, green or black, red or blue
There is only the truth of an experience and the pleasure of our
experience of it!
Beauty and truth and pleasure
Curiosity and continual discovery
Of what is
This Here Now
I You Us

MAGIC AND MEDICINE

Can we open up to the wonder of the world? Can we suspend our disbelief and recall the open, enchanted mind of our childhood? The magical is right here in the middle of our Monday mundane messiness, waiting for us to notice . . .

We sometimes forget that we do have choice and our imagination can never be taken away from us, not even in a prison cell. We all have the gift of perception and expression, and are artists of one medium or another. Nobody is unimaginative. We are all many things, more than just one label or job title. No one is only an accountant, plumber, salesperson or software engineer. We are all limitless creators that all possess the ingenuity to shape our lives in small as well as big ways.

How do we access the magical? Children are often naturally already there. Some adults rely on psychotropic drugs, but we don't really need to take something extra to perceive deeper reality. Activating MAGIC is a process of reintegrating the fragmented aspects we discussed in MESS.

The MEDICINES in the next section of this book offer seven sequential, kind and effective ways to access the magical through a series of ideas and exercises. We will gently explore each medicine as a new territory, both philosophically and practically, that can help us to activate a profound shift in ourselves towards magic, taking us from the closed mundane into the full spectrum of pleasure.

In the next part of the book, you are free to travel at your own preferred speed of exploration and practice. You can, of course, read as much as you would like and put the book down whenever you wish to contemplate. You can read it alone or with friends, at home or out in a cafe or park. It is your process and pace. I hope the medicines in Part Three of this book will take you closer to the true you and the wise and sensual pleasure of the Universe of Deliciousness.

Part 3

Medicine

SEVEN MEDICINES FOR MODERN TIMES

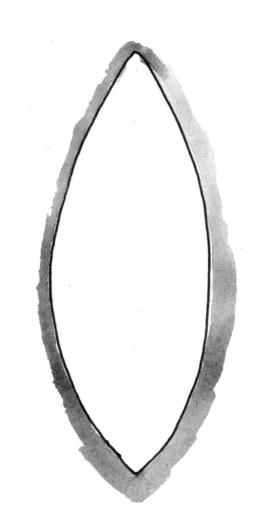

*"The quality of life is in proportion,
always, to the capacity for delight.
The capacity for delight is the gift of paying attention."*[30]
Julia Cameron, author, artist, poet

"Healing is a gift. It is the restoration of order."[31]
Bert Hellinger, theologist and psychologist

"What we learn with pleasure we never forget."[32]
Alfred Mercier, physician and writer

It's a somewhat painful discovery to realize the mess we are in. We have become so used to being stressed, distracted and polluted that we hardly notice it. We are living a life of narrow conformity, in the mistaken hope it will bring us acceptance, love and a sense of belonging.

Now that we recognize the real possibility of expansive magic existing, beyond this immediate situation, we are ready to begin to travel, via the medicines in this part of the book, into the Universe of Deliciousness. Our route is through the perspective and practice of seven paradigm-shift medicines: Slow, Body, Depth, Relationship, Pleasure, Power and Potency.

As you progress through the chapters that follow, notice what interests you and what you enjoy. Experiment and trust your own intuitive responses. The work of healing oneself is a detective story, tracking down the missing pieces of information and energy we need. The aim is not to be self-obsessed, but to gather enough resources, enough ballast, to be able to experience what one couldn't before – feelings, sensations and thoughts of difficult times past. In this way, we restore our healthy vitality, fragments are pieced together, and the liquid light of pleasure, power, potency flows again.

1
Slow
the medicine of slowing

"Anything worth doing is worth doing slowly."[33]
Mae West, legendary film actress

"Adopt the pace of nature: her secret is patience."[34]
Ralph Waldo Emerson, philosopher and poet

"Attention is the blessing we have to give."[35]
Roger Housden, spiritual writer

In an attempt to keep up in an increasingly fast world, we are always on the go, non-stop doing, grabbing coffees and rushing lunches . . . We are in constant motion, fingers active if not our whole body, while our mind is split between various things. We are distracted. Very few people, often not even ourselves, are gifted with our undivided attention.

Slowing down does not necessarily mean physically slowing down and stopping. It means vibrational slowing, so that mind and body can connect at a similar pace and together work well.

This is slowing down out of the fastness of stress, of agitated nerves, speeding thoughts and tensed muscles. Slowing into a more unified focus, a calmer experience that is more satisfying for ourselves and others. When we stop rushing, we become aware of the presence of the present.

Here, we are talking about slowing to access that which is already present, beneath the surface flurry. Like pulling back the arrow against a bow and pausing to take aim in a moment of focused preparation . . . the success of the shot is determined in that moment of slow.

Now at the intersection of inner and outer worlds, as I sit writing this in the park, a large and beautiful butterfly arrives to sit still, wings folded shut, on my notes next to me. Enjoying it, I pause too.

ARTIFICIAL ACTIVITY

We live in a super-fast, highly pressured world, where time is considered money. Most of us live constantly switched on to high alert, ready to respond. We may physically tense ourselves, hold our breath and rush our actions, pushing ourselves on! In urban modernity, non-stop doing is seen as a good thing. But it is unnatural and unhealthy. In order to keep going, we can override our impulse for rest, movement, food, sunlight or sociability. Many people have problems with their sleep, energy, digestion and happiness, and some people are literally dying from overwork.

Non-stop stressful activity can lead to nervous system burnout. Our biological capacity for fight or flight is important and useful; it ensures our survival and gets the urgent jobs done. But we also need to be able to be flexible, to switch off sometimes, wind down and relax without guilt.

Learning to slow down may be more productive in the long run. Like the tortoise in Aesop's fable *"The Tortoise and the Hare"*, slow may be effective. Research suggests that workers who take more breaks actually get more accomplished.[36]

THE ILLUSION OF TIME

As a culture, we are obsessed with the illusion of time.

We tend to focus on either the past or the future, and to think about the things that have happened which caused the current moment and to feel blame or pride in relation to them. We may also think about anticipated outcomes that we hope or fear. In this way, the present moment barely exists for us. It has become a diminished nothingness, a fragment of time to be rushed through, a means to an end, a line between past and future. We ignore right now and turn the series of present moments – now, now and now – into linked-up stories that have a causative beginning, middle and resultant end. We falsely believe that because of this, that.

Such an illusion of time denies us life. We miss out on a lot of what is on offer now.

In actuality, every moment is full of value. Just writing that sentence, my body breathes more deeply than it has for a few moments and relaxes . . .

For the present moment is a present.

Below the expectant rushing is an ever-present, deep-running stream of slowness. When we really experience the now, we experience a quality of realness that is impactful and valuable.

TIME IS RELATIVE

Time is not absolute; it passes at the speed of the observer.

The Ancient Greeks had two words to describe distinct experiences of time: chronos and kairos. We know clock time as chronos. This is chronological, sequential time: it is 3 o'clock and we are meeting for fifteen minutes. We all agree on this understanding of time.

Kairos, on the other hand, is the appropriate time for action, an "appointed" time, a personal opportunity. It lasts as long as is needed and the experience can feel as if time stands still. We become present to what is here and now.

Our transition between these two experiences of time is mediated by the body's chemical messengers. Under stress, the hormones adrenalin, cortisol and norepinephrine increase our blood pressure and blood flow to our sense organs and muscles; our nervous system activates, our perception and behaviour speed up, and we are ready to react quickly. We return from kairos to chronos.

CHOOSING TO SLOW

When we are living full-on fast and busy, we need to remember to slow down sometimes and experience the realness of eternally present time – to return from chronos to kairos. If we don't intentionally relax and wind ourselves down, we will stay activated. We need to consciously interrupt our go, go, go with a glass of wine, a cup of tea, a movie, dance or meditation. Slowing is what every therapist, healer, shaman or mystic does. Slowing is what I offer when I work with individuals and groups. This is a slowing out of our anxious thoughts, agitated emotions and fraught nervous system; it is a slowing out of the stories about what has happened and what might happen, and a slowing down into the simple sensate feeling of what is happening this moment now. Slowing down can provide a holding space for a while, so that agitated vibrations can pass through a transformational still point and become rearranged into a new movement and frequency.

We might imagine stressed nervous activity as a line on a chart. When we are anxious, our emotional vibrations move faster and the line is agitated, showing sharp excited peaks and steep depressed troughs. Slowing down is calming vibrationally from agitation to relaxation. The line on the chart softens. Stepping down the voltage or vibration of the energy in this way, we deeply slow, entering a realm of more realness, a different and truer dimension. Perspective, relaxation and enjoyment arrive.

It doesn't need to take a long time to do this. Slowing right down can happen quickly, as we learn to move down through the gears. When we do, sacred multi-dimensional space is always present and available to us.

RHYTHM OF LIFE

Natural rhythms underpin our lives, but in the twenty-first century we often override their call within us and around us. Instead, we tend to live out of tune with our environment and the constant changeability of life. Darkness, which naturally invites pause, has become almost always lit by light, during both the night and the winter. Midwinter, once a time of deep rest, has become a time of upbeat partying and shopping before returning to work in January. This can feel exhausting and soul-destroying!

Slowing is a return to the rhythms of the natural world we live in. Daylight to dark night. Waxing and waning of the moon. Seasonal changes in light, temperature, colour, plants and animals, and in our energy and mood as we move from summery expansion to wintry internal retreat. We live according to the rhythms of heartbeat and breath, appetite and tiredness, desire and creativity.

These natural rhythms are part of our physical make-up: just like animals, birds and insects, the human body's circadian rhythm responds to external fluctuations of light and temperature. We all generally have more energy between 9am and 12 noon, and less around 3pm; more energy in summer and less in winter. Similarly, a woman's fertile years are governed by her body's active preparations through a 28-day womb cycle; if her egg is not fertilized the cycle ends with the womb lining bleeding, a time of release, rest and pause. This rhythm informed the traditional calendar of thirteen moons, each made up of twenty-eight days, which was used before the newer twelve-month (plus leap year every fourth year) Gregorian calendar. A woman's cycle takes her through the four seasons of spring, summer, autumn and winter each month.

We move within a lifetime through the seven stages of man: from baby to toddler to child, teenager to adult to elder to death. Traditionally, there were many rituals to act as pauses marking these life transitions.

And within all of the natural rhythms there are similarly many pauses, between the in-breath and the out-breath, between out-breath and in-breath. A pause of harmony at sunrise and sunset, when the light is soft between the harsh brightness of day and the total darkness of night. A pause at the full circular moons of light in the dark night skies, a cycle obviously complete; and we can pause again at the half moon and no moon too. The ancient pagan calendar marked the seasons at their high points and their transition points, the solstices and the equinoxes, signifying ritualized pauses and moments of change through the year.

Human life is rooted in the earth and connected to the sky; the rhythms of nature pulse through our bodies and lives. There is ebb and flow in everything, all of the time. We are wise to align ourselves with this pulse, its movement and pauses.

PAUSING IS PRODUCTIVE

We can begin to slow down by interrupting our non-stop motion through building in some pauses. There is no music without a pause and no visual art without some empty space. Our body is not built of non-stop strings of nerves, but with spaces between them. Without gaps there is chaos.

In pauses and gaps, new data integrates with the old. Healing takes place in the spaces between sessions, not during the treatment or programme. It is the same at the gym, where personal trainers say that muscle builds not during the active repetitions, but in the rest period afterwards.

Ants work very hard and achieve a lot considering their small size and short life. They don't sleep at night or hibernate in winter; unusually, they frequently sleep in fractions of seconds, pausing often. Might we learn something from this model?

It is useful to interrupt our non-stop doing and consciously pause. This does not mean reaching a state of unconscious collapse, but simply allowing a little space and time for ourselves, a moment of not-doing, of emptiness and potential. When we consciously pause, nothing is lost. Rather, there is a gathering of energy and focus. A pause is a refresh button, a mini-transformation point. As we pause, we are contained; we can reorganize and shift; the pattern changes, opening into something new.

Slowing and pausing doesn't change anything . . . and yet it changes everything – habit, perception and experience.

SLOWING AND OPENING

When a mother looks like she is doing nothing, just sitting still with her baby, she is actually silently attuning to her little one, so she can care for it even though the baby is not able to ask for what it needs.[37] The mother is opening up her perception and learning to listen in another way.

When we similarly slow down our racing thoughts and release tensions, we also begin to relate to others from our whole body, not just our heads. This way of listening creates healthy intimate relationships. Singer Naomi Judd recommends that we slow down, simplify and be kind.[38]

In this slow state, we can sense more deeply into the emotional information that is always present, feeling into what is there and what is needed. We all want to feel truly seen, heard and understood; we want to feel "met". When we slow down or someone else slows down enough to be able to attune to us on a deep level, the effect is very soothing. Simply a touch, look or breath can say to us everything is ok, I'm right here with you, you are safe. We can then relax, open up and connect . . .

When I'm working with a client, and they move through shifts and insights into new energy, what I'm doing is meeting them vibrationally where they are and inviting them to go even deeper, even slower, into their truth, energy and expansion. I attune to their soul as they slow vibrationally and move through a transformational still point . . . emerging the other side into a new healthier state. As we vibrationally slow, as we become less ego-agitation and more soul-essence, we open up to a more nuanced field of information, gain perspective and a richer, more pleasurable experience. I can hear the sound in the silence right now.

ATTENTION CREATES REWARD

Paying attention can seem unnecessarily hard work. Some of us don't want to pay attention; it is something we "have" to do at school or work. On the other hand, many of us feel starved of attention, both from others and from ourselves. Attention is about being completely present with something or somebody. It is special care, the gift we have to give. It is about honouring, listening, witnessing, sensing and appreciating. It happens from a state of slow.

Where attention goes, energy flows . . . Attention is a wisdom that is often overlooked because it is receptive, subtle and hidden, and our culture usually only values what is visible, obvious and loud.

But who or what is doing the attending? From where within ourselves do we pay attention?

Attention means allowing ourselves to be with the unknown. To be present without imposing or demanding, to hold a space where something can arise and unfold, where we may be surprised. Attention is consideration, concentration and care. It is a state of arousal. Attention comes not from the head, but the heart and the body. It occurs in the present moment now and is a choice.

We can choose to attend to what is happening in ourselves, others and the world around us. We can also attend to how it is happening, the energy behind words, actions and objects. We do this without prejudice or agenda. The listening of the heart is always love. As Llewellyn Vaughan-Lee, a Sufi teacher in the Naqshbandiyya-Mujadidiyya Sufi Order, says, "Without the lover how can the song of the beloved be heard?"[39]

Attention is the key. The price it asks of us is sensitivity and responsibility. The reward is increased pleasure.

Putting the Brakes On

In a world gone mad drunk on speed
Fast is the answer to get to the achievement
For temporary respite from the list of things to do
And a fleeting application of sweet-treat when we are done.
But contained within it all, in ever-present possibility,
Is the pleasure
If you can just slow down enough to feel it
To really feel it
Not chase it
But feel into it,
It comes to you
Slow is not overwhelming
Slow is not too much
Slow is satisfying
And sensitively real.

Practices for Sensitivity

Not bothering to pay attention and staying unconscious in the present moment may seem to be the easiest, safest option. But to enter the Universe of Deliciousness, we will need to slow down and use our attention. Buddhist scholar Joanna Macy said that in the space between despair and fake optimism is the beauty of the present moment, where love resides. We must attend to our body, to our needs and wants – and to those of other people near us. We must learn to slow down . . .[40]

Productive pausing

A pause is a mini-ritual, a mini-reset. It marks the end of one activity and beginning of the next.

How can you begin to build-in pauses in your life? Right now stop reading . . . Does it feel good to briefly halt?

It is good to pause between activities. For example, after a journey before getting out of the car, or off the train or bus, after a piece of work, before or after a phone call, when preparing a meal, etc. In the middle of a busy working day, you can even turn going to the bathroom into a private pause. It can become a conscious moment out of activity, allowing you to return to yourself, to breathe, think or stretch. If you would like to explore pausing at a deeper level, you can try dancing, creating within it many frequent stops and interrupting your motion. Does this increase your energy levels?

Try to enjoy a moment of restorative pause at transitional moments, to gather your thoughts and energy and to sense your body, before continuing your activities. How does that feel? Do you notice more energy, focus and relaxed satisfaction?

Pausing in daily life is good practice for pausing in lovemaking, to fully relish the enjoyment.

Train your attention

Many people are constantly on scanning mode for the next new thing. Attention is something we need to train. This is not appreciated by our culture and is not taught in most schools or workplaces.

The classic technique for developing attention is to meditate. There are many meditation resources online, apps and probably classes in your local area, and it is a practice with significant benefits, such as finding calm and improving performance. Many businesspeople use meditation to increase their efficiency.

A simple meditation technique is to concentrate on something such as a candle flame, mantra (meditative chant), yantra (meditative picture), body part or beloved's face. Choose something that feels right for you, then focus on the object, and whenever your attention wanders off, which it will inevitably do, gently and repeatedly bring it back to the subject of your concentration. Keep returning your attention and focus without pressure.

Choose a time of day; morning is often a good time to sit and focus your attention. Begin with a short amount of time that is realistic for you to achieve, such as five or ten minutes. Try to extend your attention practice to twenty minutes a day and over time, if you can, an hour.

When you have practised for a while, consider what effect the practice has on your mind and on your living.

You can also experiment with giving your attention to the people around you, pausing activity to really look at and listen to them, even if only for a few moments. Allow your body to become like theirs while you attend to them, attuning to what they are saying and how they are saying it. What is it that is needed? Consider your attention to be a delightful gift that you can give to yourself and others.

Breathe intentionally

Breath is life. Without breath we would not be alive: we are literally inspired. Breath is a bridge to pleasure, opening our capacity to enjoyment, connecting us to the world. If we stop breathing, we stop living. With every breath we bring the oxygen we need to be alive into our blood and body. Yet most of us breathe without really noticing we are doing so.

Breath connects our interior and exterior, spirit and matter, soul and body, life and death. As we breathe in, we draw the world into us; as we breathe out, we offer ourselves to the world. Paying attention to the breath is an incredibly simple practice and seems obvious. However, doing it makes a subtle but palpable difference, immediately combining mind and body. We feel more substantial.

When we are stressed, we tend to hold our breath and breathe shallowly into the top of our chest. When we are more relaxed, our breath is fuller, slower, down into our lungs, belly and whole body.

Notice how you uniquely usually breathe. Through your nose or mouth? What other parts of your body move? Is your breath smooth or jerky? Warm or cold? Do you breathe more easily in or out?

To practise breathing intentionally, first make sure you physically ground yourself with both feet flat on the ground, and, if you can, both hands flat on the armrests or seat of your chair. Take a moment to feel into the sensations of your feet and hands, the physical solidity underneath you.

Set a timer. It can be enough to begin with just five minutes of conscious breathing. As you breathe in, allow your belly to expand. As you breathe out, let your belly flatten.

Begin to experiment with breathing into different areas. Can you breathe into your lungs and your belly? Can you breathe into the heart area, making the chest rise and fall with each breath? Can you breathe into the sides of your lungs, either side of your diaphragm, making them expand and contract side to side with each breath? Can you breathe into your whole body?

Try noticing your breath first thing in the morning. How is that? Try pausing to notice it during your day, maybe five times daily.

Try combining breathing and moving your pelvis, tilting your hips backwards as you inhale and releasing your hips forward as you exhale. Try this sitting, standing or on all fours. What do you notice?

If you would like to, you can also combine breathing with expressing the name of God. Mystical Judaism describes the secret name of God, Yahweh, as the sound of exhalation and inhalation. Yah Weh. God as a three-dimensional, body-infused reality. There is a similar mystical Islamic Sufi practice of saying Al-lah on the out- and in-breaths.

Experiment with expressing the English version of the Hebrew name of God as "I am that" on the out-breath and "that I am" on the in-breath; or, of course, use God's name in the language that comes naturally to you.

Live rhythmically

Pleasure is to be found by tuning in to a natural rhythmic relationship with the world. Although it may at first seem counterintuitive, consider planning your life to work with – and not despite – the natural changes of the day, month or year. Try to live as a part of the ecosystem.

Wear natural fabrics as much as you can, so that daylight – and the different-coloured wavelengths within it – can reach through to your body at different times of the day and affect your subtle energy.

Experiment with planning key tasks and meetings for the times of the day when humans are biologically expected to have most focus and energy, which are in the mid-morning and late afternoon. This utilizes the circadian rhythm, a biological response in humans, animals, plants, fungi and cyanobacteria to temperature and light fluctuations. How effective and enjoyable do you find this? Did you notice less stress, less of a "push" energy and more of a spacious, creative flow?

Divided into its weeks, each month contains four quarterly moods – we can call them "child", "teenager", "adult" and "elder". The "child" has new, playful, initiatory energy. The "teenager" is expansive, dynamic and creative. The "adult" is unexpected, critical and releasing. The "elder" is inward, reflective and still. Try planning cyclically for the month's changing energy with these phases in mind. Which task might be good to do when? Plan for the moon's cycle from new to full, or, as a menstruating woman, after your period until the end of the next one.

Sense into the rhythm of the year: how can you live in tune with the seasonal changes?

- Spring: life is bursting with potent fertility. Invest fresh energy into your business and life. Find what puts a bounce in your step. Renew connections with people and with what gives you joy.

- Summer: life is in full flower. Act on your passion and purpose. Interact with many others, such as your customers, colleagues, supervisors, friends and lovers, and show off your stuff. This is the time for creative freedom!

- Autumn: harvest. Appreciate the bounty of your life. Attend to problems and jobs that need completion. Let go of people and tasks that no longer serve. Be open to unexpected change.

- Winter: the life force goes underground. The natural impulse is to rest. Try to avoid major deadlines, allow yourself to work more slowly and to start later in the morning. Reflect on what you have achieved and allow space for the seeds of ideas to come through for next year's development.

Where are you within your lifetime? A woman moves through her life seasons, from girl to mother, queen to crone (or you might say "wise woman"), while a man move through similar seasons, from page to prince, king to elder.

Take a somatic snapshot

There is a tremendously simple pleasure in being fully oneself in the moment, in contact with all the sensations and feelings in your body. It's an experience of authenticity and aliveness.

How are you right now? Do you already know? Or would you like to find out? To find out, take a somatic snapshot.

Slow down, cease activity, sit still and turn your attention inwards, noticing the state of your body.

Scan your body and see what you notice; it is a bit like taking a sensory photograph of yourself. Do you notice any sensations in your body? Is something happening or nothing? What is happening and where? Is there a strong sensation like an ache or a light sensation like an itch?

What interests you? Is there a sensation you do not really want to notice? Is there a numbness?

Does the sensation change as you notice it? When you notice one sensation, do you then notice others?

How do you feel now that you are in touch with more of your sensual self in this moment?

The body is always in reality. The question is where are you . . . in somatic contact with your body?

Discover your response

When you slow down, you may begin to notice in more detail how you respond to the different people that you meet.

To get yourself started, try this exercise with someone who you encounter on the street, at work or in cafe (but not your partner, parent or child). Rather than just glancing at them, take a moment to really look at them and then explore your reaction.

What happens in your body when you look at this person? Do your shoulders rise and does your body tense? Do you feel soft and calm? Or do you have butterflies in your tummy?

If you speak with them, what then? And, if appropriate, if you reach out and touch?

Do you want to turn towards them or would you rather turn away?

This week, take a moment to register your unique in-the-moment response to a person or situation in this way at least once a day. How is it to slow down for a moment in everyday life? Does it drag you down or free you up to make different decisions and take better action? Do you realize there is something you want or need? Does slowing make the moment more interesting and fun?

Slowly connect with pleasure

When we slow, we begin to notice that pleasure is always present. It might not be what we usually think of as pleasure, but something that is pleasurable nonetheless. Perhaps the touch of your clothes on your skin or the contact of your legs on the chair right now. We can increase our capacity for pleasure by practising paying attention to small pleasures that already exist.

Right now, find a part of your body that feels good. You might find pleasure already present – perhaps in your thumb, arm, back or leg – and then follow this sensation and attend to it by giving it your attention. Begin to move it, sensing into the pleasure that is already there, expanding that feeling. Follow the pleasure until it changes or until another area of your body comes into your field of attention, then you can sense and move to follow that.[41] You can generate a good feeling in the body too by smiling – even a fake smile – and by imagining pleasure.

"Put the body in motion and the psyche will heal itself,"[42] said Gabrielle Roth, dancer, musician and creator of 5Rhythms Dance. In silence or with music, allow yourself to move playfully, following spontaneous impulses, sensations, feelings and movements. High, low, left, right, twist, flop, shake and stretch – you cannot get it wrong!

I invite you to use this book slowly and creatively. Reading it is not the same as using it. This is a workbook, a space for intellectual consideration, emotional reflection and practical embodiment, where each of the seven Medicines builds on the previous one, week by week.

Pause to consider which practices from SLOW you would like to try this week. As an experiment, choose three that appeal to you or that you resist. (And the rest are there for you to use later.) Choose when and where, and for how long, you might like to do each one. Maybe on Tuesday at 7.30am, sitting on the sofa, for five minutes, or perhaps 8pm, in the garden, for ten minutes. Afterwards, enjoy giving yourself an achievement tick or star!

What?	When and where?	How long for?	Done?

CONNECTING WITH THE BODY

The first medicine of SLOW – pausing, attending, breathing, living rhythmically, observing our response and expanding our pleasure – brings us into contact with ourselves in this moment. We need to practise slowing to be able to access the second medicine of BODY.

2

Body
the medicine of embodying

"If you cannot find it in your own body,
where will you go to find it?"

The Upanishads, Hindu text

"We will never again have the chance
to be born into a body like this one."[43]

Kalu Rinpoche, Buddhist lama

"There is a voice that doesn't use words. Listen."[44]

Rumi, Sufi mystical poet

Can I remind you of what you already know? Body is where life is lived, your life and mine. Here, now, we are alive. In this three-dimensional, fleshy, messy, smelly, dripping and feeling form.

Yet modern life encourages us to become separated from our bodies and desensitized to our physical feeling selves. The way we live today binds our body for hours, first to school chairs and later to office chairs and seats on transport. So that when we do really allow ourselves to move again, it is often in the crush of an overstimulating, mechanical gym. Rarely do we allow ourselves to move freely and naturally, without imposing ideas onto the body, such as running in an open field, climbing a tree or dancing for pleasure not performance. Rarely do we listen respectfully and act on the arising wise feelings, sensations and knowings of our body.

Many of us as children were criticized for being "too full" of ourselves, for inhabiting our bodies too fully, for being too much alive, sensual and sexual. As adults most of us are in closer touch with ideas of ourselves – created in selfies, self-images and self-identities – than with the wild selves of our lived experience. Our attention is taken away from the wonderful richness of interior sensations, feelings and knowings, away from our immediate wisdom. We become diminished.

Often we are busy thinking about one thing while our bodies are doing another. We eat while looking at our phones without tasting our food. We exercise while watching TV. We have sex while worrying about our to-do list or fantasizing about someone other than the person we are physically intimate with. This is a dislocation, a fragmentation, a split.

YOUR BODY IS NOT AN OBJECT

We may believe that our self – the identity we know as "I" – is something separate from the body, like individual software located in empty fleshy hardware. We value our sophisticated thinking capacity and disregard the body that houses it, as if it were a cumbersome piece of meat with a pump and electrical circuit.

We have been taught that our body is a thing we have, a functional object that takes us places. We judge it according to others' ideas of our being too thin or too fat, and then we starve it or pump it, dress it to impress or neglect it in shame. We treat our body as just another mechanical object, to be fed, exercised, rested and sexed, often without real care. We ignore the body's signals, pushing it on according to our ideas, treating it with a lack of interest and respect. We think of the body as being our servant and are suspicious of it. If we take this approach, we tend to look energetically like lollipops, with a huge ball of energy surrounding our heads and narrow thin bodies, impoverished without attention, merely a vehicle to transport our precious inflated heads!

Yet the body is far more mysterious than we think. Given the right resources, it is self-healing. The ancient Greek physician Hippocrates said the healing nature within us is the greatest force in our getting well.

Each person's experience of their body is unique. It is the most personal thing we have.

The body is intelligent, it knows, it feels. Contrary to popular belief, we are not going to get to heaven by transcending the body, but through fully feeling, inhabiting our body. To access the body's considerable wisdom, we need to value it as being worthy of attention. This chapter is an invitation to respect and appreciate the amazingness of the body and to celebrate it.

A Living History Map

Everything that has ever happened to us, happened to us in our body. The body registers everything; good or bad, it keeps the score. Tension patterns develop to "hold" our uncomfortable experiences, to keep us safe from pain, fear and discomfort, and to protect us from being overwhelmed. These patterns are held at different levels in the body, a nervous pattern of thought and response, a tension pattern of muscle and connective tissue, an energetic patterning of life force, a cellular pattern of hormones, neurotransmitters and more.

We do not "have" a body, we *are* our body. Stanley Keleman, author of *Your Body Speaks Its Mind*, says that our different body movements, shapes and postures are directly related to our emotional history.[45] Some people's chests (and confidence) are collapsed or puffed-up, while the heads (and opinions) of others jut forward or their bellies (and emotions) flop out.

How we use our bodies helps to create how we think, feel and act. We evolve within our lifetime to embody ourselves, forming and reforming.

I loved my journey with a naturopath who helped me to look at my health at a cellular level. When we can actually see our blood under a microscope, we can see if it is stagnant or flowing. At first my blood cells appeared dull, crinkled and pointed, with a background serum polluted with food particles and parasites. Over time, as I took different supplements and detoxed at a mitochondrial level, I watched it transform into well-formed bright blood cells moving in a clear serum. This detailed picture showed me the impact of our choices on our cells.

No part of the body is unconnected to any other part of the body. No part of the body is disconnected from our history and present experience. Both are present in our flesh. Yet many of us do not fully inhabit our fleshy form, but exist somewhere else, sometimes out of it.

The Body Can Be Hurt

We learn early on in our lives that the body is vulnerable. It sometimes gets damaged and when that happens, it can be painful. We don't want to feel hurt, so we move away from our experience. If the discomfort is really bad, sometimes we move right away from our bodily sensations. Most of us, most of the time, are quite disembodied.

But it wasn't always like this. At birth our body was whole and we were fully in it, if we were lucky enough to have had a good conception, gestation and birth. From childhood onwards, we become less physically sensitive. We learnt, each of us for various reasons, to distance ourselves from our uncomfortable experiences. Many of us were shut down by critical parents or school or simply shut ourselves off from our bodies to fit in with polite society.

We may have shut ourselves off from our bodies because of trauma. Trauma brings a feeling of hopeless and helpless inaction, freezing our confidence and preventing our imagination from creating other possibilities. After the initial traumatic event, it can show up again from time to time or not show itself at all. We can be shocked by a major event such as war, the death of a parent or being in a car accident, but even small events can have a traumatic impact, such as going to the doctor's and being held down for an injection. We can even inherit "invisible" trauma passed down to us because of events that happened to our ancestors decades or more ago. Shock can knock us "out" of our physical body. We can be floating somewhere above or to the side, our physical nervous system overloaded. The technical term for this is disassociation.

Frequently, after strong experiences, we develop new coping mechanisms. We might even develop internal splits, which can be called personae, gestalts or characters within a personality. Schizophrenia is in some respects an extreme version of this. Most of us so-called healthy people contain several sub-personalities or internally divided selves. They can represent us at different ages, including our inner child (speaking of which, pause for a moment: how old do you feel?), or come into play in different circumstances.

After a trauma we are driven to re-enact, to repeat, to try to find a resolution for the nervous system activation that began in the traumatic event, but which did not complete with it. We need to be resourced and well supported to come out of a trauma state. With the right support and guidance, we can then re-experience the overwhelming scenario that was originally too much. We can respond with action, rather than collapse. Survival isolation becomes replaced with social reconnection. Anatomically, healing trauma reawakens the frozen nervous system and the shut-down areas of the brain that usually deal with non-essential activities of language and reasoning.

Peter A. Levine, author of *Waking the Tiger*, says that when the primitive hindbrain, emotional midbrain and cognitive frontal cortex can work together, then we are fully human.[46]

With my birth by forceps, trauma and brain damage, I have lived through intensely difficult times . . . Sometimes I would literally feel myself moving up and out of my body. It was quite scary and I didn't know how to "be" with this, when I was amongst other people. It was a silent, invisible, private occurrence I couldn't talk about, because no one else would understand. However, the hidden treasure of my trauma has been the development of a body-based way of being. Without a cognitive brain that functioned well, I relied on my body's instinctual, intuitive intelligence. Most of the time, I sense my body first and then "translate" arising sensations and feelings into language, words and paragraphs, in order to communicate with other people. It is the opposite of how most people function. It's rich, deep and real.

LIFE HAPPENS HERE

We have elevated a survival strategy into a way of life. Collectively, we believe "being in our heads" to be simply the way that people are and that society is – shrill and ungrounded, reactive rather than responsive, defensive rather than inclusive, and conceptual rather than sensual.

As we have seen, being a body can sometimes be an uncomfortable, vulnerable and raw experience. It is easy to understand why we might "leave" our bodily home for easier-to-bear, abstract, disembodied thoughts. It can feel better being in a warm "floaty" state than stuck down in a "boring" or "painful" body.

But life happens here and now, lived through each of our physical bodies, yours and mine. Life happens whether we are really experiencing it or not. Let us include ourselves in creation by bothering to make the return journey to full inhabitation of our flesh. Let us sense our arms, legs, belly, back and head, and every other part of ourselves from which we are split off and separated.

To do this will take inspiration and courage. We can create a heaven on earth, but we have to participate, be co-creative, to bring the possibility alive. Now, like this, here in our bodies.

We have to descend from the lofty heights of being correct, free and innocent, into the humble reality of pelvis, paunch and imperfection, personal responsibility and passion. In this body we truly live. Life unfolds through our small body, just one within the cosmos of other interrelating bodies, all experiencing physical and emotional aliveness.

Let us remember how amazing this physical home of ours is . . .

FORM IS FUNCTION

The human body is beautiful. Have you ever considered the incredible shapes of our important inner organs, the bones, muscles, nerves and microscopic cells? You are a design masterpiece!

I'm going to share a poetic biological description in this section to encourage your body awareness. We usually take it all for granted, the body's secret somatic symphony, hidden beneath smooth skin. Health arises from good order and a healthy body is a complex system, working beautifully at every level. Microscopic cells, tissues, organs and the whole organism interact in a series of amazing non-stop orchestrated physical, biochemical and electrical interactions . . .

It's often a small shock when we cut ourselves and red liquid oozes out or we bite our cheek and taste the iron tang. We forget our own organic substance. Quite unlike how we think of the body based on a dry skeleton, everything inside is red, wet, dense and noisy. Each part is a uniquely different colour, texture, movement and rhythm. There's no wastage or spare empty space. Everything resounds with heartbeats and liquids sloshing . . .

Heart

At the organ level, we rely on our heart to pump oxygenated blood around our body and our lungs to inhale oxygen-rich air and to exhale carbon-dioxide-rich air as waste.

Liver

This large organ is responsible for detoxification and biochemical transformation. It works with the gall bladder and pancreas to produce digestive chemicals for the small intestine.

Gut

This important organ enables the digestion of food and the absorption of nutrients. The stomach is filled with acidic liquid and microscopic organisms. The small intestine is a long tube with many protruding "fingers" to absorb the partially digested food. Food particles are rushed to the liver to be cleaned and checked, and to the brain. The large intestine stores food pulp without nutrients before excretion.

Brain

This organ receives messages via biofeedback from every other organ and tissue in the body. Everything is talking together at the same time. The main routes of communication are the nervous system, a "hardwired" network of nerves, and the hormones, chemical messengers in the blood. These work separately and together, a kind of belt-and-braces double security system, ensuring messages reach their destination organ to protect us.

Nervous system

This complex collection of nerves and specialized cells has two important functions: one to alert us to action, the other to calm us down.

Mitochondria

At the microscopic level, let's appreciate these tiny ancient powerhouses, which create energy, circulate oxygen and contain reproductive data. Hundreds of mitochondria exist within all our cell nuclei, except for in short-lived blood cells. They are responsible for cell health.

The structure of our moving body is a series of interconnected bones, joints, connective tissue ligaments and tendons, and muscles. The skeleton itself works like a series of pulleys and levers. The soft centres of big bones are factories for the creation of new blood cells, and the body is protected from infection by the white blood cells produced in our bone marrow. When these areas are in balance we will feel healthy.

Health is also influenced by our genetics. We may have DNA mutated or DNA switched on or off by our diet, lifestyle and other factors.

Beyond all this, we are 60 per cent water. Water is in our blood, lymph and cerebrospinal fluid, bathing the nerves and the brain. All cells are in constant communication with each other via messages of light called biophotons, according to the recent science.[47] According to the science of osteopathy, light is dissolved and carried in the water surrounding and within all of our cells[48] and mitochondria. The quality of the light within us is felt as our energy, vitality or life force.

I hope you are impressed with your own awesome physiology!

GREAT SENSITIVITY

Do you know that the whole body is an antennae of responsive, quivering perception? We are exquisitely sensitive, wired for life by our nerves. Our skin, muscle, organs and bones can all feel. That's a lot of information to absorb. Fortunately, we have a huge capability for sensual emotional responses.

Yet when people are distracted, overwhelmed and shut down, their capacity to notice their own sensate data is reduced. Many people do not have the five basic senses fully open – of sight, sound, taste, smell and touch. In the chapter on pleasure we will explore opening our senses.

Rudolf Steiner, the nineteenth-century Austrian philosopher and social reformer, described the existence of twelve human senses.[49] He included movement, temperature, balance, texture and imagination. Perhaps reflect on this for a moment: when did you last notice the simple pleasure of moving and balancing? The delight of being touched by mud, flowers, air, feathers, clothes or wood? Or making contact with your elbows, wrists, legs and hair? Imagination is a sensual spirituality we will explore in the chapter on potency.

The body deals with our sensitivity physically, emotionally and energetically. Seven bodily areas contain interrelated endocrine glands that secrete physically controlling hormones, and these also house nerve clusters busy with electrical activity, as well as the major chakras of subtle energy defined in ancient esoteric practices. These processing areas are represented by the seven "stations" on the caduceus, the symbolic staff carried by Hermes in Greek mythology.

The genitals are a particularly sensitive area of the body. We receive a great deal of somatic information through our genitals all the time, wherever we are, however we are. But can we consciously increase our attention to this part of our body while in work or at the supermarket? Can we allow a subtle stream of sensually sexual information to inform us all of the time? Is that information only sexual or to be acted upon in some other way? How might it affect us to sense into the intelligent sensate information from our genitals?

Every sensation is a doorway to depth, to a further discovery about who we really are.

INSTINCTUAL INTELLIGENCE

The body is always communicating with us. Sensation is not just an experience, it is information. Tension, relaxation, a headache or fidgeting are forms of information for us about our environment. We need to assess others for only seven seconds, body to body, to know if they are a threat or not.[50] We unconsciously know something about their intelligence, health, honesty and attitude. Painful symptoms are signals for us to pay attention. Often we will experience accidents or certain issues repeatedly if we don't listen to the message of the body the first time.

Instinct is not just a form of crude, mechanistic, survival selfishness. Instinct is refined, accessing our deepest soul-knowing in ordinary life. Love at first sight, for example, is an instinctual response. Instincts are intelligent, usually giving rise to good decisions in every area of life. Successful businesspeople use instinct, as do parents of well-adjusted children. Common sense is healthy instinct. A whole-body instinctual choice is often better than an overthought decision.

Yet this does not mean that instinct is somehow better than rational thought. As Daniel Kahneman says in *Thinking Fast and Slow*, we need both fast instinctual/emotional thinking and slow cognitive logic.[51] Instinct bypasses the rational mind, operating via spinal segments, as very fast response. There are no reasonable reasons and qualifications, just raw information and fast impulse.

We've all had a gut impulse to do or not do something. More than once I've moved away from unseen falling objects. I "know" stuff, but it's not learnt knowledge. It is a form of arising in-the-moment, person- or situation-specific, knowingness. I navigate by instinctual intelligence.

Listening to our instinct saves lives. Apparently General Eisenhower, famed for his instinct, knew not to take his troops across a bridge that later fell down. Many people have had an experience of this, sensing something is different and not right, feeling appropriately alert and able to deal with an unsafe situation. Doctors, nurses and healers have instincts about their patients' health, as do parents about their children's well-being. And sometimes instinct heralds that something lovely is about to happen, such as meeting a beloved partner.

Most of us know the experience of having a gut instinct, but often the difficulty, when it is not a life-or-death situation, is "listening" to it and taking appropriate action based on that impulse. Sadly, our habit is often

75

to override our sensate instinctual intelligence in the moment . . .

Instinct is a wild and protective body response. It is a type of deeply authentic body intelligence. It is our own, in-the-moment responsive wisdom, not learnt ideas from parents, school or tribe. Can we trust it and take action on it? Instinct is our own wild god, dare we live in harmony with it?

Instinct is a kind of body thinking, from a brain that most of us may be unfamiliar with.

THREE-BRAINED BEINGS

According to ancient wisdom traditions and modern science, the body has not one but three "brains" – in the head, heart and belly.[52] Each has a similarly large anatomical nerve cluster, called a plexus. But each brain has a different function. The head centre takes care of our thinking, the heart centre our feeling and the belly centre our movement. The head discerns, the heart engages and the belly embodies.

Head

We are already familiar with our head centre and the way that it usually functions. It has the potential to work with clarity, precision and insight, and to be brilliant.

Heart

The HeartMath Institute, a non-profit organization that helps people reconnect with their heart, says that the heart responds before the head, often before events happen. Heart sends messages to the brain, which then sends messages to the body.

Our heart beats. We grew in the wombs of our mothers, fed at her breast (whether breast- or bottle-fed) and slept on her chest, always listening to the beat of her heart. Steady, constant, vital, the heartbeat is the rhythm of life, there until it is not. Life is essentially and lovingly rhythmic. People who dance regularly to the rhythm of music reduce their risk of heart disease and other physical health problems, as well as mental ones.

The heart is a portal to the beyond. In a growing embryo, the heart first appears at the top of the head. The baby, in its innate knowing, bends over itself and implants its heart from the top of its head into its own chest.

There is something beautiful about this primal gestational movement. It seems to carry an encoded wisdom, like a dance gesture, swirl of paint or musical movement, signifying that sacred life is not above, but here in the centre of the body.

Love is not just a feeling, it is a behaviour. Falling in love is a passive falling into a pool of neurochemicals. Stepping up to love is doing something positive and compassionate.

The heart's intelligence is relational, connecting our soul with a variety of other people.

Belly

The intelligence of the belly is embodied and grounded, informing our actions from reality.

In this moment, my body is dense with sensation; I know through visceral sensation that there's something of value here. A delight in my heart, a melting awake, a whole body yearning yes. My body is prompting me, all our bodies are prompting us . . . but are we listening?

There are 100 million nerve cells in the gut, which is equivalent to the number in the brain.

The gut communicates with the brain by hormones in the blood and enteroendocrine cells signalling via the vagus nerve, which runs the length of the body from the brain down to the belly/pelvis, and runs both left and right of the spine. This process quickly alerts us to both the pleasures and dangers of eating.

The belly centre is where we experience butterflies of excitement, gut feelings and instinct. It's where we experience our physical centre to be; like toys that wobble, our fulcrum is here. When we are aware of not just our head but our whole body – our belly, heart and head – we gain an active sense of alignment, participation in and guidance from life.

APPRECIATING THE BODY

The body responds well to our appreciation. When we eat, drink and exercise well, our flesh responds. When we consider it, think and talk about it, touch it and allow others to touch it with kindness, it glows in response. Thought, feeling and function become intertwined.

When my sister was a little girl, she used to spontaneously and randomly kiss her own arms and legs . . . Our body, its cells and organs, can "hear" how we tend to it or criticize it. Experiments show plants respond to love or hate by thriving or dying, and in his book *Messages from Water*, Japanese researcher Dr Masaru Emoto shows that water molecules respond by changing shape;[53] given that this is so, how might our soul-body respond to our criticism? How can we criticize it for not being like people on the TV, from another part of the world, twenty years younger than us?

The body does so very much for us, but when was the last time you appreciated it? Said thank you to it, for all that it does for you all day and every day? Apologized to it for banging it when you bump into something? Talked to it with kindness and respect?

How do you feel reading this? I notice a wave of relaxation in my body as I write it.

Where is our humility in front of the great orchestration of the body's functions? I can follow instructions to bake a cake but I can't simply decide to create a baby: my body does that. All of our bodies do the most amazing things every day. Might we live more relaxed lives, with more breath, and more energy, if we appreciated the beyond-intelligence-and-creativity workings of our body?

We love it when a lover appreciates our body, and makes us feel beautiful or trustworthy. Is this something we can easily do for ourselves? Loving ourselves as physical body?

Listening to Our Body

We hear with our whole body. We directly perceive the vibrations of everything – musical instruments, other people's voices, emotional moods, physical tensions and mental attitudes – with our body.

Pause now: what do you register in your whole being? Can you listen out from your body to other people, animals, plants, elements? (As a toddler, my daughter would dance to the sounds of water tumbling out of the tap.) Can you listen with your body to your own sensations, feelings and knowings?

Can you hear the cosmic concert?

The world of matter does not lie; it shows us in solidity what is happening energetically. Bodies express our truth. They shape, move and reveal the terrain of our inner world. To access the knowing of the body, we need to shift into attentive listening to our flesh.

Listening to our body is a form of being kind to ourselves. When we are cruel, our body feels tense, but when we are kind to ourselves or others, our whole body softens and we relax. Scientist Dr David Hamilton says that when we are kind, our bodies produce more oxytocin and nitric oxide, and fewer free radicals – unstable atoms that can damage cells, causing illness and ageing; our blood vessels expand, blood flow increases, blood pressure reduces and our immunity is boosted. It is a biological positive feedback loop: kindness literally make our hearts healthier and slows our ageing.[54]

Listening to ourselves in this way is a wisdom that is often ignored. It is receptive, patient and hidden in a culture that values only what is visible, useful and fast. Listening comes from our ears, hearts and hands, present and empty, holding space for something unknown to unfold . . . Listening is a tuning-in that requires our attention – hearkening, heeding what is. When we listen in this way, sometimes thoughts arrive unbidden in already formed sentences, melodies, feelings or sensations, images or knowings. We do nothing active to create them.

We have been taught that attending to ourselves is selfish, but when we receive spontaneous "gifts" in this way, it is sensitive and sensible of us to act on them. True listening requires an open attentiveness without an agenda for a particular outcome. It's a practice of awareness to the self without the self-consciousness of "how do I look?" but instead with a curious, "what is here now?"

There is always some phenomenon happening in our body: sadness or anger, neck pain or cold feet, love or irritation, uncomfortable upper arms or a big exhalation, itchy or tense . . . there is never nothing here. Numbness or blankness are not nothing. Every experience is an experience. It is truly fascinating, to notice how we are right now . . . It is often not what we expect. What sensations, feelings and thoughts are you now? We are kaleidoscopic beings in constant evolution, experiences unfolding without pause. Everything in the body is always changing. Popular science neatly says that the body is rebuilt every seven years. But really red blood cells live for about four months, white blood cells for a year, skin cells for three weeks and gut cells for only four days. Bone and fat cells live about ten years, and nerve cells for a lifetime. Our experience of being this body is constantly changing.

Our task is to sense, listen and observe ourselves, as life unfolds, happening in this body.

The world is constantly coming into creation and being created anew. We are like winking lights, off and on, off and on, off and on again without pause, a bit like the pixels on a screen, coming into form again and again, creating the impression of a solid fixed object.

The human body contains all the patterns of creation, it is a blueprint for living. Digestion and regeneration. Breath in and breath out. Foundation and expression. Eyes blinking open and shut, and yet we see a continuous stream of apparently steady information.

OUR UNIQUE AND UNIVERSAL BEAUTY

What is happening in us matters, just as much as what is happening out there. We are each unique, precious and valuable experiments in creativity, consciousness and form. Each of us – and my heart is blazing now as I write – are delicious flavours, like a chocolate in a chocolate box, or a buttery flavourful sauce over a meal, or whichever flavoursome food appeals most to you.

We are each a delicious note of music, an exquisite dance, a beautiful pattern of tapestry, a fragrant bouquet of delight. We are particulars in a vast universe of expanse, contraction, rhythm and variety. We are uniquely Fiona or Avi, Valentina or Dayo, Reshma or Abeer, each one quite exceptionally unique.

And how we show up, the colours, fragrances, feelings, thoughts and sensations that pass through us, the swirl of internal and external experience, is the detail within the whole of us. Each of us constantly changing, winking in and out of existence, every second everything possible, in any possible combination with other life forms too.

Attending to ourselves means attending to the universal within us. Attending to the universal as a specific, here and now. My foot feels cold. A shiver is passing through me. I'm thinking about what I need to do this afternoon. My spine feels alive. I'm aware of my head. A good breath in. Aware of my bum on the seat. Enjoying myself sharing this moment with you (future reader). A smile on my face. A glow in my heart. A sensation at the back of my neck . . . Sometimes it is just a feeling or a knowing: everything will be ok. Go left. I need to be there now. Say hello to that person . . . All this despite the many distractions in life, seeming to indicate they are more important, pulling our attention away from our experiential bodily intelligence.

Like the many digital distractions in our lives, tension gets in the way of us being in contact with the great wisdom of the body. Relaxation is therefore a good thing for all of us to do. It is not about simply collapsing and doing nothing, but can be an active practice to release tension. We practise slowness and depth to be able to sense the wisdom of the body, in preparation for relationships and pleasure. Unlike what we may think or feel is happening, our body reveals to us what is really going on. Without paying it attention, we do not know how we are.

We cannot sustain the earth without sustaining our own bodies. We cannot cooperate with others without being in touch with ourselves. The skill of instinctual intelligence is not a selfish activity for the benefit of ourselves, but for the good of our community and world. To reconnect with our whole body heals a huge split in our consciousness, for us as individuals and together as a collective. The world needs us to act from our embodied state. We need all of the intelligence, wisdom and knowingness, all the sensitivity, empathy and creativity, contained within our bodies.

This Body Now

My personal shape
this home of flesh
is sensible
it knows how to do
a lot of really amazing things

Hills and valleys, landscapes and terrains
I am variously
solid and flexible, wet and dry, hairy and smooth,
strong and vulnerable, painful or pleasurable
all this sensorality is me
an incredible unfolding infinite experiencing

I say I and point to my chest
but this whole solid me
is in constant rapid change
responding and regenerating
my body does not stay the same

This sensate physicality is alive
in relationship with substantial bodies everywhere
hidden inside by my smooth skin
forgotten organ structures
remembered familiar in elemental nature

This body now is mine
to breathe, feed and water, wash and clothe
To rest and exercise
To love and cherish
From this day forth

Practices for Embodiment

Becoming embodied increases our stability, balance, flow and grace. Embodiment enables us to hold steady in ourselves when all around is chaos. It is the foundation of a good life. The more we practise listening to ourselves, to our bodies, the more it becomes a natural everyday way of life.

At the simplest level, move your body regularly. Choose an exercise or sport class that you enjoy and do it. Even five minutes a day stretching or fifteen minutes walking, running or dancing will release stress and viscerally improve your life experience.

Daily life is noisy. To hear our own inner sense, we need to take time for ourselves, to be by ourselves. Alone, we are better able to tune in to the genius of our body. We can be intimate with our sensations and feelings, and with our unfolding, wise knowing.

The body is our own personal home, for pleasure, wisdom and intimate interaction with the world. David Abram, philosopher and ecologist, says, "Other animals, in a constant and mostly unmediated relation with their sensory surroundings, think with the whole of their bodies."[55]

The following exercises begin the process of increasing whole-body sensuality.

A journey of somatic discovery

Begin by noticing your own personal landscape of sensate flesh. How does your body feel right now? What do you notice? Where? Can you feel your bottom on the chair? Do you sense your feet on the ground? Are your jaw, shoulders and back tense or relaxed? Do both the left and right side of your body – both arms and legs, hands and feet – feel the same as each other?

What temperature, movement or sensation do you experience emerging from inside your body? What thoughts or feelings are occurring? What is your body revealing to you?

Do different areas feel as if they are made of different things? Feel free to use words you might not usually associate with your body – plastic or wood, glass, wool, moss or jelly.

Now pay attention to what is emerging from outside. What do you notice happening around you? What sounds, colours, movements attract your attention? How does the air feel on your skin? Does the environment encourage you to relax and expand or contract?

Do you feel solidly right inside your body? Or not? Maybe above or beside the body? Do you care?

What barriers do you face to being in your body – which memories, sensations or feelings? Any tension or numbness? Often we respond to discomfort by judging ourselves; but now try to approach it with kind curiosity. This is an ancient spiritual practice, sometimes called focusing, enquiry or self-enquiry.

Approach what's going on in your body with an open curiosity, interested to find out.

What do you notice? You can include everything, any thoughts, feelings, sensations, images, memories, fears, hopes, questions, expectations, insights, connections... Anything that comes into your awareness that is happening within your personal field.

Try to put words to the felt experience. Inaccurate words will not feel right. Resonant words will. There may be a felt shift, an insight, perhaps a healing ... and your next steps may be obvious.

Set a timer for five or ten minutes. Allow yourself to speak about your body in an open-ended exploration without any agenda. There can be pauses or non-stop verbal exploration. Alternate between sensing your body and speaking your experience. Be kind to yourself. For example: Right now I am feeling tired, my feet are cold, my lower ribs feel a bit tight like a corset, squashed, stuck . . . I feel a bit sad and grumpy, my eyes are heavy, my shoulders ache, energy stuck, wants to expand . . . now my heart feels warm, heat in my spine . . . I feel wide . . .

Whatever you can do to be in your body, inside yourself is great! Try scanning your body before you get out of bed in the morning for a few minutes and then let your attention go. This exercise creates a defined time and space for you to sense into a deeper experience of yourself.

Sensing practice

This is a simple exercise to bring mind and body together. Attend to your body by slowly sensing one body part at a time. Sense your right arm for a few minutes and then sense your right leg; move across to sense your left leg and then your left arm; sense your pelvis, belly and lower back; chest and upper back; and head. You can also choose another order.[56] Does anything change? Do you feel a pleasing warmth?

Tense and let go

Often we think we are relaxed without realizing quite how much tension we are holding. The following is a great exercise found in schools of bodywork, psychotherapy and healing.

First, try increasing tension in one part of your body, like a hand, slowly clenching and then releasing it. Then you can try slowly clenching and raising both shoulders, holding and then releasing them.

Next, tense any part of the body, such as an arm, leg, back or your face. A part with a particular sensation or no particular sensation. Slowly build the tension while continuing to breathe. Hold the tension at the peak; then release at once with some big breaths. Sense your body. Is there any movement that wants to be made? Enjoy the relaxation!

You can also amplify emotional tension, such as anger, frustration or shyness. Notice what you are feeling, dare to really feel it, and to exaggerate it. Keep breathing steadily. Make the body shape of the feeling as clearly as you can. Slowly intensify the shape and the feeling, more and more intense, then suddenly release, taking big breaths, allowing a new freedom of movement and sensation.[57]

Shake to release

Animals in the wild shake to release intense fear after being chased by a predator. Human conditioning teaches us not to show our shakiness, but maintaining tension traps fear and shock in the body. You can experiment with or without music, encouraging bounces and shakes of different tempos and sizes through the knees and hips, shaking for release and relaxation.

If you would like to explore this further, see the practical details in the Resources section. Try Osho's dynamic meditation, William Reich's bioenergetics, David Berceli's trauma release exercises or the chaos section of 5Rhythms dance.

Creating balanced well-being

Many traditional healing and spiritual paths teach that our physical form, personality and soul are all interconnected. We can look at ourselves as being made up of elements, such as Earth, Water, Fire, Air and Ether. Each has a different energy, character and home in the body, and each person is a unique mix of these elements in their unique soul potential and in their actual everyday reality.

Body: the medicine of embodying

AIR	
Associated Body Areas	Head, neck, nervous system, brain, spinal cord, the sense organs of eyes, ears, nose and mouth and the skin.
Functions and Qualities	Perception and communication, making connections, understanding, thinking, brainstorming, communicating, creativity, insight; fast, light, detailed, precise, quickly moving, in many directions and shapes, expansive, spreading out across big distances, cool.
Practical Embodiment	• Can you think clearly? • How do you perceive life? Are you visual, auditory, gustatory, olfactory or kinaesthetic? Do you enjoy looking, hearing, smelling, tasting or feeling sensations? • We need to distance ourselves from our inner critic. It may tell us we're wrong and disaster looms... but it is not telling the truth. We can defend ourselves from it, and tell it to back off! • For clear thinking, we need clear living/working spaces. Decluttering, tidying and organizing are practical tasks.

FIRE	
Associated Body Areas	Heart, lungs, arms, hands, upper back, chest, blood and muscles.
Functions and Qualities	Relationship and action, dynamic, active, changeable, creative, relational, warm, fast, assertive, protective, loving, passionate, purposeful, adventurous, empathic, opening and closing, generosity, containment, courage, anger, boundaries.
Practical Embodiment	• Can you express yourself in relationships? • Try standing tall, chest out, shoulders wide and back with big breaths. • How do you feel? • Squeeze yourself small, then open up big again. • How do these physical changes make you feel? • Notice how "Yes" and "No" show up as body signals: for example, what's your response to mouldy food? Arguments? Sunsets? • Express clearly your "Yes" and "No" for others to understand.

WATER	
Associated Body Areas	Belly and mid-lower back, stomach, liver, spleen, gallbladder, pancreas, small intestine, kidneys and bladder; fluids including saliva and digestive liquid, tears, urine, menstrual flow, blood, lymph and cerebrospinal fluid.
Functions and Qualities	Digestion and absorption of food/ drink, also of feelings and experiences; flow, fluidity, freshness, circular, spiral movements, dots and circles, ripples, relaxation, connection.
Practical Embodiment	• Can your feelings flow? • Notice where things in your life are stuck and stagnant, and where things are flowing. • How often do you relieve yourself? Does your period flow? Do you allow your tears to fall freely? • If stuck, try drinking more water, taking a bath or being near water. Ions released by oceans and showers are healing. Make sure water flows in sinks, baths and toilets in the home. • Water naturally moves in spirals. Try moving your body in spirally, non-linear ways. • Declutter, so the energy in water droplets found in air can easily move around.

EARTH	
Associated Body Areas	Bones (bone's internal structure is a lattice), spine, pelvis, hips, legs and feet, large intestine, genitals, womb.
Functions and Qualities	Foundation, security, survival, sex, excretion and reproduction; organized, precise, slow and steady, rhythmical, warm, protective, determined.
Practical Embodiment	• Do you have what you need? What habits support you? • Finance: do your income and outgoings balance? • Nourishment: what kind of food and drink is best for you? When? How much? • Body: what's uncomfortable or numb that needs healing? • Rest: how much sleep do you need? Do you have an evening wind-down routine? • Exercise: what exercise do you enjoy? How much a day? • Temperature: how hot or cold do you need to be? • Social: how much solitude and connection suits you? • Sex: is your sexual blueprint slowly energetic, beautifully sensual, sexual fun, kinky play, shapeshifting alchemy?

Managing history

What happened to us in the past often affects how we respond today. How do you find yourself responding, for example, to the sound of a ticking clock, a red traffic light, someone cancelling an appointment, a man shouting, a woman crying, a couple arguing or a loud noise? Your knee-jerk responses may have hidden origins in your past.

Each person's nervous system has a unique capacity. Is it easy for you to be in touch with your body or does it somehow feel far away and distant? Do you have any resistance to sensing your body? Does your resistance affect your capacity for sensations, impulses and feelings?

Can you be kind with yourself? Can you allow yourself to feel exactly what you are feeling right now? Can you allow yourself to feel your physical pain, fearfulness or anger?

Do you recognize when your historical stress physiology is activated? This is when your heart beats fast and your body feels charged with surprisingly strong energy. You are not responding to a present event, but triggered into an automatic reaction to an old event. It is useful, then, to slow yourself down, to breathe deeply and sense into your body, to bring adult containment to the child's raw hurt reaction. This is responding to biology with biology.

Do you have a physical weak spot that flares up repeatedly when you're under stress? For some, it's their gums, for others their lower back. Where and how do you feel under attack? When your spot hurts, can you recognize you are probably exhausted and need to rest? We all need to be able to give ourselves what we need to express our emotions, soothe ourselves and calm down. Here are some simple techniques to help calm you back "into" your body:

- Slowly rise onto your toes, then drop back onto your flat feet rhythmically.

- Go out into nature and walk barefoot on the earth.

- Take Rescue Remedy drops.

Reaching out to other people for support is important when we feel overwhelmed. It can take courage to connect with others. Who might you ask for help, and what might you say?

What helps you to feel good? Maybe taking big breaths, stretching your body, bashing pillows, shouting, dancing, wiggling, singing, painting or writing? Perhaps enjoying a bath, eating chocolate or drinking tea?

Letting the body choose

The body responds super fast. No brain-processing time is required for it to analyze and weigh pros and cons to deduce best outcome. The nervous system responds with a very simple and fast binary yes or no, I like or I don't like, muscles tighten or loosen. This is a response at the soul level of self. Try these ways of listening to what your soul-body has to say to you:

Connect your left thumb with your left little finger in a loop. Make another loop with your right thumb and index finger inside it. Ask a question and then pull the right hand out. If the left-hand loop breaks, the answer is No. If it's strong, it is a Yes.

Use a pendulum, crystal or basic metal nut on a piece of string. "Set it up" by saying something true, such as your name or the date, and see which way it turns for your "yes" (this is usually clockwise). Then say something patently untrue for your "no". Then ask any question and allow it to answer.

Set your whole body up as a pendulum by first saying something true and then something untrue to test your "yes" and "no" responses. The body usually rocks forward for "yes" and back for "no". Once you have established your test, ask any question that has a yes or no answer.

Pelvic floor exercise

The pelvic floor is an important area of the body for foundation, stability and sexuality. These muscles hold in our organs and thus contain our subtle energy. When we are young, not much needs to be done to look after this area of the body, but anyone over the age of forty needs to exercise their pelvic floor weekly, if not daily, to maintain healthy tone. (Some women have over-toned muscles. It can be useful to have a professional evaluation.)

You can do this easily by squeezing inwards and pulling up the muscles you usually use to stop the flow of urine. Squeeze for a count of ten and then release for a count of ten. Do this a few times to create a set of repetitions. With practice, women can isolate their urinary, vaginal and anal muscles. Within the vagina are three rings of muscles that can contract inwards and upwards, from the entrance of the vagina up to the cervix.

Pelvic floor exercises are fun and juicy, reconnecting us with vitality, desire and competence. Squats and lunges are also good exercises for this part of the body.

This Power of Pleasure journey is not just thoughts and feelings, but inhabiting your full sensate bodily experience. Which BODY practices would you like to playfully try out this second week? Choose three practices for yourself. When, where and for how long will you do them?

What?	When and where?	How long for?	Done?

At the end of this second week, notice which you most enjoyed doing and what you feel changed.

LEARNING TO EMBODY OUR POWER

We all have our own ways of perceiving data: for some of us it is primarily a form of sensate kinaesthetic knowing; for others it is visual, sound or smell information to which their bodily instruments of perception are most attuned.

As may be clear by now, the medicine of the body is an important, everyday basic for good health and well-being. We feel happier and calmer when we are in sensate contact with ourselves. Only when we are at home "in" our body are we capable of connecting with other people. A healthy and pleasurable relationship is based on two (or more) people who are calm and at home enough in their own bodies, and aware enough of the depth of life, to be able to really see, hear and feel each other . . .

American teacher and writer Hilary Hart says that embodiment is the next spiritual frontier in our collective evolution, and it includes human, animal, and all that is within the shared body of Earth. So much energy and power awaits us through this web of embodied life, and it is released and available as we are humble before its beauty and grandeur. Collectively we have yet to understand how the instinctual world is spiritual. Only those who hold no prejudice against the physical, material dimension of life will pass through that gateway.[58]

Are you aware of the vibrant depth of existence?

3
Depth
the medicine of deepening

"There is another world, but it is in this one."[59]

W.B. Yeats, poet

"In all things of nature there is something of the marvellous."

Aristotle, philosopher and scientist

"There is nothing that exists that is not God."[60]

Lee Lozowick, Tantric guru

The physical body is real. If we knock our body it hurts; if we don't eat, we get hungry and will eventually die. Our body seems to be an irrefutably solid entity and we a solid personal identity. Aren't we?

According to science, at a subatomic level, 99.99 per cent of matter is actually empty space.[61] Apparently, if all the solid matter in our body were to be compressed, it would take up less space than one dot of a dust particle! If all the solid matter in the human race was compressed, we would take up less space than a sugar cube. Quite a humbling thought.

Welcome to the medicine of depth, where things are not quite what they first seem.

Life is not the way we are taught it is. It is deeper and more mysterious than we will ever know. Underneath the surface appearance is a constant essential reality. What some people call our higher self is what I call our deeper self. It is not floating above, it is deeply within us.

Let us go now, you and I, on a dive into the delicious deep . . .

ADDICTED TO THE SURFACE VENEER

It can sometimes appear as if surface is all there is. We live and die, go to work and have relationships, and try to make enough money and friends to feel secure in this insecure world. End of, nothing more.

Cars and houses, shoes and dresses, plastic and concrete, make-up and mobile phones . . . It is incredibly easy to think all that matters is keeping up with the latest fashions. Health, wellness and spirituality can also become a shopping spree, keeping up with those apparently amazing workshops and teachers that friends rave about. Not necessarily any depth to be found there. Perhaps, however, there is a desperate need for personal healing, beyond the need for financial security.

Everything can become urgent in our bid to survive. Anxiety reduces everything to this-minute panic and all that matters is getting our immediate needs me . . . time and space seem to shrink, proportion is lost and we find ourselves trapped in knee-jerk reactions and a state of me, me, me.

When we live on the surface of life, things can appear deceptively simple. We can easily stay trapped there to avoid the pain of blame and responsibility. It's much easier to talk about "hating" dogs, for example, than to admit the truth of our fear and vulnerability when we are around dogs. But living on the surface is not just about language and semantics. It is an orientation to dwelling only on the surface and the illusion that we can control and manipulate this level of existence.

VENTURING BEYOND THE SURFACE

Where can we find meaning beyond the seeming superficiality of existence? Often spiritual life is conceived as something vertical and hierarchical, something to aim for that is above and beyond our small selves and little lives. We may hope to rise above the mundane ordinariness of our uncomfortable reality – to be glamorously elevated, superior, enlightened. The truth is that spiritual depth is horizontal, not vertical.

A lifetime's experience has taught me that the material world and the spiritual world are intrinsically interconnected, like nested eggs or Russian dolls, one inside the other, one touching the other. It is as if we are in the middle of a huge frisbee. The centre is the most superficial part of existence, where we can only see a short distance ahead. We participate in this superficial centre as if everything there matters greatly; and it is here that we make a big effort, we struggle and tense.

Yet depth is all around us horizontally. Everything we can see, hear, smell or touch is physical, but it is not just physical. It is imbued with something much more – something that we might call intelligence, or energy, or being. The further we relax back, outwards, the more possibility, truth and perspective we would find; the more powerful this realness and the greater the relaxation of the self and trust in the whole.

Can you feel this depth around your body? Can you feel it pressing gently on the surface of your skin? On your limbs? Can you sense the "more to life" that is unseen all around you, right here and now? The deeper our contact with Life, the less disturbed we are by occurrences at the surface of life. The more settled we are in the depths, the clearer an overview we have of what is happening.

DEPTH INFORMS EVERYTHING

According to Ilya Prigogine, Russian Nobel Prize winner in Chemistry: "Matter is not inert. It is alive and active. Life is constantly changing in order to adapt to conditions of non-equilibrium."[62] When we think like this, we recognize that the sacred is not far away. We remember to respect.

The soul exists in the deep, in the space behind, around and within our physical body. We are informed by information coming through us from beyond us: our ancestors and our deeper self are here, and they have got our back.

This perspective can change how we see ourselves: we are active participants in the big, wide, deep, multi-dimensional reality of space and stillness, existence and void, solid and non-existent. When we realize there is so much more going on than meets the eye or ear or hand, we become engaged with life, aware we are acted upon as well as acting. We regain perspective on our relative position in relation to the immense, wide and deep Universe of Deliciousness.

Another way of thinking about this is to imagine viewing the world through an old-fashioned camera lens that allows you to adjust the depth of field and thereby shift elements of the picture in or out of focus. Most usually, we have a foreshortened perspective on life. We see mostly just what is immediately in front of us. We concentrate on the foreground. Often the subject. But just as we can change the focal length of a lens on a camera, we can become more aware of the depth of life that already exists, for example through practices such as meditation or healing work.

PLEASURE IS A FUNCTION OF DEPTH

We spend most of our time and energy on the surface of life. In our day-to-day lives, we usually cope by becoming more tense, fast and nervous, rather than slowing down and exploring depth. We escalate speed both internally and externally. We want to keep up and we want to "arrive"; we want to beat all the others, in order to succeed, get attention and validate our very right to existence. However, the route to finding pleasure actually lies in relaxation, in knowing that we are already more than good enough and have every right to relax and be, and to enjoy ourselves . . .

When we are tense, we are literally capable of feeling less. There is less empty space in the body and less responsiveness as a result. Our capacity to feel pleasure and to be conscious is greatly reduced. Our capacity to notice the true depth of the world is reduced. We shut down. We see, feel and hear less. We are aware of less.

The truth is that it can be temporarily uncomfortable for us to go deeper because it is unfamiliar and means confronting things we would rather not. But most of us can bear some discomfort. We can bear much more reality than we think we can. And when we do, pleasure opens up for us, along with beauty and truth, because truthfulness, beauty and pleasure are different refractions, experiences, expressions of the same thing.

Life is essentially pleasurable when we fearlessly live it in its full depth. Jesus expressed this as, "I have come that you may have life in all its fullness" (John 10:10).[63] Heaven is not separate above us or separate in the future – but is right here now, just under the unexplored surface.

Another way of thinking about depth is to visualize the waves on the ocean: we can only see waves but the ocean extends far beneath and in between the apparently separate waves. My name Julia means "Wave of God" in Hebrew, a meaning that I love.[64] When we individual waves forget our connection with the vastness of the ocean, we lose access to the fullness of life that is possible.

The Democracy of Depth

Traditionally, religion and spirituality have been regarded as the domain of depth. For those who follow a particular cultural or spiritual path, it is easy to get sucked into the specifics of their tradition, to identify only with their path or believe their team to be better than others. There is a bad habit in some alternative healing and spiritual circles of talking about people as being "spiritual" or "not spiritual". It's a ridiculous snobby shorthand that suggests there is any such thing as a non-spiritual person. Everyone has equal spiritual potential. We don't need a priest or priestess, shaman, imam, rabbi or minister. Everyone has equal access to the deep.

Some people are more wounded than others. Some people have more resources than others. We all have different destinies. But essentially, each human is made alike of soul-imbued flesh. Similarly, all spiritual and religious paths are of value. Each is a different route into deeper truer reality. Each has their own unique symbols, maps and vocabulary and a slightly different crystallization.

We are each a unique refraction of the depth, informed by the light or intelligence behind us. It is as if we each have a personal soul crystal that imbues us with a particular colour, tone and intensity – as if there is a prism or crystal that holds the unique shape of Sharon, Nadya, Deepak or Alfredo, this aloe vera plant or that jaguar, the individuality of each of us, as we shine out and radiate into life.

The medicine path in this book is deeply personal and is designed for you to put together for yourself, rather than you having to rely on the second-hand reportage of others on what works or doesn't work for them.

A Vision of Depth

Imagine God as a ginormous, vast octopus-type being. There is a solid central body and emanating from it billions and billions of "tentacles". Imagine that each person, each animal, insect, plant and rock is but the tip of one of those emanations. Every possible combination or combinations of meeting are possible. For moments or lifetimes. For stillness or dancing. For looking at or touching or talking or lovemaking. Anything goes.

We see the superficial reality of an encounter as two separate entities meeting. When we change the depth of field, we feel the interconnection, and we are informed by that which is behind us, which comes through us as "us". It lives, speaks, behaves and dresses us. Sometimes we can feel the shift "backwards" in our perception in ourselves as we deepen into reality and accurate perspective.

The point is the spark of electricity that comes in the relationship, in the meeting point, between any two or more things. The moment of meeting. Creativity occurs when we put together two or more things that have not been put together before. Creativity is the fun of the juxtaposition between one thing and another, or between space or silence. From this perspective, the world is a huge creativity kit – with not just images, sounds and language to create with, but a vast selection of fauna and flora and apparently inanimate objects too. Big and small. From microbe to elephant, from earth to lily, the colours, materials, tastes, the sheer variety of life on Earth is fantastic! What a palette to play with.

Life is relational and fundamentally creative. It is a dynamic interplay of variety, playfulness and humanness, toughness and softness, masculine and feminine, light and dark . . . It is delicious!

The intelligence or Great Spirit or God or source or any of the hundreds of names of divinity is behind or underneath everything that we see on the surface.

HOW DO WE GO DEEPER?
DOORWAYS TO DEPTH

There are several everyday ways in which we can plug ourselves back in to depth, away from the surface of existence. The deep is not so very far away.

Attention and mindfulness

Attention and mindfulness can both take us deeper when we bother to apply our focus. The washing-up may always need to be done, but when done with attention to ourselves, the dishes and the water and the soap, the act is transformed from a simple unpleasant chore to be gotten-over-as-quickly-as-possible, into a sensual meditation. We can notice the delightful sensation of warm water on our hands and the playful fluffy rainbows of the suds, the feel of the cloth, brush or sponge on the solid curve of the bowls, the sounds of the crockery and the patter of the rain outside, for example. The mundane transforms into the sacred just like that. All we need do is switch our attention on.

Attention transforms the daily objects we use. An object that has been loved and used over time has a patina that makes it glow, like well-worn books handed down to us from our grandparents or the velveteen rabbit toy in the story, loved into being real.[65] Our grandparents used to live like this, handling items with reverential attention. Think of the musician who loves his wooden instrument and cares for it lovingly through many years, the maker who loves her knitting needles or sewing machine, the craftsperson's relationship with their tools or a chef's relationship with saucepans and ladles.

With the advent of everything digital, and touchscreen, objects function with built-in obsolescence, and we have lost our love and care for our tools. We may touch our screens more, but with less sense of love and honour. With all of this non-stop activity, especially on digital devices, our attention spans are becoming shorter and we are becoming more impatient. Many people are constantly in "scanning" mode.

The medicine of depth is to give of our precious resource, our attention. To listen to everything, not just with our ears but with all of our body. This attention, once given, reawakens our natural state of wonder, reconnecting us with the soul of the world – the *anima mundi*.

Imagination

The imagination is another doorway readily available to us. Native American traditions speak of the world as "all my relations". Through imagination, we can visualize everything in relationship, all things arising from the same deep background. Tiokasin Ghosthorse is a spiritual activist, shaman and musician from the Cheyenne River Lakota (Sioux) Nation of South Dakota, USA. He suggests we imagine the sun as Grandfather Sun, the earth as Grandmother Earth and the trees as our brothers; although at first this may seem forced, in time it becomes easier and natural.[66]

Anthroposophic education, founded by nineteenth-century philosopher and mystic Rudolf Steiner, teaches children this perspective. It seems to them totally natural. When I "bother" to play with my young daughter, allowing her to lead the play, it is always enriching, widening my perspective and experience of myself and her. We can borrow play from our children; it legitimizes us not taking ourselves so seriously for a little while, enabling us to experiment and be playful.

Reflection

This is yet another opening into the deep. We looked at some fascinating scientific facts earlier in MAGIC and again at the start of this chapter – about how solid matter is 99.99 per cent space and 80 per cent of reality is invisible microorganisms. When we reflect on these and other discoveries from science, they can "blow our mind", opening us up to what we hadn't realized was true and expanding our thinking, curiosity and heart.

Enquiry

Enquiry takes us deeper into reality by asking questions, being curious about others, situations and ourselves. Take a moment to question yourself now. How am I? What am I thinking, sensing and feeling? What is really true?

At the Diamond Approach psycho-spiritual school, I immediately felt a sense of homecoming, as it resonated with my own natural way of enquiry, including my sensations, feelings, thoughts and imagination. Enquiry – or self-enquiry as it is also known – is popular in the teachings of Byron Katie, AA, Collective Awakening and other contemporary spiritual paths that use elements of an enquiring approach in their teachings.

Our experience of life, the ups and the downs, opens us from contentment with the mere surface appearance to the truer depths. When we experience love, grief or suffering, we discover there is a great deal more to life than we thought. Maturity arrives as we experience suffering and challenges. The great life events of, for example, losing a parent and having a baby can impact us far more than we might think they would beforehand. They take us deeper into the current of a life. New experiences, having courage, taking risks and getting out of our comfort zones all give us fresh perspectives and richer experiences. We are the wiser for trying something new, whether that's broccoli or windsurfing.

Love

Love in all its forms opens us. Romantic love is heart-opening, but so is the love of a parent or caregiver for a baby, of a therapist for a client, of a child for a dying parent. Love as a practice of loving-kindness, empathy and compassion reveals to us life's depths. It changes both our heart and our perspective as we learn to stay steady, to give to another or others, come what may. We learn we're not the centre of the universe. Love is literally all around us. Air is full of water and within that water is light or love. Space is not empty, it is full of subtle information: love. In the Bible, Psalm 139 speaks of this in the words: "You hem me in, before and behind."[67]

Longing

Longing taps us into a deeper vein of life. Whether we are longing for God, an intimate partner, a home, health, or peace and stability . . . whatever it is, longing is a heart's desire for something more, stemming not from a selfish want, but a real deep wish from the depths of our being. Through sustained longing we open our hearts and minds to depth. Suffering has a redeeming quality when we can stay with the pain of the suffering and the longing for something more. Suffering adds weight to our soul. As eleventh-century Afghani spiritual scholar Al-Ansari said, "Strive to be the true human being, one who knows love, one who knows pain, be the bowl of wine passed from hand to hand."[68]

Trauma

As we have already seen, trauma can be a gateway into depth. The great difficulty of being can motivate us to find healing. Being traumatized often means we have to negotiate our movement in and out of very sensitive states of being. We seek resources in order to better be able to be with our own delicate states. We seek to restore ourselves to the internal sense of potential and wholeness we instinctively have about ourselves, even if we don't know, identify with or use the word trauma. The intensity of suffering can be transformed into an intensity of wholeness, into a deeper experience of reality.

Rituals

These practices can enable us to get out of our own way, opening us to the deeper space always present. Practices such as drumming, chanting, dancing, walking and meditating are very practical ways to change our vibration.

Sometimes we live at the real depths and sometimes we are on the surface. There will always be days when the depth seems inaccessible, for whatever reasons, however "advanced" you may be in your practice . . .

Into the Deep

Pleasure: the meeting place of this and that
It is to consume each other,
to consummate the relationship.
Not to orally consume each other,
but to take each other in totally,
and in so doing to transform each other.
Both people relaxed back into the depths of their being,
able to meet as two souls inhabiting their flesh,
(rather than two personalities hunched forward
to try to please, manipulate).
Remembering the living context beyond our sight
accessed through slowness
trusting in relationship
two bodies imbued with the radiance of depth.

Practices for Presence

What if everything we interact with is imbued with love from the beyond?.
. . How can we touch into the depths every day? How do we stabilize
depth?

We have hints from Rumi, the thirteenth-century Persian poet; he
wrote, "Make everything in you an ear, each atom of your being . . .
listen and your whole life will become a conversation."[69]

Here are a few ways to help you access it yourself.

Notice love

It is not that we lack anything and need to do something to "get" it –
love is actually already here, around us. This exercise is very simple
and can be subtly powerful. Normally we think that we are in empty
space, but space is invisibly full of Love. Something changes when we
acknowledge this.

Pause what you are doing, so that you can have a few minutes of
quietude for yourself. Then open yourself up to receiving the love that
is invisibly everywhere all around us. Switch on your incoming channel,
imagine and viscerally feel the subtle sense of love moving, curving
towards you, flowing in.

What if anything changes for you? What do you notice? Is the love
palpable? Can you feel love touching your body? Can you breathe it in?
Do you feel a deep relaxation, more melted, softened and resting? Do
you perhaps feel a change from being a separate entity within empty
space – to feeling held within a web of interconnection?

Honouring the world

We are so used to being disrespectful to people and objects that this
practice may at first feel strange.

Experiment with the notion that everything is worthy of being given
your loving attention. With this approach, almost all our ordinary tasks

can be transformed into a practice that takes us deeper – and the task becomes transformative for us.

It's best to begin with a small practical activity that involves the hands and heart. Perhaps start in an outdoor place, listening, waiting and sensing as you connect with a tree, stone, flower, earth, wind or rain. What happens when you simply do that?

Then, at home, notice the small objects around you, maybe a phone, radio, cup, kettle or sofa, pausing to simply notice them and yourself. The Buddhist monk and peace activist Thich Nhat Hanh suggests we give our attention to something for a few moments before taking action, for example to the ringing doorbell before we answer it.

Try silently giving grateful touch to objects you've interacted with thousands of times, such as the wooden table you eat on, the bed you sleep in, maybe a kettle you frequently use or a lamp that belonged to your grandparents. Valued objects give a home a palpable depth of presence: can you feel it?

Sing praise to the water, appreciating it for cleaning your plates and body and being nourishing. Be glad for your favourite clothes as you put them on. Does the physical world respond in some subtle way to your attention?

You can also try this practice of grateful attention at work, although it is harder to do if you are sat at a computer and under pressure.

Nevertheless, all substance is sacred, including manmade metal and plastic, as well as wood, wool and stone. What do you notice? Does a dull office and colleagues become imbued with a sense of aliveness?

Gardening

Growing things is an ancient activity, and it can be humbling, reconnecting us with the life cycle of birth, growth, reproduction and death, and the changeable elements of sunshine, rain and wind through the seasons. It plugs us into the visceral life of the planet as we plunge our fingers into dark soil and feel the aliveness of it, full of seeds, insects, microbes and minerals. It is psychologically and physically healthy for us to get a bit messy and dirty in the earth. It's inspiring to nurture a plant on a windowsill, or turn a small unwelcoming area into glory, just as much as it is to tend a big garden.

Connect with the abundance of life in your patch of land, whatever size plot you are working with. Tune in to the responsiveness of everything. How do you bring yourself to the garden? Do you rush through spring planting or pause to sense the potential of each seed?

Appreciate all the stages of growth - germinating, sprouting, growing, flowering, fruiting, seeding and dying. Do you water and weed as an obligation or feel drawn into the dance of the elements, the sun warming you, water soothing you, slugs calling you to action, bees doing the essential work of pollination? As you touch and attend, can you listen to what the garden is telling you – when is it time to prepare the ground, fertilize, cut back, pick the lettuce or allow fallow time?

Delight in the abundance of the peas, tomatoes or raspberries, the surprising finds that lie hidden. Notice the deep relationship of exchange, for as we nourish the earth, so she nourishes us. We too are like seeds: what do we need in order to bloom?[70]

Cooking

Often our heads say one thing while our hands, hearts and bodies communicate another. A friend says that although a part of her thinks, "Oh no, another meal to make for the family for supper!" another part of her absolutely loves handling the vegetables and other foods in preparing dinner for her loved ones. Food responds to the love in us while we cook; it opens in response with more deliciousness somehow, nourishing us much more deeply. This is a kind of ancient magic.

Love is alive and it grows as it is shared. As you prepare to cook, let yourself feel the love that you have for the person or people you are cooking for, and let your feeling of love infuse your cooking.

It is a real act of self-care and generosity to others to let your love inform their food. Let it flow from your heart, down your arms and into your hands. Let it flow through your eyes, into your nose and mouth. Take your time, don't rush, so you can touch, smell and feel each of your ingredients – the tang of the cinnamon, the hiss of the boiling water, the taste of the chopped courgette. Remember the chicken or cow, the earth and sky this food has come from. Enjoy the creative experimental process. You are just one part of the Earth's creative abundance, and you are participating in the planetary generosity and passing it on.

Cleaning

Cleaning is a foundational practice for accessing the deep. Cleaning our homes and ourselves, physically and psychologically, is important as we need the clear space to be able to sense depth. Everything responds to our care and love, not just people, animals and plants, but also the furniture, books, carpets, clothes, crockery, sinks and toilets. Everything matters. Everything deserves our appreciation, and in return loves and cares for us too. Often we clean with carelessness, haste and toxic products, even with disdain, but if we clean with care, we notice that our home really feels like our sanctuary. My heart sings after tidying and cleaning. Does yours?

Most areas can be cleaned well with different combinations of vinegar, baking powder and lemon juice. Begin by looking around at your home with honest receptive awareness. Do you have spiders' webs, dirty floors, windows, fridge, oven or floors? What needs to be cleaned? Appreciate the physical environment and objects that facilitate your life. As you clean, bring your full attention to the materials you are touching, to your breath and hands as you move with loving attentiveness. Notice how things feel before and after you clean.

Do recycle excess clutter, things you have not used in months or years. Do you feel lighter when you have less stuff? Do you prefer to clear out each week or month, or each New Year, spring or autumn, or when the energy of change inspires? Daily dish-washing, bed-making and tidying up keeps the outer home and inner life in good order. These tasks are not unimportant.

You can also take an overview of your diary, to see the tasks and people you feel are cluttering up your days and wasting your time. Clean out and simplify your time and your environment to what you really need.

Walking in nature

Enjoy a walk outdoors, most days if you can, whether it be for ten minutes or an hour. Notice the changing light and landscape. Enjoy the physical rhythms of your feet on the earth, your legs and hips moving, your arms swinging, your breath quickening.

Perhaps you can walk without knowing necessarily where you are going . . . dropping into the rhythmic movements of body and nature . . .

allowing yourself to feel a part of something much bigger than you, part of the living natural world.

Humans were all originally nomadic people, who would walk many hours each day for food and shelter. Walking reconnects us with our biological, ancestral and tribal depth of being. Walking for about two hours, equivalent to about ten thousand steps a day, creates a palpable sense of bodily well-being. Walking for very many hours a day, on a trek, can have a profound deepening effect.

Walking often allows worries to get unpacked, inspiration to be accessed and health maintained.

Travelling deeper

Choose a place where you feel comfortable and safe, perhaps a quiet bedroom or living room. Put on a timer for five or ten minutes to create a container in time.

Allow yourself to open up to your feeling state. It can be any feeling at all, perhaps shyness or anxiety, excitement or nervousness, fear, anger, hatred or blame. What is present right now?

This is about receiving yourself as you actually are. It is an act of kindness to yourself, an embrace, offering yourself permission to be simply as you are . . . While this process can at times be unfamiliar or uncomfortable, simply allow yourself to be with yourself, as you would with a small child perhaps. To be curious and kind towards yourself.

This is often how I work with clients in sessions, as travelling into the depth of the current experience creates changes and opens dimensions. The process is always unexpected. You can move your body with what you feel, or you can speak it aloud, you can write or draw or sing or play it on an instrument or hum or growl, including all your somatic sensory information, feelings, images and thoughts. All of these expressions are portals to other deeper dimensions and states.

I want to encourage you to not just skim the surface of this book, but to really deepen, by doing your practices. Which DEPTH practices would you like to explore for yourself this third week?

What?	When and where?	How long for?	Done?

What if anything did you notice was subtly different during and after this week?

TOWARDS A DEPTH OF RELATIONSHIP

We move now from the medicine of depth to the medicine of relationship. This is about relationship with the full depth of a person, not just interacting with their surface presentation, which is often designed to make us think they are who we want them to be. It sees past our smart suits, aftershave, make-up, push-up bra or whatever and however else we try to manipulate our external appearance and behaviour to please.

Here is how Kabir, the fifteenth-century Indian mystic and poet, evokes deepening: "Inside this clay jug there are canyons and pine mountains, and the maker of canyons and pine mountains! All seven oceans are inside, and hundreds of millions of stars. The acid that tests gold is there, and the one who judges jewels. And the music that comes from the strings that no one touches, and the source of all water. If you want the truth, I will tell you the truth. Friend, listen: the God whom I love is inside."[71]

There is a great deal more to any person than just their surface, and a relationship of depth is a living thing of beauty, satisfaction and pleasure, an important component of the Universe of Deliciousness. So, let's keep on moving, through the next medicine doorway, on our journey onwards.

4
Relationship
the medicine of relating

"Connection is why we are here."[72]
Brené Brown, professor and author

"We need four hugs a day for survival.
We need eight hugs a day for maintenance.
We need twelve hugs a day for growth."[73]
Virginia Satir, therapist and author

"When two people relate together authentically and humanly,
God is the electricity that surges between them."[74]
Martin Buber, Nobel philosopher, quoting Talmud, Jewish sacred text

As we travel through the galaxies of SLOW, BODY and DEPTH, we realize we are already in many different relationships, with ourselves, others and our god or gods. We are never not in relationship. I glance up this moment, thinking myself alone, to see a large grey-pink pigeon, sat looking down at me from a neighbour's high wooden ledge. Life is teeming with relationships. Everything is in relationship with us and we are in responsive relationship with everything. The world was created so we could relate . . .

Relationships create our sense of self and how we see the world. They can squash and limit us, or they can be doorways, through which we can experience and see ourselves more clearly.

THE ILLUSION OF SEPARATION

We are confused between "relating", which is a verb, and having a "relationship", which is a noun. We usually think of ourselves as independent individuals in an empty space. We imagine we as people stop where the edges of our bodies stop. From this isolated perspective, relationship is something we make an effort to create, rather than something that we are already naturally held within.

Relationships are very important to our health and happiness. But we tend to elevate the importance of a primary, personal, romantic relationship above all other relationships with other people and beings, thinking that only an intimate love will satisfy our need for contact and connection. Yet however many people are trying to get into a romantic relationship, there are just as many trying to get out of one. Intimate relationships are complex, fulfilling and frustrating. Other people are often unpredictable. Despite our best intentions, we can keep repeating unhelpful behaviour patterns with our partner. It is more supportive of our happiness for us to have a web of several different loving relationships, including with our family, friends, colleagues and others, rather than only one. We need community, we are a tribal species, and our loving relationships reflect this.

The ancient Greeks had eight words to describe different types of love. *Eros* is erotic love between lovers; *philia* is affectionate love between friends; *storge* is kinship or familial love; *ludus* is playful early romantic love; *mania* is obsessive love; *pragma* is enduring love in couples or friends; *philautia* is self-love as healthy self-compassion; *agape* is selfless, spiritual, loving kindness for truth and others.

These forms of love cannot exist without our interactions with each other; it is we who bring our relationships to life. Through our relationships we find out more about who we are, whether the relationship lasts for a moment or a lifetime. Relationship is a unit of evolution, a sacred crucible for healing, pleasure and creative possibility.

RELATIONSHIP AROUND AND WITHIN US

If we are fortunate, we usually live as part of a local network of family, friends, enemies and colleagues, and we all live in the world as one part of a big global story unfolding through us. We were conceived, born and nurtured in relationship, created from the relationships of our parents, family and ancestral tribe. But we often forget all that. We tend to think of ourselves as just "me".

Beyond relationships with other people, we are in direct physical relationship with everything all of the time, whether we are aware of it or not. We are in contact with the chair we sit on, the ground we walk on, the air we breathe and all that flies, crawls, walks, swims and grows in the environments around us. We are connected by water moving through us, from the sky into rivers, entering our bodies as drinking water and coming out as urine, tears or sweat, evaporated into moisture in the air. The seemingly empty air is full of water and dust from our own and our neighbours' dead skin – breathed in and out by us and them. Our personal bodies are inhabited by many other forms of life, such as the vast communities of microbes in our gut.

We are constantly exchanging information with others in all of these many different relationships. In a human relationship, especially an intimate relationship, there is a huge volume of information exchange. I imagine the exchange as forming an infinity sign, a non-stop movement back and forth between us of visual information, feelings, spoken words and the exchange of oxygen, carbon dioxide and water. Information is being exchanged by us all as we breathe air in and out, air that contains evaporated water. We can all immediately read the atmosphere of a room when we walk in; for example, is it heavy or bright? We have seen how water can respond to emotion: perhaps "psychic" phenomena are actually us responding to the information in the water in the air of a room?

Just as I wrote this, sitting in a cafe, a drop of water fell from the ceiling directly onto my laptop. It must have come from the air-conditioning unit above, although the baffled cafe owner said that had never happened before. (The laptop was not damaged and I knew it would not be.) I find this happens frequently: I have a thought or feeling as I write, and there's a direct response from my body or from the world around me. Something happens, someone turns up, I see a message . . . The connection is precise. Each time, I engage with this information, to try to understand what is being reflected or invited, and how this leads me further into understanding what I'm writing about. For me, this is the stuff of everyday life: constantly translating and transcribing the sensations, thoughts, feeling, occurrences that arise; using Life, you might say, or allowing myself to be included in Life as we co-create together and as I allow Life to lead me . . .

We are never alone. Be alive to synchronicity interweaving the material and spiritual in everyday life.

REALITY IS RELATIONAL

The surface of life appears to be many separate entities interacting. At depth, all is one. We're not alone even if we believe we are. Looking from different perspectives, we see that relationship is everywhere, and that all is interconnected. We can tap into deep universal energy and "know" everything.

Here are a few examples from different worlds and traditions: enjoy those that resonate with you.

- Native American traditions such as the Lakota tribe of Dakota in North America do not use nouns for the names of people and things, only verbs. So you would not be Dave or Priscilla but Daveing or Priscillaing. There is no table, only a table-ing; no river, only a river-ing. This language emphasizes that we are not one fixed finished thing; we are continually finding out who we are through our relationships with others. We are constantly becoming.

- All physical matter is affected by relationship.[75] Subatomic particles behave as a continuous wave or a discreet particle or both, according to the observer. This is known as the wave-particle duality. When two things have been in contact and are then separated, apparently even to opposite ends of the universe, they remain in relationship and communication. What happens to one affects the other. This is known as quantum entanglement. Science is just beginning to acknowledge what spirituality has known for centuries.

- Cells from a gestating baby are found in a mother's brain, bones and blood, and cells from the mother are found in the baby.[76] This is known as foetal-maternal microchimerism. It means we are biologically interconnected with our children, mothers, grandmothers, and perhaps sisters too. Our DNA was present inside our grandma, who was carrying in her womb our mother as a foetus, whose ovaries already contained in utero the egg that became us. Amazing to realize!

- The new science of epigenetics shows how the experiences of our ancestors can affect us and our DNA for generations; some say for seven generations, some much longer. Stress and other experiences switch different genes on and off in ways not yet entirely clear to us. Trauma can be inherited, and we see this in the children and grandchildren of those who have suffered as war victims.

- Healing techniques access the "field" of energy. American well-being educator Bonnie Bainbridge Cohen says that the space within and around us "holds the information"; it contains consciousness, which is both everything and nothing. The energy field can be seen in action in the modality of constellations, where a client's intention "sets" people or objects to "represent" other people, organizations, plants or animals, and through representatives' sensing of somatic and subtle sensations, useful information becomes accessible for healing interventions.

- Psychometry involves "reading" objects at a distance.[77] This usually takes the form of sensing, drawing or free-associating-words in connection with an unseen subject. This is described as reading the soul of things.[78]

- Memes are units of cultural transmission (ideas, behaviour, styles) that spread quickly, as described by biologist Richard Dawkins.[79] Scientist Rupert Sheldrake suggests new generations come into life knowing more than their predecessors by "picking up" memes.[80]

- We can, without knowing, it channel information. Once when my daughter was four years old, she came out with a sentence including the long word "consciousness", perfectly pronounced and in context.

- Dreams can come true. As one amongst many examples, one morning my dad told my mum about his dream of a blue Rolls-Royce and that same evening he came home in a chauffeur-driven blue Rolls-Royce: one of his clients that day had surprised him by offering him a luxury lift home!

- Sometimes we just know something, an intuitive capacity I call "knowing without knowing". Once my daughter's dad moved a ladder away from the back door, which we rarely use, just before I opened it. If he hadn't, it would have fallen, hurting our daughter, who was then a crawling baby.

IMAGES OF INTER-RELATIONSHIP

As we touched upon in the poem "This Body Now" (see page 82), everything is made-up of fractals, holographic repeating patterns "nesting" inside each other at different levels.[81] Everything repeats and everything contains everything else.

The ancient Buddhists used the simile of a giant three-dimensional spider's web, known as Indra's Net, to describe their concept of the interconnections within reality.[82] Imagine a web extending in every possible direction, covered at each juncture in reflective dewdrops, each reflecting everything else. Everything that has existed, every idea that can be thought about, is a pearl in Indra's Net.

This symbol of complex coexistence is similar to descriptions in other spiritual traditions. In Christianity, Paul refers to everyone in the Church as being part of the body of Christ. Using the metaphor of the human body, he explains how different body parts have different functions, as do different individuals.[83] The Tantric tradition says everything is interlinked consciousness and energy; that just as every cell in our body has intelligence and health, so we are each a cell in the whole of life, involved on the levels of both the local microcosm and as a part of the whole macrocosm. The Ridhwan psycho-spiritual school describes the awake state of Unilocality. This is the experience of being in more than one place at a time, accessing something of the lived experiences of others. When this state arises, it feels surprisingly natural, even though it sounds impossible if you haven't experienced it.

Science also now recognizes that, amazingly, atoms can exist in more than one place at a time. Dr Rupert Sheldrake has hypothesized that morphic fields exist, as the connection between everything, such that wild animals know to migrate and pets know when their owner is on their way home.[84] On another level, the internet is a modern image of interconnectedness. It forms a planetary neural network transcending local, national and international barriers and divides according to gender, race, sexuality or ability. It is a symbol of our essential equality and our very many real-time relationships with each other.

How Awareness of the Interrelationship of Life Affects Our Own Relationships

How does being aware of our individual place within the wild-world-web of interrelationships affect us in our personal relating? Is interconnection just an idea? Does it change our behaviour?

We can imagine relationships as ripples from pebbles dropped in water, the ripples interacting, creating a new pattern. The Nguni Bantu term for "humanity", *ubuntu*, is often used in a philosophical sense to suggest how we all influence each other.

Because we usually think of ourselves as separate, we may not realize the impact we have on others. If we've had a bad day and dump our anger on our partner or a person in the supermarket, we usually think that is that. We might feel a little better for releasing our "charge" and perhaps pleased temporarily to see them suffer. We think it's a private matter, between us and them. But when we remember the contextual web of interrelationship, we will naturally consider how our behaviour might affect others. If we rage and blame at a stranger in a supermarket, they might feel upset and stressed. Perhaps they will fail at work and get fired, or have a foolish accident and twist an ankle, or their blood pressure will increase, lowering resistance to a virus, or they shout at their colleagues, who are also affected badly, who then take their stress out on the people or animals they meet . . .

It is mind-blowing to realize we do have an effect on everyone we relate with during our day – not just the people we talk to, but the effect we have as we walk past someone on the street. Do we knock into them by accident or give them a compliment? A dirty look or a smile? Does the way we walk stir the air around us with gentleness or hatred? Might other people actually feel that emotion? Could we really have such a big silent effect on other people, animals, birds, plants and insects? If we invite others into a sweetness of heart and deliciousness of body, how might they spread that on through their day? If a simple passing-by temporary relationship can create such a powerful positive ripple through the street, how important is it to cultivate easy delightful relationships with our family, friends and lovers?

I hear the depth of silence now and a bird singing outside. As in this moment, as I sit listening to birdsong, we can find inspiration in the natural world, hearing and seeing the interactions of different organisms. It helps us to realize we are but a speck in the great expanses of history and geography. We can feel more humility, respect for and cooperation with others, and kindness to our sometimes struggling self.

When we remember we are not separated from the many varied relationships all around us, we can behave with greater awareness of our impact on others (and sense into their impact on us). We can more consciously craft our relational dance with the whole.

PERSONAL RELATIONSHIPS ARE COMPLEX

We have already touched upon the challenges of personal relationships, and about how just as many people find themselves trying to leave a relationship as to enter one. We might think we need a relationship to "complete" us, as a structure for our happiness. We can then be disappointed and confused when, after the initial honeymoon period, arguments arise. There is a myth about romantic love being somehow pretty, but in reality, however wonderful it is, it is also sometimes demanding and messy. It takes attention, effort and maturity to create a good relationship.

Most of us in the West tend to take it for granted we can choose who we will be intimate with. But in the past, and in some cultures today, relationships could be chosen for economic stability, social elevation and reproduction. Some relationships are still based on practicality, as are some phases of our relationships, but many people also want romance, elusive chemistry and emotional compatibility.

With so much choice today, there is often an inevitable sense of having made "the wrong" decision at some point – of there perhaps still being a better partner option out there for us!

Unconsciously, most people are inclined to view each other as functional objects that should fulfil our needs, listen to us, look at us, touch us, hug us, make love to us, cook for us, clean for us, organize us, etc. But that's not an accurate or healthy foundation for the possible fullness of a relationship. Similarly, our addiction to orgasm as self-medication for stress can prevent the deliciousness of relationship.

Every human relationship is unique, as we all differently affect and alchemize each other. Each person has their own individual history, style, interests, abilities, likes/dislikes, moods, maturity and potential. Each moment in relationship is unknown. How will we act and react to each other?

In many respects, how we interact is beyond us on some levels, beyond the mind and our conscious thought, beyond our attempt to control. Often despite our best intentions, response arises in the body. A friend tells me how every day he decides to be kind with his wife and children, but the moment he walks in the door from work, something happens and the rows begin again . . . Despite himself, he can't relate differently, and feels sad and frustrated.

We sometimes believe our thoughts, feelings and behaviours are caused in us by something that someone else does . . . but that's not the full truth. Whatever we are feeling is caused by something somewhere deep in us, from our history, even if another person is the immediate catalyst in that moment. The only way through is to be totally responsible for our experiences and behaviour, not blaming anyone else for them.

The question for many of us in our relationships with others is whether we stay with ourselves or lose ourselves. Are we authentic, responsive and responsible? Do we compromise, shut down, become false to ourselves in order to keep the peace or the relationship? How much of ourselves do we bring to the relationship? How generously do we share our honest feelings? How available are we really?

A BASIC NEED TO BE SEEN AND WITNESSED

Until we receive true soul witnessing, we will have a need for someone else to provide it for us and our relationships will become focal points for our projected feelings. We will want to get our needs met from our favourite people, and when they disappoint us, they will turn into our psychological triggers. We keep repeating our historical experiences, until we can find a deep healing resolution, in life or therapy.

The truth is that everyone needs to be really seen and witnessed in some way. As babies we need to be seen in our joy and distress by our mother, or the person who fills that role for us. Our capacity to relate well with others as adults depends on how well we were cared for as babies and children, and on how well we have healed any wounds we may have from that time. This is known in psychology as attachment, a theory first proposed by John Bowlby.[85] Is a person securely attached, insecurely attached or ambivalent? Even the most well-intentioned caregiver can of course still get it wrong for the baby they are looking after, or the baby might feel unloved due to having a condition that isn't resolved.

Ideas about best baby care have changed greatly over time. Some have advocated leaving babies to cry in prams in the garden, feeding them on a strict schedule, and children being seen and not heard. Many more variations on this approach ignore the natural arising needs of this unique baby, here and now.

Attunement is there in the quality of the mother's glance, touch of her hand and body, her timing, talk and song. Breastfeeding enables mothers and babies to gaze at each other at an optimal distance for connection for both. This gaze offers soul contact. A mother's love radiates through her eyes, heart, nipples and milk. A mother provides nourishment and is the equivalent of a god for the baby.

When a baby has not been really seen, there is a great sense of loneliness and abandonment. Many of us have unseen children inside of us crying out for attention, the walking wounded. The zombies are not out there, but in here. Many do not feel it's possible to fill their inner void of emotional need. We all want and need to be seen, to feel ourselves safe, in happy relationship with another . . .

INTERPLAY OF MASCULINE AND FEMININE ENERGY

In our everyday life, in the pairing of masculine and feminine, we usually regard the feminine as being the more passive and the masculine as the more active of the two. We tend to see men as playing active roles in the world, good at focusing, fixing and achieving things, while women are more in touch with feelings, details and food.

But if we zoom out to the bigger picture, we can see that in the cosmos, masculine and feminine are huge natural elemental forces, not the same thing at all as men and women, boys and girls. Masculine is the context, as constant awareness, emptiness, stillness and knowledge. Feminine is the manifestation, as changing form, energy, sensuality and aliveness. The masculine simply is, while the feminine is dynamic movement. The interplay between these essential energies is the essence of creativity and life!

In human relationships, there is attraction between the magnetic opposite poles that creates a sexual spark – and between similar poles as we seek what mirrors us in our desire to know ourselves and grow. Feminine energy leads by invitation. Masculine energy follows that up with penetration. Because our culture does not value the feminine, it does not see the feminine invitation as leadership. It only acknowledges masculine action as leadership. We are missing out on seeing the equal dance of difference.

People are born with clear natural tendencies irrespective of their gender. Shamanic cultures have long recognized that there are more than two genders. Each of us is a combination of masculine and feminine in our three different aspects: a physically gendered body with external genitalia, an inner sense of self as a gendered identity and sexual orientation of attraction to others as a gender. Every human being contains both archetypal masculine and feminine energies. These show up in different ways in different areas of our lives; for example, how we are at work is often not the same as how we are in the bedroom. The nineteenth-century psychotherapist Carl Jung[86] called our inner masculine and feminine energy our Animus and Anima, while the ancient Chinese Taoists called these principles Yin and Yang.

We are attracted to someone who reminds us of our inner spiritual self. In traditional genders, a man is attracted to a woman whose feminine aspect reminds him of his own inner feminine, while a woman is attracted to a man whose masculine aspect reminds her of her own inner masculine. In this way we deeply recognize each other – a phenomenon we call falling in love. It is a mysterious process not organized by logic, time or space, but by significance, soul reflection and completion. When we see someone in love, we recognize their bright soul light shining.

A CONTAINER FOR HEALING

We learn about ourselves mostly through our relationships with other people. A relationship is a healing opportunity, a playground for exploring new pleasures and transforming old patterns. Very often, when choosing a partner, at an unconscious level we choose someone who is deeply familiar, meaning that they remind us of the difficulties we had with our parents. They often trigger our childhood wounds, but they also offer us the possibility of healing or retrieving a part of ourselves through owning our true feelings and taking responsibility for our actions. A relationship is really an opportunity that is less about the other and more about fully experiencing ourselves.

In relationship we move through cycles of ease and challenge, either resolving a conflict and deepening our connection, or separating. Relationship is not a fixed thing; it's always changing, demanding us to grow, respond and change. What do we need now to see, feel, understand, say or do?

Being without a partner brings us different but no less valuable healing gifts. Being single does not make us "incomplete". Being single is an opportunity to expand individually, and to appreciate a wider, more complex set of relationships. The temptation when "in a relationship" is often to focus exclusively on "the other", forgetting we are in relationship with everyone and everything around us. Both circumstances, being in and being out of intimate relationship, offer healing challenges and gifts.

A RELATIONSHIP LIVES

Each relationship has a life of its own; it is alive, it has an existence. In addition to the obvious interaction between people, a relationship also has a subtle energetic field, a relationship soul. A relationship has its own particular subtle atmosphere of mood, interest, images, colour and texture, etc. We are familiar with sensing this atmosphere; when, for example, entering someone's home or room, we can often tell if there is lightness or heaviness between people before they say a word.

Just as each individual can evolve, so can each relationship. Where do we place our attention? Just on ourselves? Just on the other? Can we also attend to the shared relational field?

We need to care for the soul of our shared relationship as well as for each other as individuals. Might the grit of friction in our relationship, like in an oyster, create a "pearl" of radiance and durability?

ORDERS OF LOVE

Relationship is a dance of interaction, a play of two fundamental movements, towards and away from others. When we reach out to others, we say YES with interest, openness and energy: we want contact, relaxation, spontaneity and support. When we move away from others, we say NO, pulling back, protecting, rejecting, defending and fighting. It's important we can do both.

A romantic relationship often has three main phases: initial romance, settled togetherness and then deep commitment. We begin with feelings of "I fancy you, desire you, need you. I take you into my heart. You can have me completely. I love who you are and what you do for me." As a relationship moves into the second phase, we feel that "I love you and where you come from, everything that went into making you, your family, culture, past, child and partners who came before me." In the third phase, after many shared years together, we feel "I love you and wherever fate takes you and me."

Successful intimate relationships are characterized by an equal balance between the couple of both partners' needs, their give and take, their values shared. Adults bond over a thousand acts of exchange, cups of tea, conversations, considerations and sex, which is very bonding. In a thriving relationship, both partners refresh themselves outside of it, often with same-sex friendships.

However, conflict arises from time to time even in the best relationships. It is helpful to know that we all move between four types of feelings that have different effects on us and our partners:

Primary feelings, such as disappointment, gratitude or sadness, are honest, intense and temporary, and may be uncomfortable to admit but strengthening to express and resonant to others.

- Secondary feelings arise when we don't believe our feelings will be met with a helpful response. Instead there's chronic blame, anger or worry, often connected with past hurt. Expressing these feelings is weakening; there's a sense of stasis, a substitute for taking appropriate action.

- Systemic feelings show up in us but don't really belong to us. They may perhaps lead to us feeling unsafe, rejected, worthless or abandoned, or to have an impulse to start a family or to divorce. Due to an unconscious identification with an ancestor, these feelings may actually originate with someone else in the wider family system.

- Impersonal meta-feelings are not emotional but carry strength to act in a crisis, such as wisdom, courage, meta-anger and even cruelty, for example when a mother is moved to lift a heavy car crushing her child.

When we are in a relationship, we are in relationship with not just an individual but their family too. Happiness occurs when we include everyone in a family, honouring everyone, respecting those who came first, including previous partners, older children, elders and ancestors, acknowledging what they have given to those who come later – literally life, attention, guidance, gifts, money, etc. We also need to accept that feelings of guilt and innocence do belong to those who earned them, those responsible need to feel and own them, freeing others in the system from the burden of carrying what is not theirs to carry. These "orders" occur invisibly beneath the surface of relationships, as described by psychotherapist Bert Hellinger.[87]

From the shamanic view, an intimate relationship is a ritual that includes the upper world of souls, the middle world of everyday life together and the lower world of vulnerable and intimate secrets. A good relationship fully inhabits these three realms.

EVOLUTION FROM ENSLAVED TO EMPOWERED

There are three basic levels of human relating:

Chemical love

This is the simplest level, based on the hormonal secretions of the glands. This gives rise to the impersonal drive to procreate, where attraction is chemical and blind, and variety is seen as the spice of life.

Emotional love

This is about falling in love with another based on unconscious childhood survival strategies. The other is seen as an object who will help us to get our needs met. Such relationships of mutually entwined patterns of neurosis are demanding and controlling, involving love, hate and codependency.

Delicious love

This is empowered, genuinely vulnerable and freely expressive. It is based around considering what is best for the other, my lover. Delicious love is about allowing another person to be exactly and uniquely who and how they are. It is clear-sighted and respectful, with interest both in the other and in the self. It is based on qualities such as discipline, awareness, meditation and healthy lifestyle.

Delicious relationship occurs between two whole, fully-rounded and autonomous people, who can be independent and interdependent. My attention is caught right now by two people beautifully chatting in relationship next to me. Their quality of connection is palpable and spreads positivity. As an observer, I can feel the back and forth of the attention passing between them non-stop.

DELICIOUS INGREDIENTS

Deliciousness is a bringing of awareness to all of the ingredients of relating. It means relating with a positive intention for the best outcome for both yourself and the other, for everyone involved.

Freshness

Most of the time, we don't really perceive everything in our present circumstances; we rely on old ideas and assumptions, maps and labels, on what our parents told us, what we learnt at school, or what happened last year. It is not easy to have a good relationship when it is based on who we thought James or Fiona were five years ago, when actually, right now, they are somebody else entirely! How might it be not to define them based on past experience, but to see them again with fresh eyes, right now?

When we look afresh, we might see beyond society's ideas of attraction, perhaps to the raw data of their flesh, feelings and soul, maybe a wrinkle or pore, curve or hairiness, sensitivity or passion, and we might have no thought of "good" or "bad"; just as-it-is them.

We can begin to relate with the real them – not merely engage with information about them, such as where they were born, the colour of their eyes, their work, hobbies and opinions – but with them as they really are right now.

Allowing

Love is allowing another person to be exactly who and how they are without trying to change them to please yourself. If someone loves you, they will open themselves up to you. There is no need to intrude, manipulate or dominate, mother, father or baby them, demand or sulk. Simply be present in yourself and leave the other person alone to be themselves.

Generosity

Love is kindness, consideration, generosity to the other and for the other. It is not to forget oneself, but to attend to and give to the other, while at the same time being attentive and giving to self.

Responsiveness

A mature relationship is marked by its responsiveness to the other – by our openness, curiosity, consideration, care, trust and interaction. There is enjoyment, sincerity and authenticity: a real individual interacting with another real individual, both of us self-aware, unique and respectful. We are genuinely interested in the other, and we really want to know them, not fix them.

For a relationship to thrive, we need empathy, good contact and connection. We need to respect the other as a constantly unfolding person with their own experience, wants and needs. We keep on learning about ourselves and the other, both of us being real, respectful and responsive.

Vibrancy

There's a quality of immediacy, desire, pleasure and sensuousness; we are excited, nervous, vibrated and affected. We impact each other and are aware of this. Through our sensations, feelings, reactions and sexuality we affect each other's body and chemistry, creating a unique relational alchemy. Two people, attuned to themselves and to each other, will vibrate together, creating a kind of subtle energetic music.

Reflection

This means being constantly curious: what is this relationship? What is happening right now? I want to know myself with you – how do you feel with me, how do the two of us fit together?

We can feel our own delicacy in our responsiveness to the other, and the pleasure of our authenticity, energy, erotic nature, aliveness and love. Who am I in relationship with you? And now? And now?

Responsibility

When we rage and blame others, we give our power away, thinking other people have the agency in our life. We need to fully own our feelings. We all unconsciously generate responsive interpretations from the complexity of our internal life, and we are responsible for our own experience. Real authentic communication does take time and effort. The benefits are that it usually feels better – bothering to dig down to express what is really true – and it usually gets a better response.

124

Self

The quality of relationship we are able to have with others depends on the quality of relationship we have with ourselves. This does not mean becoming self-obsessed, but becoming familiar with the ebbing and flowing, rising and falling changeability of our experience! The more we are in good contact with the depths and widths of our own experience, the more we can be in good relationship with others. It's important to experience what you feel, need and want, and what you don't want.

HUMILITY AND DEEP LISTENING BRING RELATIONSHIPS TO LIFE

The art of relating is the art of really listening, looking and sensing the other. We are humble in relationship, affected by and affecting each other. Ancient Southern African *ubuntu* teaches, "I am because you are."

The art of creating a delicious life means recognizing we are all equals in responsive relationship. We are each an antenna of receptivity, sensing ourselves and the other, curious about what is going on in ourselves and in the other. It is a tuning in rather than zoning out. When we acknowledge the fundamental existential equality of everything, the body becomes relaxed and open, as does the heart, listening deeply to the vibrations of all of life around us.

Our language and mode of communication are different with each being. Not just with different humans, but different species. But how do we experience communication with an insect, plant or animal? If when a leaf brushes across our face, as we move a plant pot from the light of the window into the shadow, or away from its previously close-companion plant, and we feel a subtle fleeting sensation inside, a sense of not-quite-right-ness, might that be part of the way the plant is communicating with us? Once you know that, you can't just prune a plant without asking . . .

Relationships are embodied, and are about being in contact with our own body and with the body of another, listening not just from our ears and head, but with our whole bodies. Listening out to the other and to how we are impacted by them. Listening outside and inside. This moment I hear the sound within the silence. In relationship we listen to the sounds and the spaces, the place in their body where sound arises, the place in our body where sound lands and feeling arises in response. A real relationship is a balanced exchange of attention, interest and care between self and other. There is a constant exchange of information and communication. Sometimes it can be felt as a subtle, slow pendulum of attention, gathering data, swinging between those in the relationship.

We may think all communication is carried by the meaning of our words and gestures, but actually that's only a small part of the information we receive from each other in an interaction. Unconsciously we are sensing each other's bodies and our own body all of the time, making decisions and taking action based on somatic as well as rational information. Like everything in the universe, we communicate via vibration.

Relationships are vibrations. When we can tune in to ourselves and each other; we can really begin to vibrate in unison, both in resonance and in dissonance, to create beautiful music together.

MATHEMATICS OF RELATIONSHIP

Life is all about relationship and the creation of the new.

The whole is greater than the sum of its parts, said Aristotle.[88] Synthesis, integration and unity are both the potential and the "meaning" of sacred geometry – reminding us, in the mathematics and shapes of life, that the magic occurs in the meeting point between us, where everything is possible.

$$1 + 1 = 1$$

When ink meets paper, literally anything is possible. When two animals meet, who knows what will happen. Every moment, every interaction, is pregnant with infinite possibilities of final outcome.

When two people meet in relationship, a third entity is created, which is the relationship itself. As everyone knows, a relationship needs attention; it needs tending if it is to grow. It is alive itself, a new entity that emerged from two others. Two adults make a relationship. Two adults in relationship make a baby. The baby encourages the two adults to change, to hopefully become better people than they were before – more mature, focused not only on their own selfish needs, but united in care for the new third party in the relationship.

The same pattern repeats everywhere in nature. We can see it in the structure of the body, with two eyes, ears, nostrils, lungs, arms, legs and one nose, mouth, heart, stomach, womb, vulva or penis. We see it in the way we make love with each other, when two become one in pleasure.

The Seal of Solomon or hexagram, also known as the Star of David, is a symbol from ancient Egypt, India and Israel of two triangles, one pointing up and one down. These triangles, and also three-dimensional tetrahedrons, express in form masculine and feminine energies. They represent this plus that; two different things meeting in fresh creativity. These relational shapes are within the gestation of cellular life itself.

When masculine and feminine energies inside us are in balanced relationship, a mature "neutral" person is created, of greater perspective, calmness and love. Energy, glands, hormones and secretions become activated, creating a biologically enlivened "new" individual.

Life itself wants us to be in relationship. Life loves itself through every moment of relational interaction, from flirting, touching, lovemaking, all the way through to silent, distant and respectful communion. Life knows itself through every variety of relationship, every meeting of at least two, which gives rise to the creation of a third unified newness. Slow, felt, embodied relationships are a dynamic doorway to the pleasure, power and potential wisdom of the Universe of Deliciousness. Life loves Life.

You Are Not Alone [89]

Right now
Air is caressing your face
Water is awaiting your tongue
Warmth is at your back
And the earth is welcoming your feet.

The lavender plant outside knows you exist
The ants are grateful for the crumbs you drop
The kettle anticipates your frequent touch
And the apple in the bowl is ready for your bite.

You are seen and heard by the solid walls around you
While being a world of change for millions
of microorganisms inside your gut.

Parents dead or alive are wanting the best for you
Grandparents and ancestors are sending you blessings
down the family line.

Friends are speaking of you with smiles
pets are needing you
and a partner is loving you
(even if you've not yet actually met them yet)
The people you have helped along the way are grateful
remembering you, even if you've forgotten them.

You are related to those who are praying with hope
in their temples, mosques, monasteries, synagogues and churches,
those dancing the same message, others singing,
drumming or painting
some in the next street along
or on the other side of our circular world.

You are needed by the future that depends on you.

Breathe in and breathe out
we are all connected
Oxygen, carbon and hydrogen, our shared elements recycling
Loaned today for you to play.

Your body is built
from the foods you have eaten
made from the sun that shone and the rain that fell
and the insects that pollinated
and the farmers and the drivers and the shopkeepers too.

You are formed
by the impact of others
Close by, across the solid globe and the transit of time;
You are loved right now by the fullest most loving deeply empty
looking at you space;
Yes, you
Are known.

_____ Practices for Nourishment _____

Relationships are vital. Anaïs Nin, the French writer, said that each friend represents a world in us, a world possibly not born until they arrive, and it is only by this meeting that a new world is born.[90]

For mature delicious relationships, we need our whole body sense, our sensations, feelings and thoughts; awareness, curiosity and compassion; courage, sensitivity and love. It is a bad habit to neglect oneself while searching for another to give us the attention we want. What do you seek in relationship? Can you find a way to give this directly to yourself?

Our relationships can be enriched by including others in the interspecies interrelationship that is the world, including the full spectrum of data, physical, emotional and energetic.

Exploring the relational nature of life

As an experiment, imagine that everything going on around you is in some way connected. Ask a question and see what "answer" or "hint" might appear . . . Do you suddenly notice a van with something written on it, or words in a book, on a sugar packet, manhole cover, menu or shop front? Do you notice the lyrics of a song? Or do you suddenly "think" of something or does someone nearby say something that seems unexpectedly relevant? It's a fun way to open yourself up to the invisible network of connections all around you.

Coming into relationship

Is it necessary to physically touch someone or something in order to connect with them? There is a spectrum of contact, from a subtle energetic touch where bodies are not touching at all, all the way through to the direct physical touch of laying a hand on an arm or a whole-body hug, through to the intermingling of body boundaries in sexual intercourse. In all of these levels, there can be a fullness of contact.

What distance or closeness is appropriate with this person you are with now, in this moment? For yourself and them? Explore by moving your own hand closer to your other arm or slowly moving closer to whatever is nearby, a flower, cat, friend or lover. What do you feel? Do you notice different subtle sensations at different distances? When do you feel a sense of relationship? Can you trust that sensation? What happens in you as you move? Do you feel most relaxed at a certain physical distance?

Communicating love

We all communicate in different ways. How can we communicate and be best understood by others in relationship? According to Dr Gary Chapman, a counsellor and author, there are five universal languages of love: words of affirmation, quality time, receiving gifts, acts of service and physical touch. We each have a primary and secondary language, and we can enjoy all of them.[91]

Words of affirmation include "I love you" and compliments, while on the other hand criticism cuts deep. Quality time is all about giving your undivided attention, and being heard is important. Receiving gifts is a tangible and thoughtful means to make a person feel appreciated. Acts of service include lending a helping hand to show that someone really cares. Physical touch means everyday hand-holding, kissing and, of course, lovemaking.

What are your favourite love languages? What languages do you think someone else prefers? A person usually expresses love in the language they most like to receive. Can you match your friends, partner, children or parents with the love language you think they most need to hear? Experiment with giving compliments, attention, gifts, kindness and touch. The secret to a good relationship is generosity, however you choose to express it to another.

We can relate with others in many ways – in a glance, words, movement, dance, art, through silly sounds, music, touch, cuddle, throwing a ball, pushing each other, fighting, caring, lovemaking, in friendship, parenthood . . . In how many living languages can you communicate and relate to others?

Being safe and vulnerable

Our default setting is often defensive, sensibly closed to protect us from hurt; but that stance can isolate us, preventing real contact and connection with people with whom we would like to be close. In an intimate safe setting, we want to be able to be open and to show our sometimes vulnerable feelings. Can you drop the automatic mask of attitude and tension? Dare you risk showing your realness of feeling? Do you trust the other person to be interested, kind and gentle with you? Can you experiment?

This is not a blanket decision. It is a moment-by-moment choice, a calibration, according to the very particular circumstances in which you find yourself. Dare I voluntarily disclose how I am really feeling?

Dare I reveal more? How much might be too much? Am I safe to share here now?

Communicating directly

We need to be able to take care of ourselves, to sometimes say "no" and sometimes say "yes". We need to be able to sense into what we need, and to speak up and ask directly for what we want: for example, "I don't like this", "I do like this", "Please stop now", "Please continue", "I need to eat" and "I need to leave."

Your capacity for saying "no, slow down, not now, I don't like this" is really important. Practise saying "no" in various ways by yourself so you can feel fluent. Practise in small everyday situations. The ability to say "no" is like a muscle that needs to be trained. The more confident you are with saying "no", the more easily you will be able to say "yes". Practise also saying "Yes, I want you," and "I want you to want me."

It can take commitment and work to dig deeper to find your personal truthfulness beyond your daily habits. Not just the truth about who ate the biscuits, but the truthfulness about how you are feeling right now. Real intimacy is not about sex, or even about being good enough, but about sharing your personal and imperfect felt truth, whatever it is. When you feel safe in being truthful, even about something uncomfortable, then you usually feel more intimacy and pleasure.

Experiment with sentences that begin with the pronoun "I"; for example, I am feeling sad, happy, confused, awkward, delighted, sorry, frustrated, angry, sexy . . . Experiment with this in many everyday situations, so that you can become familiar and confident in expressing yourself. It is powerful self-management to be able to explain your situation clearly to someone else during a conflict, such as: I am angry and upset right now, but not with you!

Psychotherapist Virginia Satir suggests that couples practise their communication using The Daily Temperature Reading,[92] which is a short exercise to express your longing without making the other person wrong. Try creating a conversation that includes at least one of these approaches:

- An appreciation or excitement: I love it when you . . .

- A worry, concern or puzzle: I'm feeling afraid about . . .

- A complaint with possible solution: I'm frustrated, could we talk about/ explore/try . . . ?

- An update, some new information: I am going to . . .

- A wish or hope: I would love it if we could . . .

Connecting with delicious freshness

Sit with another person (although you can also do this exercise with a tree, cat or anything else). You can also do it with yourself in a mirror. Look at them (or yourself), just as they are, taking them in with a non-judgemental appreciative gaze as in an art class or when looking at a baby. The looking is acknowledging the object of your attention as it is.

Prepare for this relationship by descending out of opinionated mind. Follow the medicines, 1) slow vibrationally, 2) connect with your body sensations and 3) depth of feelings. Arrive now.

Looking is just looking. Seeing what you see, in front of you, exactly as it is. Let your attention be free. Notice where your interest goes . . .

Are you drawn (despite ideas of attractiveness) to the light in their eyes, delightful wrinkles by their eyes, their fabulous bushy eyebrows, red cheeks, uniquely shaped nose, lip colour or veined hands? What is alive in them? What do you appreciate?

Let this be concrete not abstract, physical not ideal, and real – this, here, now, you and me. Imperfect and delicious at the same time. Real physical, vibrant, raw, human person, furry cat or pine tree here and now, in this moment.

Avoid labels: not "this woman", "that tree", "those colours", good, bad, etc. But simply take it all in, imbibing the raw sensory data. Let yourself be informed by your impression of this mood, flesh and movement right now. There is no comparison or evaluation. Big nose does not mean "bad" or "unattractive". Wrinkles, grey hair or a bit of a bulge are similarly observations without interpretation. Simply focus on details of their actual specific physicality without judgement or translation into usual opinionated attitude. Just welcoming.

It is the difference between watching and looking, listening and hearing. A state of openness, a quality of innocence, receiving what is naturally visible – all beautifully real. It is delightful and satisfying to have permission, an invitation and time to be nourished through our eyes. It is also a pleasure for the person, animal or plant being looked at, to really be seen. Tiny details of freckles, pores, hairs and skin; curve of a breast, buttock, vulva or penis? Not looking in order to achieve or do anything, but looking simply because. This is a form of meditation, sanctification, honouring, awe.

Sensing the relational field

As we have seen, a relationship itself is a living entity; it has an aliveness. It can be fascinating and clarifying to tune in to not just your truth and that of the other, but also the subtle relational field between you.[93] Relationship is a sacred natural crucible for all of us to find out more about who we really are.

For this exercise, go through the process of slowing, connecting with your body and opening up to depth.

Set a timer and create a sacred space with a simple ritual opening and closing, such as ringing a bell and taking a bow.

Within an agreed timeframe of say ten to twenty minutes, both partners can explore their relating.

Look at the object of your attention; really look in their eyes, be curious about them, sense them . . . and at the same time stay with your own experience of your own sensations, feelings, thoughts, perceptions, images, memories and insights as these change: for example, "I am experiencing pain in my knees, a tightness in my left shoulder blade, sweetness in my heart . . ."

Allow time and space so that one person says one thing, pauses, and then the other may speak.

Notice how the other person impacts and affects you, and describe your response to them: for example, "After you said that, I noticed that I felt soft all over" or "I want to tell you that you can trust me."

Next, widen your perception, so you are aware not only of yourself and the other, but also of the "space" between and around you both. Is there anything in particular that you notice? Be open and receptive . . . Perhaps you perceive a particular colour or image in your imagination, or sense a mood, or maybe a reaction or a knowing. It's always a surprise what shows up as the truthful living nature of the relationship. You may see something in support of the relationship, the function of the relationship or that there is no interest in the other. There are unlimited possibilities. Each relationship is unique.

This is a kind of doing nothing together, of simply noticing what is arising with honesty, curiosity and respect. It means speaking of what you are aware is happening, within your own experience of yourself. "I can 'see' a red flower in the middle of the space between us" – "Yes, I can 'see' that too."

In this mutual exploration, there is a shared experience of the living relationship. We can both speak as "We are experiencing".[94] We are both here now, both sensing the same relational field:

"We are shy and feeling slow and gentle right now. We are melting and there is just stillness here."

Another different experimentation is to notice what you notice about the other person: how are they? Relaxed or tense? What do you notice about their body? What might they need? Is there any unexpected information about them? Something you try not to notice, a warning sign maybe?

What impulse is alive in you? How are you affected by being near to them? Do you want to know or touch more of them? Do you allow that impulse or restrict it? Do you want to share more of yourself, your thoughts, feelings and physical body? Do you feel safe and open?

Or are you uncomfortable and trying to please them? How do you act on your sense of there being an "off-note" in what they said or a discomfort in your belly? Do you ignore your intuition and carry on as usual? Do you freeze in fear?

Do you have an agenda, something that you want from that person, something you want them to give or do for you? Have you turned the other into a commodity? Do you feel they are not really seeing or hearing you, treating you as an object to provide them with ease or pleasure?

Are you in good balance, able to sense both yourself and the other? Do you feel that the giving and receiving between you is roughly in balance? Does one or the other of you dominate or control passively? Do you both feel that you are getting your needs and wants met? Is there more you want to "bring out" in the other? Perhaps more you would like to do for them? Do you need to stop them saying or doing something? Is this interaction complete for now? Is it time to leave it be?

Can you sense the movement of energy, a swinging of attention back and forth between you?

Clarifying relationships

Reflect on your relationships . . . What did you enjoy or not enjoy in relationship with your mother, father, siblings, teachers and schoolmates? What are your ideas about relationships? What did your parents believe about or long for in their own relationships? How were your early first romances?

Many of us don't really see reality as it is most of the time; we see projected images of our parents, schoolteachers and other childhood authority figures, rather than who and what is here with us now. We can often unconsciously see rejection, disapproval or judgement when there might be none.

It is good to "separate" from our images and to see the actual reality. It can be very useful to take a few moments alone quietly to imagine someone in front of you (or to focus on a representative object of them) and say aloud to them, "You are my . . . [partner; husband or wife; boss or employee], not my father, mother, brother or sister." This clears the relational field between you.

It is also useful to consider the gifts you have to offer to others through relationship.

Everything is in relationship. What is your relationship with yourself? Do you challenge yourself or indulge yourself? Which practices from this Medicine are calling you to include them this week?

What?	When and where?	How long for?	Done?

How are you, after a week of attending to your relationships with other people, things and beings?

THE INTIMACY OF PLEASURE

When someone is happy in an intimate relationship, they are open in their relationships with everything else – their relationships are relaxed, communicative, bright, interested and wise. In this way, relationship is a doorway into the universe. By fine-tuning our relational ability and heightening our sensitivity, we can sense people, animals, plants and places more deeply emotionally and vibrationally. We enter into a deeper intimacy with life.

When a relationship is built not on being "good enough" but on being "real", then it is delicious. Esther Perel, therapist and author, says that eroticism thrives in the space between the self and the other.[95]

The next medicine is pleasure. We are conditioned to think of pleasure in a relationship as being about sex and orgasm, but pleasure can be so much richer, wider, subtler and more profound . . .

When we bring our curiosity, authenticity and embodiment, life becomes deeply enjoyable, pleasure becomes quietly, deeply, satisfyingly delicious, in our intimacy and ordinary daily life.

5

Pleasure

the medicine of sensing

"We are hardwired from birth for sexual pleasure."[96]
Dr Christiane Northrup, women's health expert

"Beauty is truth, truth beauty."[97]
John Keats, physician and poet

"Soul is the source of the erotic."[98]
Roger Housden, spiritual writer

In the last chapter we discovered how a personal relationship is really a container for our evolution. Now, we are going to explore the reality of pleasure as something essential. Not a satisfaction that is caused only by gratification in external stimuli, and not just a distraction to wake us up when we are exhausted. Pleasure is our true nature.

What if pleasure is already here, intrinsic to our life, and simply waiting for us to notice it?

Pleasure has become conflated with sexuality and many of the other sensual pleasures have been forgotten . . . When, for example, was the last time you bent to smell a rose? Or appreciated a glorious sunset? Or really tasted your coffee? We all need a regular pleasure practice and I don't mean masturbation. I mean a practice of paying attention to the pleasure that exists. Our noticing reveals to us the pleasure that is already within us and all around us. And so we can relax. We can each find our own unique personal enjoyment of pleasure.

Unfortunately, most of us don't even have the basic five senses of touch, taste, sight, smell and sound fully open. We usually perceive only a fraction of what is really there. We saw in MEDICINE, chapter 2: Body, how

Rudolf Steiner described twelve senses, including touch, movement, balance, warmth, language and health. This is similar to Harvard professor Howard Gardner's theory of multiple intelligences,[99] which he developed in the 1990s. As we begin to open ourselves up to a broader concept of pleasure, how much more might we wisely enjoy?

Closely related to pleasure, sensuality is expressed differently in every part of the world: in Mediterranean Europe, it's found in the sunshine, sea, food and art. In Japan, it appears in sumptuous fabrics, gardens, spaces and a cultural sensitivity to energy. In Eastern Europe, there is a creativity of original colour and music. The French have a famously sexy approach to beauty, food and humour. In the Middle East, the approach is direct and open. Who are you sensually? What lights you up? How do you live your pleasure every day?

By exploring our pleasure, we create a positive vortex, sharing nourishment, enjoyment and satisfaction.

SELF-DENIAL

Let's start with where we are now. We often think of pleasure as something we really should deny ourselves. Best to work first, enjoy later! Yet in modern Japan some people have died from overwork. For most of us, pleasure has become a fleeting future reward for all our efforts, a carrot on a stick that we strive towards, something we then absolutely deserve, like chocolate, beer, shopping, a holiday or sex.

We usually push ourselves hard now, ignoring our bodies, in order to get the work done and gain that future treat. We abandon the experience of this moment in favour of an idea of a "better" future moment. Everything is done in order to get something else. Little is done for the sake of itself. As a friend once said, "I was treating myself well in order to get better, rather than just treating myself well."

As we push ourselves harder, faster and further, to reach the always just-out-of-reach future pleasure, our tension and frustration build up. We become addicted to the anticipated reward, feeling entitled and voracious in our hunger: we demand our expectation to be fulfilled, narrowing our focus and hunting it down! This attitude is exhausting and disrespectful to everyone involved. It creates the disharmony and dissatisfaction in relationships that many people experience. Even sex then becomes a form of stress relief! How did pleasure get to be so distorted?

SHAME AND HOLINESS

The essential wholeness of life in antiquity was divided by organized religions into either good or bad facets. Pride was encouraged in the elevated masculine – in the mind, rationality, work, territory, individuality, heaven, order and god; as opposed to the apparent shamefulness of the feminine with its associations with the body, Earth, pleasure, sexuality, instinct, inclusion, chaos and the devil. We became divided against ourselves . . . and against each other.

There have been many repressive cultures throughout history and around the world. Some Buddhists and Puritan Christians regarded pleasure as bad, dangerous, dirty and primitive. Variously, dancing, drinking, card-playing, and sexuality have all been seen as sinful. A woman's hair and legs (or, in Victorian England, even a table's legs) had to be kept hidden from view. In the Catholic Church, the litmus test for sin is still the question: did you take pleasure in it? Much of the world has an implicit understanding that pleasure must be limited or stopped in order to maintain the social fabric. We think humans are not to be trusted, and it's safest for us not to be embodied in our sensuality.

Often almost as soon as we notice pleasure, we squash it back immediately. We feel guilty.

We are afraid of melting, being undone, losing control . . . and where might it lead? To natural wildness! In this way, sexual pleasure has become separated from community life, hidden away in private bedrooms, relegated to the "pure" future-after-death-reward or the "dirty" across-town red-light district. Despite the constantly titillating sexual imagery, we have become cut off from ourselves and from what is going on in our bodies. We think this sad state of being is normal. We are a most unsensual culture.

The resolution of shame comes when we can understand that the body is not just the location of our pain, but of pleasure and the whole spectrum of experience too, and that it is all wholly and intrinsically holy.

PLEASURE IS POSITIVE

A holistic view of the body is healthy. In many ancient cultures, the body was respected as the site of fertility, gestation and birth, while sexuality was appreciated as a powerful and positive force. It was understood that the earth and sky made love and produced the crops. Ancient life was not perfect, but it did integrate the material and the spiritual, the feminine and the masculine, into one whole.

Pleasure is a natural positive feedback system. We are on the right track when we feel good! Babies and children naturally seek pleasure. Breastmilk is delicious and nutritious. Hugging and touching are delightful as well as reassuring. Nature's colours and fragrances show us which nutritious foods to pick. Sexual pleasure is a great encouragement to reproduce our species. Pleasure is our birthright, a whole-body experience of relaxation and expansion, aliveness, instinct, curiosity and interest, fully present and full of energy. When we are experiencing delicious pleasure, it often has a positive immediate effect on other people's bodies. We can all relax . . .

It can be a pleasure to witness another really enjoying themselves. Pleasure is magnetic. A child's laughter is contagious. Seeing someone absorbed in a physical or creative task is compelling. We can revel in another's sexual pleasure: what is good for me, is often good for us. We all benefit. Pleasure is a form of nourishment. It is something we need on a daily basis to be healthy.

How do we behave when we don't feel safe and don't have enough? We become cranky and try to grab some from others in a win–lose dynamic. Desire is a powerful force that needs to be honoured, contained and enjoyed. It can leak out in inappropriate ways, distorting from natural flow into greedy power-over-others dominance. We are seeing an uncovering of abuse within the Church, Hollywood and spiritual organizations. If pleasure is not allowed, it gets perverted. It is not that pleasure itself is perverse. We need to acknowledge the fundamental importance of pleasure.

SELF-AUTHORITY

Very few of us grew up with parents who were not complicated in some way around sexual energy. Children love to be in bodily contact with their parents and children sometimes touch their own genitals. Often this natural behaviour is interpreted by adults as being sexual, rather than simply sensual and wholesome, an in-the-moment exploration of feel-goodness in a child's own body.

As children, we have a real need to belong. We often give up our sense of what is right and good in order to fit in with the opinions of others in authority, such as parents, teachers, adults and priests. We need them to approve and validate us. The cost of belonging – to our family, school, religion or nation – can be a reduction in our enjoyment. We learn to follow the system's rules about goodness and pleasure, guilt and innocence, rather than our own.

Most children are taught that the locus of authority lies outside them. Adults frequently tell them they are "good" or "bad" to reward or punish them, and to reinforce what suits themselves. Being "good" often means fitting in and being deserving of social approval – it is not the same as being morally good. Children come to expect praise, and be disappointed if it is absent.

In this way, we learn as babies and children that pleasure comes from outside of ourselves. We confuse our childhood authority figures with the other people around us now. As adults, we often still hang on to our early fears of being "too much" for others, if we are as fully vibrantly and dynamically alive as we naturally uninterrupted are.

As adults, we need to discover that nothing nourishes us as much as our inner capacity for pleasure. We need space to viscerally experience our satisfactions and frustrations. To sense for ourselves our interactions and interface with the world. This is how we will create freedom from a false consideration of others and from external tyranny over our naturally wild soul. To reclaim our pleasure, we need to reorient our sense of authority from the outside to ourselves. Permission to experience life is given by us to us: we become the location of our pleasure, here in our own body.

SOOTHING AND HEALING

Pleasure is a natural mechanism for healing. Many delights such as pleasing art, music, food, conversation and loving physical intimacy are soothing and healing. Laughter is particularly good! When we are enjoying ourselves, we breathe more deeply than usual, thereby relaxing muscular tension, releasing the charge of our nervous system and expelling cellular toxins.

Cultivating pleasure is a healing habit that can be used to treat trauma. When we have been traumatized, the body cannot bear the excitation of the nervous system that is sexual pleasure. What we call orgasm is often a short-lived superficial sensation reached via tension and stressful pushing, to create the desired outcome of a genital release. However, when we are traumatized, it can often seem easier and safer to shut pleasure down, not to breathe or feel deeply, rather than risk opening an old wound.

Left unhealed, trauma inevitably leads to the creation of more trauma, expanding outwards. Healing trauma is therefore positive not just for the individual but the whole community.

Many ancient goddess temples healed traumatized members of their communities through sexual ritual, reuniting splintered minds and bodies. In Ancient Egypt, Greece, Babylon and the Mediterranean, the sacred marriage rite, the Hieros Gamos, was enacted at temples and shrines dedicated to the goddess known variously as Ennana, Inanna and Ishtar.[100] The priestesses were selected for their dignity, integrity and wisdom. They guided people from brokenness and pain into pleasure, in support of harmony, health, fertility and creativity. They empowered people to be in contact with the spiritual forces within and outside themselves. Today, without widespread public temples, it is for each of us to do our own healing work, and to release the historical, social and personal conditioning that dictates that pleasure is bad, dangerous or only a reward.

It takes courage to do the deep psychological work needed for healing. We need to face our hidden history, the family shadow and cultural taboo that was the force behind our repression. This can be embarrassing, awkward, painful and demanding to do. It is work only we can do for ourselves, to reclaim our powerful natural potential for instinctual, sensual and sexual pleasure. When we are happy, satisfied and relaxed, we transmit positivity, creating happiness and relaxation in others. We become a contributing part of a mutually uplifting and healing society.

ARISING IN RELATIONSHIP

Real pleasure occurs in relationship. It is from within the crucible of a relationship between any two things that pleasure arises. Pleasure is the alchemical texture of relationship. It can be a momentary or lifelong relationship with any two or more things – people, animals, insects, plants, objects, elements, sounds, smells, archetypes, sensations, feelings . . . anything at all! Every encounter, such as a hand on the earth or a gaze resting on a tree, is a potential source of pleasure. Every impression, every contact, every sensory exchange can lead to pleasure.

There is a spark of electricity, creativity and pleasure in the meeting between two. Pleasure comes from the authenticity of the contact between them. Real me meeting real you is such a pleasure. Pleasure is personal. It defies definition, categorization and measurement. It is undeniable.

THE CAPACITY FOR SENSITIVITY

We have a very sensitive nervous system, with a tremendous capacity to receive sensory data. The whole body is a receptor – a quivering, feeling, insightful and intuitive wild antenna. Like adjusting a radio to the stations we enjoy, we can fine-tune ourselves to receive a range of pleasurable input, to hear the different signals of various sensate frequencies and bandwidths.

To do this, we need to slow down and empty the noisy interference from our heads that disturbs our attention and our ability to truly feel and sense what is going on in our body. And at the same time, we need to increase our body's ability to be sensitive to arising sensations, feelings and more . . . We need to practise sensing the whole of our body, especially our pelvis.

In this way, we increase our receptivity not only to food, sex, drugs, drink and rock and roll – the obvious stimulants, in a narrow bandwidth – but to be sensitive to a much wider range of data input, such as beauty, energy and silence. To feel it, hear it, see it, sense it, know it . . . To be fully conscious.

Consciousness is not an abstract idea. Consciousness may lie beyond form, beyond multi-dimensionality, beyond emptiness and mystery, yet our way to experience it is through the very ordinary sensual fabric of body and being. There are many different kinds of sensual pleasures: sight, smell, taste, touch, sound and also the pleasures of clarity and insight, the accomplishment of something well done, the dynamism and flow of energy, physical movement, spiritual connection, and allowing ourselves to rest and sleep. Our capacity to attune to the full range of pleasure is a key part of our capacity to live well and wisely.

PLEASURE AND PAIN

We live our lives between two opposite experiences. These are not the socially cultivated axis of heaven or earth, and right or wrong – they are poles that exist viscerally and moment by moment, as we live in hate or love, no or yes, fear or relaxation, contraction or expansion, withdrawal or reaching out. Everything in nature opens and closes, breathes in and breathes out, sleeps and wakes, eats and shits. It is a universal pattern. This is the pattern of life and death, whether for insects in a bush or planets in the universe.

As we live in a polarized world, our experiences become overlaid with labels of good and bad. Yet there is nothing not ok about hate, contraction and resistance. Everything has its place and purpose. Fear causes us to tense, to compress into a smaller space, in an attempt to stop ourselves from feeling uncomfortable. Love causes us relaxation, openness, vulnerability, expansion, risk and excitation. Both are natural and necessary. Pleasure and pain and everything in between are part of the texture of life. The amount of vitality we have depends on the health and flexibility of our nervous system, and our ability to feel and conduct energy – an energy that is, in itself, neither painful nor pleasurable in essence. All spiritual paths, as well as some forms of yoga where postures are held for a long time, and some tantric practices, enable us slowly, step by step, to cope with more energy flowing through our body. Capacity for a higher electrical conductivity is an openness to life itself, and to our experience and response in this moment without attachment or judgement.

The same nerves in our body register both pain and pleasure.[101] With our breath we can convert an experience of pain into an experience of pleasure. The only difference is having enough breath. Breath is a transformer. More breath enables relaxation, energy flow and pleasure. When we are tight, tense and holding our breath, an experience or touch feels painful. Energy is stuck. When we relax, open and breathe, the same experience can move through us as pleasure.

Our capacity for experiencing pleasure is the same as our openness to experiencing pain. The way to experiencing more pleasure is not avoiding pain, but through the pain. This doesn't mean being horrible to ourselves but, with self-care, sufficient resources and awareness, opening to feeling some painfulness. Pain can then be transformed into pleasure.

When we squash our sensitivity to pain, we squash our capacity to experience everything, not just the experiences we don't want. We numb ourselves to both pain and pleasure. We need to learn to be vulnerable and to welcome pain in order to experience pleasure.

Fully feeling something, even if it is not a pleasant feeling, is often surprisingly pleasing. All of our personal histories contain things that were sad and painful. The only way to be free from something is to allow it to be present fully, to feel it, whatever it is – anger, fear, disappointment, grief. Enfolded within everything is pleasure; in the blackness is gold.

Pleasure is a jewel, a delicacy, a delightful treasure. We orient to pleasure through our senses, our eyes, ears, mouth and flesh, our breath and sense of the subtle just beyond the immediate moment. There is a depth of pleasure available at all times. Pleasure is deliciousness in the mouth, heat in the heart and sensation in the whole body.

MELTING IN BLISS

Contrary to our usual idea of contentment, pleasure and fulfilment as being caused by something or somebody outside ourselves, what actually gives rise to our pleasure is when we are in good contact with our own self. The truth is that what leads to pleasure within a sexual occasion also leads to pleasure in daily life. The same ingredients – there are only a small number of essential patterns in life and these repeat. The body is a map for living well; it shows the way to the treasure. During a sexual occasion, we trust the container of love, our agreement of relational respect, care and communication. We relate with another, sense our genitals and await pleasure. When a similar process is activated in everyday life, we can experience pleasure in the whole body and entirety of life. We enter the Universe of Deliciousness. These are the medicines we've been moving through.

Pleasure can become something that is not just genitally located, private and only for me. It becomes an aura and glow, a radiation of pleasure, illuminating not just your own body and life, but also those with whom you are in contact, those whose lives you touch. The energy of pleasure is felt by others even if they don't know what it is that is so lovely for them to feel when they are with you.

We could describe this way of living as being balanced, living with integrity and authenticity. It comes from a deep trust in the external universe as a place of fundamental goodness, combined with a trust in the value of our own internal universe too. It is a willingness to take responsibility and explore all that's arising here in this body-soul location, this dynamic, unfolding moment of sensate, feeling truthfulness, followed by the next moment.

It is a state and a process of personal evolution. When combined with other people living in the same way, with other beings, elements, archetypes and the Earth, it produces pleasure, wisdom and harmony for all, creating a sense of heaven on Earth, of literal paradise.

Exactly as I write this, I hear suddenly on a midwinter's day birdsong close by.

This way of life is the very opposite of genital friction-plus-fantasy, intimacy-avoidant adrenalized sex. It is the opposite of using the world and people in it as a masturbatory toy to satisfy narcissistic needs and wants. It is not selfish, greedy, destructive and isolated; it is soulful, connected, creative, productive and evolutionary.

I experience a pleasurable, melting, delighting, sensual and connected aliveness in different parts of my body and all over, when alone or with another. This sensation is not dependent on touch, but is a by-product of my living with integrity and embodiment. I sense this in my tongue, mouth, forehead, the perimeter of my head; my heart, back, whole body; vagina, anus, legs; and body perimeter at a distance outside and beyond my body. Like a flower opening petals, softening, expanding, dissolving.

Pleasure is a great, big, whole-body turn-on response to what is happening in life. It is this subtle, delicious, melting sensation. When it occurs, I know it is a positive response in me to what I am thinking and participating in, to my feeling, seeing, understanding, choosing. It is a clear green-light Yes! to proceed. Sometimes it is not even a subtle physical sensation, just a clear body knowing, a deep arising yes to another person or situation.

At other times, when my body hurts or is uncomfortable, when I become hard and defensive or collapse and shrink, it is clear my soul-body is saying, "No, please pause or stop here." This is a turning-away from a person or situation, a turning-off and switching-off.

Everything happening in the body is useful information. Everything is worth us noting it, and being interested. Taking a painkiller to dull the pain and pushing through not only worsens the underlying cause of the symptom, it ignores the message of wisdom that is attempting to reach you, as your soul communicates through your body to get your attention.

PLEASURE, TRUTH AND BEAUTY

Pleasure, truth and beauty are inextricably linked. They are different refractions of the same energy.

Often when I experience truth, I experience pleasure in my whole body. A subtle palpable satisfaction. A sense of density in the atmosphere, a gentle turned-on-ness in all my flesh. Often when I experience beauty I experience pleasure. And pleasure cannot be experienced without also a sense and an appreciation of the truth and beauty present.

Truthfulness is beautiful in a person. Truthfulness is very pleasing to observe wherever defensive fakery has been released and there is more of the person visible! When false unnecessary clutter is reduced, the essential is revealed – beautiful, truthful and pleasurable. Michelangelo described the process of carving as revealing the intrinsic sculpture already present within the stone. Healing, personal development and spiritual work similarly produce visible increases in gracious beauty and handsomeness in people. Someone who is truly in their body, no longer busy defending themselves and insisting others see them in a particular way, is a turn-on! It's very attractive to see a person living well in their skin and flesh. Someone who is honest, and who has digested and metabolized their history, has arrived in themselves.

THE PLEASURE OF LOVE

When someone is in love they shine. Their soul's glow is visible. Love flows through them without limit. When we are in love we feel expanded and euphoric, released into our true essence. The place in the body where we feel the heat is around our heart and solar plexus/lower ribs. It is to be in the middle of ourself, balanced between fiery self-expression and watery vulnerable intimacy. For a few moments, months or years, we feel suspended in a harmony of deliciousness. Our vigilance centres and nervous systems calm down. We are safe to open up and feel our true buoyant hugeness, the deliciousness of an ego-free state.

Intimacy is the most powerful form of pleasure we have. However, it can mislead us into conflating pleasure with our partner, to see them as an object responsible for satisfying us. The danger of the myth of romantic love is the expectation that all of our needs will be met for us by this one other person. A healthy relationship is built on a balance of needing the other and being independent of the other. The more we resume responsibility for our own happiness and pleasure, the more we enliven our intimate relationships, enhancing them with subtle variety, freedom and joy. Pleasure is an inside job.

BEING HERE NOW

If and when we can allow ourselves to be simply and truly in the present moment, we arrive at the healing heart of a relationship. We enter, as if through a portal, a deeper dimension of expansion. A realm of sensuality and pleasure where every detail is in high definition. It is a privilege to experience life like this. It seems – and we seem – precious and pure, rich and tender, brilliant, delightful and peaceful. It is a state of deep, deep relaxation; a level of reality that is always there but which we are usually too busy to experience. Or we are too tense to dare to allow ourselves to relax into this. The silence is loud.

There are no points of reference or labels. No categories of good or bad or adequate or anything whatsoever. When our heads are clear, we are free to really see and feel. Then, we can see the other as a delightful sensual landscape as much as a person named Judy or Jasper. We can really see! We don't know what we will see, as impressions reach us unbidden. We might be struck by the colour of their eyes, the detail of their pores, the colours and textures of their skin, the flash of light reflecting on a lower eyelid rim, the beauty of a wrinkle, the glory of a large nose or whatever else is right there in front of you. There might also be a smell or a touch.

It is a state of receptivity. An opening up, or an opening out, to receiving what is there. It is deeply respectful of the other, almost reverential (without any pompous self-glory or self-abasement). It is the stillness at the heart of the whirring world. A pause in directed action that allows us to take in, inhale, receive and respond to the full sensory impression. It is to be a screen, as it were, imprinted by the image or smell or touch or sound of the other. It is to be affected by another.

It is to know nothing, in the best possible way, in order to receive something directly.

PRACTISING RECEPTIVITY

We need to reawaken our body and remove obstructions to our innate sensual intelligence. Our genitals are not tools. We all naturally know what to do when we are in good contact with our body and our inner sense – our innocence, our organic inner sensitivity.

According to Lee Lozowick,[102] the approach to real relationship and pleasure is by "becoming Woman". I understand this to mean becoming more receptive. Many great spiritual teachings contain this essential approach to becoming more feminine in relationship to the divine. This means being open to receiving, rather than grabbing – our usual orientation to getting and having. Our capacity for receiving is our capacity for experiencing pleasure. The way to a really delicious relationship is to become more receptive. It is feeling worthy of receiving and a melting of tension, resistance and control.

Pleasure is often encoded within organized monotheistic religion where it can be turned into underground practices. The name of the Kabbalah, a Jewish mystical tradition, literally means "the receiving" and Kabbalistic texts discuss seven levels of pleasure. It is said that Jesus and Mary (who were of course Jewish) learnt sex magic in Egypt. Other cultures had different ways of expressing the wisdom of sexual pleasure: in India, it manifested as tantra, while the shamanic nations had the sacred spirituality tradition of Quodoshka.

Ancient Vedic texts describe the universe and everything in it, including us, as being made of bliss. Can we imagine the food is deeply wanting to be eaten, at the same time as we are wanting to eat it? Bliss is our underlying nature, discoverable through a focus on this moment of experience.

When we attend to our own inner experience in our intimate lives, rather than being distracted by fantasy, to-do lists or resentments, our capacity for sexual pleasure here and now increases . . .

Sexual Pleasure

The way in which we have sex is often a limited version of sexuality. Many of us sense that sex holds untold mysteries, delights and opportunities, and that we have mostly tasted only surface froth. We are collectively hungry for more, having been collectively repressed for decades and centuries, if not millennia . . .

When Adam and Eve bit into the apple they experienced a loss. We fell from naturalness into socialization, from unity into fragments, divided against ourselves and each other, into so-called "good" and "evil". We now live in a world of either/or, upper and lower, better and worse, left and right, profane and sacred, secular and religious, sanity and madness, have and have not . . . We have lost our connection with the whole.

Today, sexuality has become the stuff of collective repression, sold back to us through promising advertising images, for products we then want to buy. We are a sexualized culture but we are the least sensual, embodied and happy that we have ever been. The modern sexual encounter often leaves people feeling disembodied, alone and unsatisfied. We may be fornicating more, but we are feeling truly pleasured less.

False ideas around gender and sexuality begin with thinking that men are powerful and women are not. The cultural Western myth claims that if women dress sexily and create a beautiful external image, they will have power over men, who will lust over them. But in their efforts to become the image they think they ought to be, women lose their own natural power and become disconnected from themselves. The artificial concept of "sexy", rather than real sensual sexuality, has become increasingly prominent in the world, especially in advertising; it is a hollow construct, a standardized uniform!

It is not true that women are responsible for what happens to men sexually. It is not true that men cannot control themselves and must have a release. It is not true that men are more interested in sex than women. It is not true that women's sexuality works the same as men's but is somehow a lightweight version of it.

In our search for increasing sexual satisfaction, we often increase stimulation in order to increase excitement: more online images, technical toys with higher speeds or fancy outfits! But these things can stress and numb the nervous system, making it less sensitive to people, touch and experience. The way to increased sensation and satisfaction is through less striving. Sex is not just about friction and excitement. It is potentially a meditation, a union of mind and body that opens up our head, heart and belly centres, and which in turn opens us up to the spiritual dimensions beyond.

Sex and intimacy require of us an extreme vulnerability and trust, both in the other person and in our own sexual response. Each of us responds in a unique way, unlike anyone else. We may all have similar sexual parts, biology, physiology, psychology and desires, but these are organized in our own highly personal way.[103] We are all beautifully, amazingly normal and, at the same time, quite different from each other.

Yet we all have the potential to be a cracked-open, heart-blasting body attuned to sensation, our head silent. At one with delightfulness. We can be fully and deeply with ourselves and with another. A communion of two unified beings. An experience of unity, consciousness and pleasure, emptiness and fullness, genitals and heart, person to person, is possible for every single one of us.

The body is where it all starts. Someone who is alive in their flesh, awake to themselves and not just themselves, is very attractive. Someone who is at home in their own body is a turn-on! That is what we all really want – not prettified or muscled vacant zombies, who look good but "taste" bad!

We are often surprised by who we fall in love with. We can have mental ideas and even lists of what we think we want – but this is often not the same as our bodily and soul's response to somebody's smell, shape, colour, texture and movement. Attraction is a specific response to this physical person now. After all, touching flesh that is unoccupied and unresponsive is not much fun. Far more pleasurable to touch flesh that feels, senses and responds, that is sensitive.

The physical body is a temple for devotion to our own experience, the other and beyond, where pleasure and energy engage us, unfolding, discovering, adventuring, relaxing both me and you. There is physical touch on the physical body and energetic touch in the energetic fields. Desire, feeling and creative imaginary play. An art form with many creative aspects and powerful energy!

In sexual intimacy, what really helps to increase pleasure is all that we are discussing in this book: slowing down, connecting with body, opening to trust in the loving depth and your current partner in relationship. This will enable pleasure and satisfaction to be felt. The more that you can practise these in everyday life, the more accessible they will be for you during a charged intimate occasion.

There is a world of difference between acting on the wilful "I want" and "obedience" to spontaneously arising information of body and being – between eating, having sex and sleeping out of defensive habits to relieve fear and tension – and being alive in response to the scintillatingly sensate soul in this moment. Good lovemaking happens when each of us can express moments of assertion and surrender. We need both energies: that of courageous, playful, bold, perhaps planned-in-advance thrusting, and also receptive, merging, passive, gentle, responsive unknowing. The combinations of strength and trust within us and between us create endless possibilities of interplay, all delightfully delicious.

Sex can be a wonderful sensual exploration, a mysterious soulful adventure. Delighting in our innocence, each sexual occasion can become unknown, fresh and new.

How might it unfold for you?

TOWARDS DELICIOUS INTIMACY

Instead of adrenalized sex stoked by the mental excitement of images on a one-way street towards an end-goal of explosion and collapse, the way of delicious pleasure is towards an oxytocin-fuelled sex of connection, care and love. Adrenalin is the hormone of fear and action. Oxytocin is the hormone of love, bonding parents and baby, and also bonding lovers.

Most men learn their sexual repertoire as young men, repeating the kinds of touch that worked to turn on their own bodies, and that have worked on the lovers they have previously met. Men can have an A, B, C and then D approach, an agenda that prevents them from really seeing and sensing the individual specific person in front of them. Often women are naturally more sensitive and attuned to their whole-body experience than men, but of course each individual is different, and each gender, sexuality and situation is quite unique.

It is important to learn how you yourself operate: what turns you on, what excites or delights you?

Desire is responsive and multilayered rather than a linear sequence of activities. It is a subjective and individualized combination of physiology, psychology and emotion. It includes arousal, but is much more than that too . . . To me it feels a bit like diving into the water. Or diving into the flesh. Flesh as imbued with intelligence, consciousness and aliveness. A non-judgemental, non-thinking approach.

To expand your own repertoire, learn what it is to become fascinated with each other. On one occasion, it could be the neck of your lover that you are fascinated with; at another time perhaps the knee, foot, waist, hair or any other body area that catches your attention. Become interested in everything, feeling and sensing, licking and touching, seeing and smelling, stroking and spanking. Be curious about the other's response to your touch there; to the shape, colour and texture of that part of the body; to the way this area feels to you as you touch it. To the taste of it, the sense of it, the hairiness of it, the smoothness of it, the delicious details of the part to which you are right now devoted.

As you discover their body, you are discovering their soul. As you are touched, you are sharing your soul with them. Through the heart, through devotion and attention, we connect deeply, and enter the Universe of Deliciousness.

Sex is powerful, irresistible and ensures life's continuity. It is the highest and humblest spiritual act, a universal movement. Love rests on equality of desire. Sex is a product of the connection, the conversation, the relationship between two people. Intimacy is not sex, intimacy is sharing authentic truth. Can you be vulnerably honest with each other? Can you hold each other safe? The quality of the sexual connection is an extension of the quality of the emotional connection.

There is a huge difference between using the other person as an object to satisfy one's genitals, and enjoying a whole-body sense of pleasure, which is delightful for the other person to sense too. This is not about another's orgasm being prideful evidence of our attractiveness and skill, enabling us to put guilt aside and enjoy for a few moments our own orgasm. No, absolutely not.

ORDINARY ADRENALIZED SEX	DELICIOUSLY CONNECTED OXYTOCIN INTIMACY
No consideration of who and how we are.	Be a human. A lover with joy, generosity, playfulness and kindness.
In a rush...	Cultivate gentle, caring, calm togetherness. A friendship as foundation is a good start. Create space where you feel safe to be vulnerable.
Without a foundation of good basic communication.	Take your time to talk. Check your communication channels are fully open – that you can both say yes and no to what you want or don't want. You can share your fears, loves and desires.
Careless.	Create a dedicated time and space for your honourable and precious physical intimacy.
No preparation.	Prepare to greet your beloved with perhaps a dance to awaken your body or a bath to relax.
Strategic exchange of affection for sex.	Offer authentic appreciation and soothing touch, inviting your partner to feel safe and relaxed.
Cool sex.	Encourage loving-heart connection through attention, praise, extended eye contact and kissing.
Man anxiously pursues his orgasm.	Man knows the pleasure in containing his desire. There are many ways of experiencing pleasure. His partner is free to be, experiencing her timing, feeling and sensation.
Pretence to impress.	Authentic, vulnerable, surprising, personal and fresh expression, feeling sadness, shyness, anger, pleasure... be as you are...

ORDINARY ADRENALIZED SEX	DELICIOUSLY CONNECTED OXYTOCIN INTIMACY
Expectation of man to deliver pleasure to woman.	Both partners are responsible for their own pleasure. An exchange of giving and receiving, while the giver checks-in frequently: "Like this?"
Interested only in self.	"Show me... " Be really curious to know the other essentially. Ask without words for your partner to show themselves to you as Man or Woman. Feel willing to show your own raw, primal being.
Stab in the dark.	Learn the anatomy of woman and man. The pleasure areas such as clitoris, G-spot and cervix, of glans and prostate.
Transactional exchange, tit for tat.	Touch the other as a sensual meditation, sensing into your sensate experience of their experience.
Urgency and tension for dominance and orgasm. Everything is a goal-oriented rush to reach orgasm. Most of the sensual touch is considered foreplay, not part of the real act of sex, intercourse. Sex often finishes with the man's orgasm.	Slow the dance of contact down greatly, with the emphasis on connection, communication and experience, rather than end-goal result. Seek and find the pleasurable sensations and experience in each touch and moment.
No especial attention to seeing the other person.	Take the other fully in, fresh in this moment. Open all of your senses: look to really see them, smell, listen, feel, touch, sense, taste them... Greet all of their body with all of yours.
Ignore whole body, only notice genitals/chemicals.	Listen to your whole body, to what is "required".

ORDINARY ADRENALIZED SEX	DELICIOUSLY CONNECTED OXYTOCIN INTIMACY
No especial attention to one's own breath.	Breathe more than you usually would, in order to increase sensation, activating the nervous system and energy channels. You can try breathing with an almost closed mouth as if sipping through a straw or with a wide-open mouth. Emphasize the exhale.
No especial attention to movement; often mostly either silent or performance movements.	Move more than you usually would, not as performance, but arising with your own natural impulses.
No especial attention to sound, often mostly silent.	Express your pleasure as sound or noise.
Confusion.	Be clear if giving touch is for your pleasure or the pleasure of another, if receiving touch is for your pleasure or that of the other. Practise asking: "May I... ?" "Yes, I will." "Will you... ?" "Yes, you may." Get this in an embodied way in your hands.
Focus is only on orgasm.	Allow yourself to flow, to unfold, one moment leading into another arising, like a painting, piece of music, dance, banquet or fragrance... Include conversation, song, dance, reflection, humour and imagination within the sexual occasion.
Non-stop humping action.	Pauses are fantastic to "gather" awareness. Can pause to chat.
Domination and manipulation.	Conscious power play. Surrender into each other.
Sense of separation.	Synchronize through head, heart and belly centres. Connect via foreheads, eyegaze or mouth contact. Breathe together in rhythm infused with heartbeat. Genitals are connected (but you don't always have to be face-to-face).

ORDINARY ADRENALIZED SEX	DELICIOUSLY CONNECTED OXYTOCIN INTIMACY
Tension and drive to release stress.	Relax into subtle-body conversation and exchange.
Eyes closed to focus on genitals.	Eyes open to see the heart–soul universe of the other.
Sex is primarily about the genitals.	Full-body use of your hands, eyes, mouth, hair, ears, arms, legs, feet, back, belly and all areas in lovemaking.
Breathing accelerates as excitement mounts.	Slow breathing and movement as excitement mounts – massage around genitals is relaxing.
Sex is intercourse.	Extend foreplay not just as a starter before the main event of penetration, but as an integral part of the oceanic ebb and flow of the lovemaking dance.
Repetitive sexual menu.	Experiment with sex becoming more playful e.g., sex from God rather than God from sex, so instead of hoping sex leads to enlightenment as an end-goal, try trusting all experiences are given to us from God and are a part of God. Play with extending or reducing the timeframe; explore a variety of archetypes; exaggerate polarity to increase erotic friction by playing with feminine/masculine and light/dark; experiment with talking dirty. Communicate what you like and don't like.
Fixed identity, dominant or submissive.	Open to the delightful interplay of energy – at different times both can embody the masculine or feminine, light or dark energy within the exchange.
Distracted.	Let the energy move you... let the sex be sexy...

ORDINARY ADRENALIZED SEX	DELICIOUSLY CONNECTED OXYTOCIN INTIMACY
Seeking psychological/narcissistic strokes.	Attend to and serve each other, adore each other. Lovemaking demands total attention. Devotion...
Wanting to "get" something for self. Man leads without awaiting her cues.	A man is to support, acknowledge, await and sense her, let her know how beautiful and alive she is. Her body will then lead the way for him to follow... Let the man adore the woman, so that she opens and leads the man... He leads in order to follow.
Usually when sexual intercourse is taking place, the mind is full of chatter. When verbal intercourse is taking place, the mind is full of genital intercourse.	Sensual meditation on the immediate moment. Communion with the god if you are a woman. Communion with the goddess if you are a man.
The female often seeks her masculine in the masculine other – and vice versa – instead of balancing essential energy inside ourselves.	In sex, the woman ascends from physical form into consciousness, and the man descends from consciousness into physical form. This is union. They alchemically exchange fluids and energies. Then the sexes disappear, higher glands are vitalized and greater creativity can be accessed.
Isolation and exhaustion.	Enjoy each other's pleasure, take-it-in enhancing and amplifying, generating delight and rejuvenation. Rest together in afterglow.

THE GENEROSITY OF DELICIOUS PLEASURE

The Delicious way is to really feel what we are feeling in the moment, whatever it is, whenever it is. It is not about acting out or suppressing our feelings, nor is it about trying to change those feelings or changing ourselves. Our task is to acknowledge, feel and experience the sensate feeling exactly as it is, in our body right now . . . To explore, accept, express the feeling, to have it for ourselves alive right now . . .

We do that in the steps we have taken here, SLOWing right down, sensing our BODY, trusting the true DEPTH of life, and feeling ourselves in RELATIONSHIP with the world . . . The pause is the space within which we can fully feel, rather than pushing outwards or squashing ourselves back. Without the "danger" of acting out or suppression, we gain a freedom to allow ourselves to have the full spectrum of feelings and experiences that we actually are. Nothing needs to be excluded, everything is to be included. Everything that we are is very OK. It is all just a feeling adventure.

When we include everything, the essential energy of the feeling is freed and any charge associated with the feeling is released. The pure energy of the feeling can be deeply felt, bringing us alive with vitality and dynamism, and with flowing, intelligent pleasure. Life becomes an immersive experience more interesting than any film or computer game, full of sensation, sensuality and significance.

In contact with the presence and energy of pleasure, life is a delightful interplay, for us and others. Pleasure is magnetic and contagious. We allow our flesh and nervous system to be vibrated by both our own internal arising pleasure and by the external other's pleasure radiating outwards. In this way, we are destroyed and recreated by the emanations of pleasure, the melting yet restorative delight that our cells love to bathe in.

If love is light, pleasure is all the colours of the rainbow and all their possible refractions and patterns. Pleasure is expansive. Even hours later, when walking in the street, a random passer-by can sometimes feel the subtle pleasure emanating from you and flash you a smile. There is a joyous divinity in embodied pleasure.

THE EMBODIED ENCOUNTER WITH PLEASURE

Embodied pleasure takes place at the surface of eyes to eyes, forehead to forehead, kiss to kiss, heart to heart and genitals to genitals; and at the depth of individual souls in relationship, destroyed and created again and again, in touch with the delight of the great constantly expanding width, breadth and depth of the Universe of Deliciousness.

Form and formlessness, winking in and out of existence, again and again and again, enacting the cosmic patterns of lovemaking, creation and death, at every level – individual, family and eternal. Pleasure endures throughout time, a qualitative experience that cannot be destroyed, that communicates forever the possibilities of fully embodied and enheartened living, ensouled and on Earth.

World without end. Just Love.

Delight communicates onwards in forms enriched by the experience and as traces of the energetic experience lingering in the air of the galaxy for others to breathe in and continue . . . Grounded ecstasy refracted in every direction and dimension forever and right now – you and me, us turning inside out with gratitude, respect and passionate love.

Love Making Love

Once upon a time there was a beautiful dawn
It stretched its paws up and down,
to the sides and back and felt the place there was.
And the world was born out of sensual lovemaking
the moment before.
It stretched and felt around the place it now occupied.
Yes, limits. That is good. And colours. Very good.
Oh, what fun to play . . .

Every moment something new is born.
From each thought springs live the very thing
we feared or dreamt or wasted our time
complaining or fantasizing about.
What lucky lucky creatures we are
able to create and create every moment.
To touch each other and create.
The erotic is probably the best fun in the whole world.
To touch and smell and taste and feel and sense and see and hear
and those waves of close on ecstasy
and fucking with our cunts and hearts and cocks
and nipples and hands and eyes and mouths and ears.
Yes with our ears. Every bit of us involved.

Making love is the dynamic of life.
Interaction. Exchange. Impressions.
Everything is making love with everything else.
It is all interaction, heart, touch and imagination.

_____ Practices for Fulfilment _____

Real pleasure is not selfish – it is wise. It is about relaxation, emptiness and fullness. The health benefits of pleasure as a wide and subtle whole-body sensuality in everyday life have not yet been measured, but without doubt exist. The health benefits of orgasm are already proven. We can imagine our sensitive, sensual body as a stringed musical instrument. When we are in tune, everything in life can "play" us, creating vibrant melodies, the music of pleasure. We are each responsible for tuning our own instrument. Can your "strings" vibrate freely? Can you feel the pleasure in this moment?

Rest in the arms of compassion

Imagine yourself sitting inside a big, round chair covered in soft emerald-green velvet or visualize yourself lying on a lush green lawn or in the middle of a field.

Feel the gentle softness of the green envelop you with loving-kindness, compassion and forgiveness, melting away self-criticism and self-judgement, regrets and embarrassments, shame and tension.

Feel embraced by the green. Pleasure is natural – as natural as nature, of which you too are a part. Whatever your experiences, you are accepted and acceptable; you can simply be, exactly as you are. Pleasure is goodness, and you are essentially good, worthy of enjoying relaxation, sensual delight and sexual pleasure.

Know and repeat this: I am essential goodness living this life. I can enjoy it fully.

Discover how relaxation opens you up to feeling more pleasure

Doing things with less effort is relaxing, opening up space in us to enjoy more pleasure. In what ways can you simplify? How can you do your work, parenting or gym class with less pushing, striving effort? What can you remove so there is more empty space to be filled with pleasure? Try decluttering at home or at work and enjoying the pleasurable effect of less is more. Try a physical detox. Can you experiment with doing things with 10, 20 or 30 per cent less effort? Experiment with everyday activities such as picking up a cup, walking, sitting and answering the phone. What is the least muscular effort you need to engage in order to do the task? What do you find when you turn the tension level down? Try relaxing one part of your body and seeing how that affects you as a whole. Try raising and lowering your shoulders, or shaking your jaw loose, or moving your pelvis. Is there more pleasure?

Experiment with how you switch pleasure on and off

With a friend who agrees to explore this experience, decide who will first be the "giver" and who is the "receiver". This is an experiment in discovering that pleasure and pain are actually the same energy in the body. One at a time, press a spot on the sole of the foot, or on an arm, that gives a tolerable level of pain. The "receiver" tries to breathe more than usual and to relax as much as they can. What do you notice? Do you perhaps feel the sensation change from pain to pleasure? Now swap roles.

You can also experiment with a pleasurable touch and notice how tensing dulls the sensation, while relaxation increases the sensation. What do you discover?

This is one of the ways of working I use with clients, having learnt it decades ago as the Grinberg Method.

Return to your senses

The colloquial expression "to return to your senses" suggests sensuality is sane and sensible – as opposed to us being in a state of shock, out of contact with our body and out of touch with information from our senses and sensibility.

There are simple ways we can return to our senses, such as by paying attention to sensing. This is an ancient practice. The tantric sutras encourage us to notice listening, looking, breathing, feeling, imagining, tasting, stopping, our weight, space, objects, darkness, stillness and lovemaking.

Can we enjoy the unexpected pleasure of experiencing everything in life, whatever it is – love, fun and joy, difficulty, hatred, disgust and discomfort or destruction, dung piles and insects?

For now, simply enjoy exploring your senses.

Taste

This sense is essential. It's one of the first things we explore as babies when we put objects into our mouths in order to find out about them. We have many nerve endings in our lips, mouth and tongue. The tongue is covered in thousands of papillae, each of which contains hundreds of taste buds, with a hundred taste receptor cells that respond to sweet, sour, bitter, salty and umami flavours. The mouth notices spiciness, coolness, tartness, metallic tastes, chalkiness, starch, temperature and fat.

The nourishment we receive is an alchemy of what we eat and how we eat, rushed or relaxed. What do you love to eat? What makes your mouth water in anticipation? White tablecloths and candles? Glistening juicy steak, sweet roast chicken, delicate fish, fresh green cabbage, buttery potatoes, courgettes and asparagus, with dark chocolate pudding or shiny pear and almond tart with crisp pastry, white wine or whisky? How does your mouth feel as you contemplate this? Practise bringing attention to your eating – savouring, relishing, delighting in the taste sensations.

Smell

This sense is instinctual and primitive, connected to survival, memory, food, danger and sexuality. Smell is transmitted from the mucous lining of the nose to the olfactory bulb in the survival part of the brain, which communicates directly with the emotional part of the brain.

We rely on smell to tell us about atmosphere. Anxiety, relaxation and pleasure have different smells.

What do you notice as you walk into a room? Does that deal or organization smell right?

As you come close to kiss people hello, do you like their smell or not? Are they sweet or sour, bitter, rancid or salt of the earth? Each gender has a smell and a woman's smell changes with her fertility, while everyone's smell indicates their health, diet, hygiene and mood. Someone pretentious can smell bad, while someone honest smells sweet.

My favourite smells include roses, lavender, cigar smoke, tarmac, hibiscus, cows, horses, apples, roast chicken, raspberries, wood smoke, ocean and pine trees . . . What are a few of yours? Notice the increased arousal in your nose, the pleasure in the act of smelling, as well as the smell.

Touch

This vital sense is deeply connected to feelings. Love, security, nurture and trust are conveyed through contact. Without it babies would not survive. In her 1975 book *The Continuum Concept*,[104] Jean Liedloff describes how the babies of the Yaquana Indians of Brazil are swaddled by their mothers for their first year of life, which makes them feel as if they are still in the womb, to help them to become calm compassionate adults. Similarly, many African mothers massage babies to "finish them off" by creating new neural connections.

Hands want to touch, enjoying shape, texture, temperature and more. The whole of our body contains receptors that sense temperature, pressure, vibration and threat, and which inform the body's ability to move in space. Can you feel the air on your skin, your clothes on your body, your bottom and thighs on the chair? How do you like to be touched? Notice the pleasure of the mouth kissing, the body riding a horse, swimming in the sea, playing tennis, climbing a mountain, receiving a massage, being cuddled . . . What do you like to touch? Tree bark, flower petals, feathers, a stone? Notice your palm and the length of your arm; do you feel awareness, arousal and pleasure? Do you want to reach out? Has your breathing changed? Your heart?

Hearing

The outer ear channels sound – vibrations of air – towards the eardrum, which shakes three small bones in the middle ear. This sends vibrations to another membrane, which rocks liquid in the spiral inner ear, with different frequencies reaching different locations and the vibrating hairs there sending data to the brain.

Our ancestors relied on their hearing for protection, surrounded as they were by elemental sounds, winds blowing, rain falling, fire crackling, hooves thudding, wings flapping, creatures crawling and insects buzzing. They also participated in collective listening to communal storytelling and music. We likewise need to tune in to the ordinary sounds of external life, of birds calling, washing machine spinning, train rumbling, door creaking, voices talking, keys jangling, phone ringing, furniture moving, dog barking . . .

Conversation is food, and we make love with words, where ideas rise, fall and are exchanged, enriching each other . . . interplay of silence and sound, rhythm and repetition. . . When we humans greet each other, the rise and fall of our voice sounds just like animals meeting. This is what David Abram observes in *The Spell of the Sensuous.*

Can you imagine yourself as an animal listening out to all the various sounds of the environment? Can you let sound come towards you, hear it without labelling it? Raw auditory data of planes and cars, kettle water heating, keyboard keys clicking. How do you respond? Can you hear the silence?

Sight

We discussed earlier in this book how we modern people are very visual, our eyes hard and our gaze evaluating as we check, scan and judge. We are used to being fed a non-stop stream of images on devices and billboards. But how much do we really and truly see? Sight occupies a big part of our brain, but we have forgotten how to really see each other, to be affected and impacted by what we see, to take it in . . .

Do you rush past that person on the street or serving you in the supermarket, or do you really see them? When was the last time you really looked at your lover, child or boss? Can you see the beauty of the sky, the sunrise or sunset, the plants, the architecture? Can you focus on looking at one thing at a time for a few seconds or longer? What do you see when your eyes go blurry?

Can you bring your attention to what is in front of you right now? Can you look at the shapes, colours, textures, shadows and light? Can you shift your perspective to see things in the distance, middle ground and foreground? What changes for you as you start to really look?

Take a moment to sense with all your senses combined: how do you respond now? Over the next few days, notice how your enriched sensing practice affects your body in everyday life – is it richer?

Sex is a challenging core dynamic for us all, which engages all our senses. For delicious lovemaking, a combination of charged initiation with trusting relaxation is needed. Are you "allowed" to be aggressively separate? Are you "safe" enough to receive and merge? It's an area worthy of our attention if we wish to develop it from being an automatic reaction to a sophisticated practice.

Throughout history, people have experimented sexually. Ancient polytheistic cultures had fertility stories, rites and rituals and, as we have seen, later monotheistic cultures developed underground sacred sexuality wisdom traditions. Today there's an explosion of workshops, sessions, festivals and parties, opportunities to explore conscious sexuality. While there are some excellent facilitators, there are also some dodgy, dangerous ones. Do explore and do take care. (More about this later in the Resources section.)

Prepare for pleasure

In a long-term relationship, we are often tired with managing the demands of work, children and life . . . which means that sex can become the last thing on our to-do list, eventually becoming stale.

Try a little preparation: make yourself ready physically beforehand by bathing and wearing clean underwear.

Then include a surprise element to freshen things up. What would you like to gift your partner? What would you like to explore? Don't plan it all – introduce just one new element – and discover how you both might like to play spontaneously with the surprise. For example, try involving the use of berries or chocolate, a feather, a rose, velvet scarf, an eye mask, fragrance or warm oil. What might you both do with that?!

With mutual consent, perhaps introduce a new sex toy? Or a whip for lightly bringing about a different kind of sensation? What about dressing up in a tail and cute ears, a smart suit or dress with high heels?

Or how about making love in the kitchen instead of always the bedroom? Or outdoors (if it's warm enough)?

Would a different kind of music or beat add something to the occasion? Candles? Can you dance for your partner? Would you like to offer a no-strings massage that they can simply receive? Might you write a loving sensual poem or song for your partner? Is there a part of your body you would like to touch them with? Or a part of their body you would like to touch? How generous can you be?

Create a special beautiful book and/or box where you can secretly store any sensual elements as and when you think of them, to be taken out and played with at some unknown time in the future.

Have flexible fun

The Universe of Deliciousness is not one thing. At different times, it can be any heartfelt point along a spectrum of variety. It can range from being delicate, refined, loving and sweet, to passionate, intense, wild and full of desire.

When relationship and sexual roles become fixed, and one pursues and one plays the pursuer, things always become boring quickly. We need variety, playfulness, change, curiosity and discovery.

Can you explore a more flexible freedom of personal expression? Can you inhabit the full range of your different feelings and the available archetypes? This kind of variety is the literal spice of life, bringing delight and freshness to a sexual occasion. For a woman, that might mean role-playing a range of sexy characters ranging from white angel, teenage girl, clumsy girl, compassionate nurse, tart with a heart, queen, seductress or crazy medicine woman. For a man, his characters might include romantic prince, policeman, cowboy, mechanic, stripper, king or vampire. Each of these moves, sounds, looks, interacts differently. The energy, intention, invitation, movement and opportunity of each is quite distinct.

Can you sense into these different sexual energies? Can you feel them in your body? Can you dance as these different characters? Can you intuitively express these energies when lovemaking?

Can you name your lover? See their different aspects and creatively name them to evoke that quality. A name can be a movie character, maybe a superhero or spy; playful like empress of sensuality or gentle king; a deeply heartfelt quality like shining-heart, emerald sea, clear sight or solid tree; or humorous like lady rice-cakes or your hairiness. What do you want to bring out in your partner?

We are all of those archetypes. We all contain a great variety of feeling, experience and expression. But usually we limit our behaviour and our expression to a narrow bandwidth we think of as "me". Once we open out of our usual limitations by finding our wildness and experimenting, we discover the delicious potential of the full spectrum of expressiveness. Divine sensual play!

Self-pleasure

We are each quite unique. What others think is fashionable, fantastic or cool is not necessarily what pleases you. So what are the activities, places, people, foods, art, travel, colours, textures, etc., that are naturally and easily fun for you?

Brainstorm a list, mindmap or sketch what brings you simple pleasure. Perhaps your findings include Netflix, avant-garde music, antiques, Dutch beer, pancakes, breakdancing, yoga, sweet wine, the colour purple, earrings, friends, massage, gardening, nakedness, ocean, stamps or books? What makes your body relax and your breathing increase when you engage with it? When do you melt? How can you include more of this in your life? In what ways do you already love to make love with life?

An exploration of reclaiming pleasure would not be complete without including a practice for conscious sexual pleasure. Make a date with yourself to pleasure yourself. Do this without orgasm as the goal, but to find and explore different kinds of pleasurable touch on the whole of your body. In this way, you open up your learnt sexual habits and pleasure pathways, to something new . . .

Find out what you need: where and how do you like to be touched – quickly or slowly, gently or with firmness, with pauses or non-stop? Do you like to include various elements such as fur, velvet, rubber, rope, fingernails or hair on your skin? How does combining these different elements affect you? What makes you relax more into the experience?

I hope you are really enjoying reading this book and trying out some of these exploratory practices. What will you experience for yourself this week? What pleasures might you find in your body as you practice?

What?	When and where?	How long for?	Done?

Do you notice that you sense more sensation in some parts of your body than in others?

PLEASURE AND POWER

We have seen that unlike our idea of pleasure being caused by something outside us, pleasure arises from the richness, sensuality and authenticity of being in contact with ourselves. It arrives as we accept ourselves exactly as we are right now, here in our sensitive body. As Hsi Lai writes in *The Sexual Teachings of the White Tigress*, "If you cannot face directly into your sexuality, you will never discover your true spirituality. Your earthly spirit leads to discovering your heavenly spirit."[105]

When we are trapped in feeling that we are not good enough, we fear our own power. Fear is the opposite of pleasure.

When we are at home in our own body and satisfied in our pleasure, we radiate the light of our soul. We are confident, we care less about what others think about us, and we don't need their approval to feel safe. We are released to feel, think, move and act as our true power.

6

Power

the medicine of empowering

"Our deepest fear is not that we are inadequate.
Our deepest fear is that we are powerful beyond measure."[106]

Marianne Williamson, spiritual teacher and author

"What ancient cultures knew, is that there is a primordial power,
greater than all us little humans, which is timeless . . .
female and endless."[107]

Scilla Ellworthy, peacemaker and author

"Tension is who you think you should be,
relaxation is who you are."

Chinese Proverb

We usually think of power as an external currency, something to be grabbed from others or held over others, a dominant physical strength. We think power is the freedom to get what we want, acquisitive and exhilarating, the ability to please ourselves selfishly without constraint. In this way, power can seem hedonistic and superior. But the pleasure we gain from this kind of power is short-lived, as it means we need to be constantly alert to maintain our powerfulness. We become exhausted, dissatisfied, hungry for more and more . . .

Similarly, most of us might be tempted to prostitute ourselves in some way to leverage temporary power, offering ourselves as part of the bargain to acquire transactional power – I will do this if you do that. But the accompanying loss of our personal integrity is a loss of our true personal power.

By contrast, Delicious personal power is self-sourced. Grounded in the body, it depends on our openness, trust and respect. What is naturally pleasurable is naturally powerful.

True powerfulness is relational. It's a responsiveness in tune with the natural cycles of our body and life. Powerfulness is our being in relationship with a greater life intelligence, and being infused with Life's power. It is the freedom to be oneself in a responsive relationship with other people, trees, rocks, animals and all. It is the dynamic exchange of energy and the magic of the depth of life.

We feel powerful when we can be honest. We enjoy ourselves when we are being fully expressed. This is authentic powerful pleasure.

MISUNDERSTANDING

We often think of power as a quality associated with army generals or muscly individuals, frequently men, perhaps in political or military situations, possibly influential, effective and capable. Philosopher Thomas Hobbes argued that the power to subdue others was essential for security.[108]

So is the world a tough, dangerous and threatening place? Do we need to be dominant in order to survive in it? For thousands of years, the idea of power over others has caused severe imbalances and threatened the very survival of life on the planet. Power over others usually comes with a secret undertow of a nagging, often unacknowledged, uncomfortable feeling.

Real Delicious power is me in my power and you in yours – both of us cooperating in relationship together. It means being respectful of each other and responsible both for ourselves and for sustaining part of the relationship. It is the capacity to be stable when life is complex and demanding, pulling in different directions at different times. Like those old-fashioned toys with a rounded base that wobbled but did not fall, always regaining their balance.

Power is the ability to be in touch with all of our many different capabilities: our thoughts, imagination, creativity, feelings, sensations and what it is that we need. Power is when we can regulate ourselves, communicate well with others and create equal relationships where everyone involved is happy. We can express our love, strength, intelligence, sensitivity and boundary.

In our attempts to fit in, to have our place, we often give our personal power away. The nineteenth-century mystic George Ivanovich Gurdjieff talked about "false consideration" for others.[109] The Gnostic Kabbalah talks about the lies we tell. Real power is the freedom to be, to express our self regardless of others.

Our current understanding of power as being a force that is wielded over others is not the only meaning and expression of this quality. There are other forms of power that humans have expressed in different cultures. Let's explore some historical perspectives . . . (By the way, the word "history" comes from the Greek *histōr*, meaning "a learned, wise man". But history does not just belong to men. Whose perspective and what information might have been left out?)

HOW POWER HAS CHANGED OVER TIME

In very ancient times, life was organized around the survival of the tribe. The essential life-giving power of the feminine was appreciated, the goddess was worshipped, women were viewed as social and spiritual authorities, and ownership was shared. It was understood that everything is alive, contains spirit and interacts with everything else – everything and everyone included.

When monotheistic religion took hold, spirituality became separated from social and economic life, and men became the holders of power. Life moved from being matriarchal and matrilineal to patriarchal and patrilineal. Individual men now owned wealth, possessions, wives and children. Life came to be about competition and individual success. For almost all of us, this is the context of our modern lives. Our sense of power is modelled according to this prevailing patriarchal paradigm. (There are a few ancient villages still organized without clocks, top-down directives and male leaders, but they are very few indeed. I visited one in New Mexico years ago, and life functioned well.)

We are now in a significant time of massive global change. The way things have been for the last several hundreds of years is rapidly changing in every sphere of climate, government, economy, media, relationships, definition of gender, and probably more. Our civilization is changing . . . and with it our ideas about currency, power and community. We are redefining what power means to us and what kind of power we want to have. We are rediscovering the true value of the power of authenticity, transparency and community, and a combination of feminine and masculine attitudes and actions.

TIME TO GROW UP

Throughout history, most people have given away their power to select others. Perhaps at first this was to the priestess, and then to the priest, and in more recent times to gurus, celebrities, banks, governments and advertisers. We have given our power away in an attempt not to realize how powerful we actually are. We have avoided our responsibility.

We can understand this as a natural part of human history. There is a parallel between the personal maturation process of an individual over time and the collective human maturation process over history. In personal maturation, there is a stage where a client gives their power away to the therapist, teacher or other authority figure. This is a transference from the client of the missing good parent/caregiver that they didn't have as a child. The client invests the practitioner with their own love, power and responsibility, projected out onto the other. It is a necessary stage in the healing process – to move through "lost" parts of ourselves in order to gain full possession of ourselves. It's a healing principle. And collectively we have invested our own powerfulness in certain apparently special others, priests, celebrities, et al, in order to have the experience of our own powerlessness.

Now it is time to reclaim our pleasure, power and potential. To step up to the role of co-creators in a variety of different situations. The internet enables us to find out more of what is really going on around the world and to contribute our voices to situations where previously only government officials or other experts would be able to intervene. We all together now have much more agency.

We all have the opportunity now to do our own personal healing and spiritual work. Whether this takes the form of expensive individual sessions with practitioners, group workshops or free-of-charge online programmes, there are a wealth of resources available today. We can become powerfully connected to ourselves and to others.

Power can be an expression of our soul self. This is a feminine version of power, used to create win–win positive outcomes for all. This new power is about alignment, integrity, openness, vulnerability and love. It is about creating and maintaining good relationships, with each other and the world around us.

Not just for survival, but for a flowering of compassion, creativity, cooperation and consciousness.

DISCOVERING WHO WE ARE

Why do we fear tasting our own power and owning it?

We often seem to prefer living in the murky middle, a constructed and occluded greyness of false ok-ness. Neither facing our power nor our powerlessness, not wildly bold or softly surrendered.

We need to go down into the specifics of where and how we lost our power. It can be painful and demanding to explore those awkward places of humiliation, confusion and tenderness. Those are the shadows we prefer not to examine too closely, not our proudest moments, so perhaps it feels better to gloss over and move on . . . But if we do descend, the gain is worth it: the reclamation of our real authentic power.

There are powerful forces and pressures to remain a victim of circumstances or of ourselves. We have become contorted and distorted out of alignment, out of our natural shape, to try to please others – who, in turn, are also contorted and distorted in their own individual ways. We try so very hard to please each other, to get the narcissistic supplies we crave, the attention we crave, to be reassured we exist!

Enemies are rarely external these days. Most of us live in suburbia. Mostly what we are fighting are our own internal unconscious historical patterns; those habits and voices we didn't choose, but are compelled to live with. By becoming aware of these, we can move out of their shadow and shine brightly as our true selves.

Stepping into the light of our own power requires courage and conviction, but why is it so hard? Because when we reclaim our power, we then have to live constantly from our depths. There is no putting our feet up and zoning out. No more fantasy, addiction or excuses. We are truly responsible for our actions without the option of taking an escape route or get-out clause. While there is a tremendous relief in letting go of old patterns, to do so requires a demanding step up in terms of our responsibility, attention and accountability. There is no one else to blame for anything any longer. Not society, our parents, partners, bosses, children . . .

We have to turn to face the darkness inside ourselves, in order to be able to face the light. By turning to face what we tried to ignore, our unconscious, we reclaim all of the power tied up there for ourselves. The better we can know ourselves, the more powerful we become. Personal power is aligned with personal truthfulness. We gain self-authority and freedom from the triggers, reactivity and narcissism that once kept us tied.

VULNERABILITY IS STRENGTH

Vulnerability is a real strength. We are powerful when we stand firmly in the truth of our personal integrity. Even if this feels uncomfortable at times, we can relax and stand strong on honest ground.

Standing in the power of our vulnerability is not about collapsing into a floppy heap. It is about being well-toned and flexible, so we can be both softly open and strongly contained in our truth. We can hold ourselves, as both form and content. We can attune to ourselves with a dollop of pure kindness.

Exercising power means behaving appropriately to our immediate situation. It is the ability to correctly discern what is needed here and now, by both me and you, and to turn the dial in ourselves to access our full repertoire of qualities and behaviours. This is about being responsible, sensitive and responsive to our own felt truth – and is respectful of others too. It is not an acting out of our feelings as if others are our willing audience, nor suppressing our feelings as if others are our critical judge.

Sometimes we need to be strongly boundaried and at other times to let another in. Sometimes we need to say, "No, stop, I'm angry", and at others to say, "I'm sad, I don't understand, I need your help." Our vulnerability is our willingness to be with whatever is happening for us. It is our acknowledgment of everything exactly as it is and whatever it is – boredom, panic, excitement, desire, irritation, open-heartedness or closed-heartedness, all our thoughts, emotions and sensations. Everything in our experience is to be welcomed as relevant and included. There is no such thing as good and bad, right and wrong, moral or immoral. There is only loving our experience, finding pleasure in it and owning our personal power.

This means that no status is fixed in stone. As parents we are the authority, yet sometimes it's our children who know better than us and they show us the way, leading from their perception and wisdom. We best maintain our power by allowing this to occur, rather than squashing them.

Indeed we all need to find a healthy balance of feeling sometimes in control and sometimes out of control. Interestingly, most of the clients of sexual dominatrixes are CEOs. These people spend most of their time in positions of authority, yet they have a basic need to surrender sometimes, release control and let go of the need for active vigilance. This is how they maintain power, by moderating their nervous system's need for both activity and passivity.

The Eastern traditions talk about the concept of *wu wei*, or "inaction". Sometimes giving way is stronger than standing stiff, limited and perhaps brittle. There are many koans, short poems, about bamboo bending in the wind being stronger than a fixed tree that will eventually be blown down by the wind, or of solid stone worn away by moving water. The martial arts demonstrate this principle too, in that sometimes giving way to your opponent, rather than resisting them, topples them over. Sometimes surrendering is more powerful than fighting . . .

FREEDOM AND CHOICE

Power is choice – the choice to act from fear or from love. That choice might be easy when everything is going well, but when we get upset – and we all sometimes get upset – what do we do?

Choosing to lash out at others often does make us feel kind of better. It offers a release of nervous-system electrical charge, punishing those we think caused us to feel bad; an action that seems to redress the imbalance we feel. *It isn't fair!* Lashing out seems to make it feel fair, as we temporarily experience the satisfaction of a power surge.

Much of the evil that is done in the world actually stems from the wish to create justice. The person or people who do such terrible things are often not seeing clearly, as their internal motivation is to redress an apparent wrong. However, even if we are feeling bad, can we choose not to hurt others?

It doesn't really matter what arises for us; what matters is what we are going to do with it. There is a moment of choice.

Real self-control is not about damming up our feelings. It is about allowing our feelings to have the time and space to be felt and expressed safely, so we can transmute them into something easier and flowing. The first step is to acknowledge total ownership of our own feelings without blaming others or projection onto another for "causing" our emotions to arise in us. It can often feel that another individual is responsible through their words or actions, or lack of actions, for our feeling uncomfortable.

But the truth is that our feelings are our feelings. No one else really "causes" them to arise. When we blame another, we are giving up our own power. When we accept 100 per cent responsibility for our thoughts, feelings and actions, we reclaim our power. The real triggers for our reactions lie within us, perhaps unconsciously so, but nonetheless inside us. Often we are triggered and reacting to things that have already happened further back in our personal or collective past.

Power means being conscious of the choices we are making in a dynamic response to this moment. Who do I want to be in this situation? Despite the way that we usually think, our identity is not really fixed. As we have already seen, we are not just one thing, such as a bank manager, sales clerk, a woman or a man. We have the potential to be everything . . . We can be much more playful in choosing how we want to respond – and why. We can dance with the world: playful choosing is powerful!

Viktor Frankl, the Austrian neurologist and psychiatrist, wrote about choice in the Nazi concentration camps in his book *Man's Search for Meaning*: "Everything can be taken from a man but one thing: the last of the human freedoms – to choose one's attitude in any given set of circumstances, to choose one's own way."[110] The human experience is not really defined by the situation. There is a very small gap between stimulus and action. Our freedom and power lie in our capacity to choose for ourselves how to respond, rather than to react automatically, by reflex, programmed by external stimulus.

The more we become conscious and aware of ourselves, our body and behaviour, thoughts and feelings, breath and desire, the more we develop ourselves as a powerful presence. We all have our own behaviour traits, typical tensions, usual attitudes, and habits. These form our individual ways of defending, responding and trying to cope with the challenges of life. We organize ourselves into a personality shaped by behavioural patterns and habits, a learnt and often repeated response to the demands of the environment. This shaping of our free-flowing essential soul is called our conditioning. It is made from the same stuff as our power, with very different results. Our power is the substance with which we strive to protect ourselves. Our life force literally "holds" our difficult experiences so that we are not overwhelmed.

To live one's real self requires power. Power to break free, step by step, from conditioning, to live "out and proud", expressing our soul in this body, in this world. It is to be constantly attentive, loving and responsive to our arising, sensitive, sensate self. It is a very delicious way to live, unfolding this and then that, in this moment and then the next one too.

SELF-LOVE

For most of us, a major challenge we face is the internal dialogue of our inner critic. This is the "voice" of self-protection that we learnt from those who cared for and protected us when we were children. Much of our judgement, criticism and hatred, of both ourselves and others, comes from here. This critical and opinionated mind, which developed in a childhood context, is now often unconsciously applied in a quite different grown-up setting. What was once relevant may now no longer be. In this way, the ghosts that the mind chases make it "a liar", preventing us from seeing reality.

Often we think of all of our mind's commentary as being an integral part of us. Our task is to begin to develop an awareness of our monkey mind chatter and the voice of our superego; to begin to notice when "it" has an opinion on us or on others that is just plain old repetition of a stale, programmed, unkind attitude. It may be our mother's anger at men or our father's hatred of weakness, or Aunt Nellie's fear of mess, or our teacher's strictness against silliness. Adapting to our childhood environmental rules kept us safe back then from transgression, punishment and rejection. It kept us out of trouble. But our old adaptation now keeps us prisoner.

The way out of our cage is to reject, ignore or see through the lie of our mind's hateful assertion that this or that is unacceptable, or not good enough. This is why it is useful to explore the roots of our conditioned guilt, repression and self-doubt. Is it ours? Or does it really belong to our parents or schoolteachers? Or even to our grandparents or great-grandparents or our distant ancestors? Is it national or cultural? Is it a remnant from previous lifetimes and old accumulated karma?

Once we recognize that this part of us is in control, we can begin to separate from it. Using whatever means is best – strength, compassion or humour – we can diminish its power, and we can tell it to stop. We can shout at it, hold up our hand, make a joke about it or simply recognize that what it is telling us is not the truth. It is a life-affirming practice that will allow us to distance ourselves from the superego.

Then we can start to be free of our "false gods" and more able to enjoy the delightful delicious reality of this moment here now. We can perceive and behave with power rather than borrowed prejudice.

The answer is always love.

DEEP LISTENING

It is a radical act of self-direction and self-empowerment to choose for ourselves what we give our attention to. As we have seen earlier in this book, attention is the key that unlocks the treasure of the Universe of Deliciousness. The cost is a small increase in effort and responsibility, but it is worth it.

We are so used to forging ahead, determining, dominating, competing and adhering to a predominantly masculine way of being, that we weaponize our own attention. Deep listening is, in contrast, a feminine way of being, listening from the heart and from the body, and attuning to subtle signals. Very simply, it means following where our attention naturally goes. This might be a fragment of a song, or an image, or a particular sensation or feeling. It is about being open to the unknown; to being moved, to being the horse and not the rider.

What if our intellect were not the ultimate intelligence in the universe? What if there is an intelligence bigger than us and we are already sitting within it and are moved by it? Could we allow ourselves to be guided by it? Dare we allow our instincts to guide us? What happens if we are curious and obedient to our arising sensations, feelings and knowing, to our wise impulses?

INSTINCTUAL DIVINE POWER

To be powerful is to inhabit our body fully. To sense into all of the feelings and sensations in our fingertips and our back, chest, neck, pelvis, arms and feet. One unified body, a stream of consciousness in sensual information; for instinct and intuition arise from the body, not the mind. Our task is to respond to these impulses in our real-time interactions with others.

We have been told the animal part of us is low, bestial and far away from the spiritual part of ourselves, but that's not really true. Primal sensual energy contains awareness of flesh and of more than flesh – there is no split into physical and spiritual, no duality. All really is one.

Our instincts are powerful and connect us to our divinity. There is no separation of flesh and spirit. We are divine animals, not dangerous wild animals that are not to be trusted. (Actually, wild animals are not constantly tearing each other to pieces, only when hungry or threatened, and they are not non-stop sexual. Wild animals are intelligent, compassionate and responsive.)

We belong not to the world of our conditioning, not to our parents, school or tribe. We belong to our own bodies and hearts. To our destiny. Do we dare to live that? Our instincts guide us, subtly, sensibly, sensitively to where we need to go . . .

Procreative energy is a manifestation of the creative energy of God. This energy, which is the most powerful thing in human beings, men and women alike, is needed for our individual and collective evolution. Instinctual energy can be experienced as passion and power. Often cultures allow one or the other. Can we experience both – sensuality and aggression – as life-enhancing forces?

Instincts can be used to fulfil the driving needs of the ego, but they can also be used in the service of something much bigger and more beautiful – something awakening and enlivening. Something that makes life really worth living, really enjoyable; that leads to soulfully embodied love. Whole-body power is the flesh-saturated satisfaction of being here now, fully in our body and soul. This power is owning ourselves, our body, our feelings, our unique potential, our desires and experience in this moment! Power is not abandoning our true selves to try to please others. Sometimes, like now, my heart blasts out glowing hot heat. Radiance.

SENSING OUR BELLY

Real power is humble. It is located in the lower body, in the belly, hips and pelvis, not in the ideas in our head. The lower body includes our biggest bones, strongest muscles, creative genitals and soft belly. In the belly is a small area that is the root of our power, creativity and sexuality. An inch below the tummy button and an inch into the body, this spot is the location of our capacity to be fully ourselves and in our body. When we connect with this place we feel more secure.

This place is a sacred spot known by many cultures and traditions around the globe and in history. In the *Fourth Way* teaching of Gurdjieff it is called the moving centre; in Central Asian Sufism it is known as the kath centre; in Japanese medical and martial arts it is known as the hara centre; and in Traditional Chinese Medicine and martial arts as the dan tien. Others just call it the belly centre.

Placing our attention on this spot makes us stronger and calls us into our body. New life begins in the womb, located nearby, while the cervix is a place of powerful pleasure. Modern personal fitness trainers talk about the importance of core strength and stability. A warrior with a strong hara is said to be unstoppable.

Being in contact with this mysterious place provides a great sense of groundedness and power. It encourages embodiment, practical body wisdom and a flow of energy that the Chinese call chi, Indians call prana and Western esoteric traditions call life force. When this is circulating freely we feel like a well-tuned instrument.

Movement from this place happens with elegance. You may have seen people practising tai chi or dance, their unified movement a delight to see. It is a real pleasure to move from the belly. The doer melts into the doing . . . something else is possible, beyond the ordinary. One feels really "here" and the grace of gesture is palpable.

Ideally we should sense into this place as a meditation practice for a few minutes or longer each day. The aim is for us to keep our attention constantly in and at the belly centre. It provides us with ballast, a fulcrum, an assemblage point.

The mystic Gurdjieff said that it was important to begin waking up the energy of the body here in the lowest of the three energy centres, the foundational belly centre. Everything we do in life depends on us having a solid stable foundation on which we can build. Over time, sensing the belly centre produces an enlarged experience of the whole body and an opening in the head centre of greater perception and vision. All this increases our personal power.

Reclaiming our power means paying attention to ourselves, and including ourselves in our attention. When we attend to sensing our belly centre and, as we have seen, to sensing our whole body, the body becomes a powerful and sensitive antenna. We become more open to receiving information from Life; our life is informed by that information and we feel more plugged in and powerful. We feel more at home.

The more we are psychically and energetically "in" our body, the more powerful we are. If you ever find yourself in a situation of conflict, immediately sense into your belly centre, so you become rooted.

DELICIOUS POWER IS RELATIONAL

The prevailing modern myth is that each person is a separate unit. We are encouraged to be falsely "powerful" by overriding our "weak" feelings or needs. This false idea of power brings to mind an individual who is tensed and holding their breath, and who just keeps on going regardless of how they feel, who they are with or what else is going on . . . The result of this attitude is that many previously powerful people become ill from stress with burnout, inflammation and exhaustion. We are not meant to carry on non-stop like machines.

Happily, there is a more essential power possible, and that is the power that informs our relationship with nature, people and God. Our true powerfulness comes from being relational and responsive, sensitive to the ups and downs of our energies and our exchanges with others. When we align ourselves to these changes, daily, weekly, monthly, seasonally, yearly, and in each new decade, we are more powerful because we are in tune with life. We do not exist in isolation. Acknowledging, adapting, being context-appropriate is power.

The first step towards this is, as we saw in SLOW, acknowledging that the nature of life is cyclical and interconnected. We are stronger when we live and work together, when we collaborate and cooperate. Power comes when we move together, sing together or act together. When we help each other. Then, power flows between us, through us, as a reliable current of energy. It is simply true that we all need each other. We need many people in our lives, not just one partner. We need a variety of different exchanges that we can only gain when we live in community. We are naturally social and tribal; we are pack animals.

When we support and encourage others instead of seeking attention and admiration for ourselves, we feel better about ourselves. The physical body biologically responds to and rewards our kindness to others with better health.[111] We are literally more powerful when we relate together, and often happier too.

LOVE IS POWERFUL

As we saw in DEPTH, we live our lives within the context of a much bigger loving intelligence. When we align with that force, divine power flows through us. The halo we see around images of saints and gurus is not just poetic, it is the practical reality of elevated energy. Those who are spiritually "plugged in" have an obvious sense of radiance, graciousness and quiet power that is palpable. This power is available to us all for the asking, inviting the power of that bigger reality to flow through us, to live us, dress us, speak us, write us, dance us . . .

Ultimately, and I hope without sounding corny, love is the currency of power. We are all our own inner healers. When we can really accept and love ourselves unconditionally, loving every bit of ourselves, including our so-called flaws and mistakes, body and soul, then we are powerful beyond measure.

Despite what many of us learnt from experience and our conditioning, we are all of us already perfect, perfectly imperfect, normal, vulnerable and capable humans. We have seen how often the thoughts, feelings, beliefs and patterns that we carry are not really "ours", just something we have brought with us from a time beyond time.

Loving ourselves passionately is empowering and relaxing. Then, nothing can be taken away from us, can divide us against ourselves or threaten us with self-doubt. Let us consciously choose to love ourselves, again and again and again. In our mistakes and our fat, our spots and wrinkles, our laziness and tiredness, our fear and sadness, our mature age and illness, our desires and lack of discipline, let us love.

We are all already worthy of our own wild love. We bless our own selves when we fully live the responsibility of our life, by loving ourselves whole, empowering ourselves totally. I am that I am.

Turning Up

Real relationship is a challenge with love,
of both swords drawn and fighting to the death,
not to kill anyone,
but to bring fully each of us
our power, passion, purpose and pleasure.

I want to be safe enough to be,
all of me, fully me, utterly me,
engaged, dynamically, in parry and thrust,
forward and back, dominant and submissive, delight and defiance,
humour and seriousness, every colour in the box,
every shade in the palette, from light to dark and up to down,
from soft with childlike innocence and relaxation
to forthright, challenge of my strength and capability.

I want to turn up fully
without worry that you can't handle me
or that I might be too much . . .
Without worry that you will believe the drama
in the gigantic play that is this life
where in reality neither of us can really die
and all is to be played full-out;

give me all that you are and all that you can be
and in fair exchange and return I will give you my all,
my heart and body, my sex and juices,
literally, my hair and my sweat, my joy and delight,
a kaleidoscope of ever-changingness
like the light upon the sea.

—— Practices for Powerfulness ——

Most people are trying to change their external world in order to change their internal feelings. They think that if they "have" this object or person, then they will feel better . . .

I am suggesting that if you devote your attention to what is already here inside you, and what is already outside you – including a sense of a deeper power than any of us – your own unique powerfulness will emerge. It takes time to practise and develop this new kind of power, as it entails a paradigm shift. Let these suggestions be your starting point.

> "Considering that, all hatred driven hence,
> The soul recovers radical innocence
> And learns at last that it is self-delighting,
> Self-appeasing, self-affrighting,
> And that its own sweet will is Heaven's will;
> She can, though every face should scowl
> And every windy quarter howl
> Or every bellows burst, be happy still."

W.B. Yeats

Step into a power pose

When we are feeling powerful, we naturally expand and take up more physical space. We stand taller, we spread our arms and our legs out, hands on hips, and we hold our heads higher and take bigger breaths.

Social psychologist Amy Cuddy[112] suggests that we regularly and intentionally hold a big "power pose" for a few minutes. This posture communicates to others, and most importantly to your own nervous system, that you are safe and powerful. (This posture is in contrast to the small postures we instinctively assume when we feel insecure.)

Very simply, for a power pose, you stand in a tall and wide way. Arms can be raised up or your hands can rest on your hips. You powerfully take up physical three-dimensional space. Feel into it, feel powerful.

This simple exercise is a great mini-reset, better than a coffee for a quick simple on-the-go boost! What do you notice when you try it?

Move the body, especially the hips

As we have seen, the lower part of the body contains our seat of power, along with the strength of our legs, hips and genitals and our desire, violence and security. Because most of us spend a lot of time sitting, we are usually out of contact with this power area, yet being in touch with it is invaluable.

To reconnect with it, move your hips, legs, pelvis, lower back, belly and bottom deliberately, experimenting with fast and slow movements, pelvic circles and rocking. Take five minutes to stand and, with or without music, play with movement.

Which movements do you like? What does it feel like to push your bottom out and tuck it under? Do you like bending your knees and crouching down for a change? What do you notice? Do you have an awakening sense of sexual sensation and personal physical power? Try moving freely for a few moments in this way each day. Be creative, emotional and authentic. Put music on and simply move. Your eyes can be closed or open. You can be sitting down, on all fours, standing up or lying down. It doesn't matter how you begin.

Concentrate on sensations and feelings. Experiment with big and small movements, curves and straight lines. You can move just a finger or hand, an arm or leg, or you can move your whole body.

Do you experience a sense of freedom? Can you feel your blood and lymph circulating, as you breathe more deeply, and your cells being enlivened by oxygen? Do you feel more sensually, physically, powerfully alive?

When we break up our automatic habits of stasis and movement we find our physical power.

Connect with your personal power centre

As we saw earlier, our personal power centre is situated about an inch below the tummy button and an inch into the body. It is best found by sensing into the belly and pelvis in general, before focusing in on that spot. The exact location of this energetic centre varies slightly from person to person. For some people it is a place that is easily sensed, while for others it takes a lot of practice to feel into it. It can feel good to focus here, bringing attention back into the body, calming frantic thoughts, and creating a sense of gathering scattered energy. Be patient, though, as it might not feel like this on your first try!

Sensing this place is not so much a matter of thinking of it or imagining it, but as if the area is sensing itself. It is grounding to sense and breathe into your belly centre, yet it takes practice to do this! To help you locate your power centre in your belly, you might like to try one of the popular movement classes that encourage attention to this area of the body, such as a conscious dance practice like 5Rhythms or martial arts such as tai chi, aikido or kung fu.

To begin now, simply practise sensing into the area by breathing in and out to the belly centre while standing. Gradually combine this with an awareness of the different areas of the body; for example, "breathe" into the belly first from the lower body, hips, legs and feet, and then from the upper body, head, chest and solar plexus; from the left and then the right; from the front surface of the body and then from the back.

Another way to connect with this area is through a sitting meditation practice, sensing and breathing into your belly. Your thoughts will wander, which is natural and to be expected, so keep returning your attention to the belly. Is that difficult or easy for you? As you breathe in and out to the belly, perhaps you notice a small natural pause between the in- and out-breaths?

Whichever type of practice you prefer, begin with five minutes, and over time increase this to ten and then twenty minutes a day. Ideally, attention is to be kept in the belly all of the time throughout the day, but this is an advanced practice. Even if you do achieve this your attention will naturally wander, and the challenge is to return to it, again and again.

This practice works because the belly is the fulcrum of our energy body. The energy body is shaped like a huge doughnut (sometimes called a torus) with an empty central vertical channel. Sensing the belly activates the flow of energy in and out of the centre point of our energy field. Placing attention here connects the physical body with clarity, then connects heart and spirituality.

Those interested in biology may like to know the important vagus nerve runs from the brain to this belly centre point. The vagus nerve supplies the heart, lungs, upper digestive tract and other organs in the abdomen, linking up digestion and sexuality.

Those interested in physics may like to know the belly centre is a zero-point field[113] of infinite possibility, a still point within a constantly moving field of energy. It is a black hole next to a white hole, the place where personal energy is recycled and renewed. Fascinating, huh?

Enjoy!

Start an intuition diary

Everyone has powerful natural internal guidance in the form of their arising intuition and instinct. However, our upbringing and work environments usually do not encourage us to be in touch with this.

Experiment with keeping a diary of your intuition and instincts, and track how they uniquely show up in you . . . How exactly do you know that you know something? Do you feel it or sense it, see it or smell it? Where in your body does intuition appear? Does it arrive as words in your head? Do you dream it? Do you notice synchronicities in your environment? Observe yourself . . .

For example, I have truth burps! Comically, they occur when I hear truth, think truth, touch a client in exactly the right place or complete a process in myself. I've learnt to trust the funny way my body communicates with me; I know its language and navigate in life by it.

Do you trust the way your intuition shows up in you? Do you act on it? This practice is about developing your confidence, trusting in your own capabilities, rather than looking out to others for validation. In this way, your self-confidence and sense of your own power develops. You learn to trust your intuition, the guidance that comes to you from within you.

Love what's in the way of your power

What makes you put the brakes on your self-expression? What grinds you to a frozen halt? Or propels you into empty action? It is well worth investigating the resistance to your powerfulness.

Consider how you have thought, felt and behaved, repeatedly, in your relationships and work.

Right now, what unkind, undermining, and attacking storylines can you find? Have you failed again? Are you doomed to never get it right? Has someone misunderstood you again? Not seen you in the way you would like to be seen? Is there something fundamentally and existentially wrong with you quite unlike there is with anyone else? Do you want to moan about your life or complain about someone else?

Slow the panic right down . . . and create some space. Before you abandon yourself as broken and rush straight into disaster and catastrophizing, believing there only to be hopelessness, shame, blame, collapse and destruction, slow yourself right down . . .

This is a special opportunity to care for and love yourself in a powerful way. You can clean your perception of yourself with space, kindness and acceptance, and can encode a new neural pathway.

With increased breath and awareness of your sensations, shift your awareness out of the overwhelming narrative, for it is no longer safe there. Ask yourself, "How can I care for vulnerable, tender, shaky me? How can I look after myself instead of aggressively criticizing and abandoning myself?" Will you rescue your childhood hurt self? Can you show up for yourself as a strong adult self? The meeting of yourself by yourself is a powerful transformational alchemy: things will change.

Return from self-criticism to respecting your embodied vulnerability and your own power of kindness. While it may seem that you need the support of someone or something from outside, what you really need is your own loving attentive presence. You need you. You may shake or ache or cry and you will be ok. Remember your own truth and love that is healing.

Your capacity to show up in powerful relationship with others is proportional to the depths you have travelled within your own darkness. We all share the human qualities of being vulnerable and powerful.

Communicate responsibly

One aspect of remaining in your power involves not giving your own power away by blaming others. When something upsetting happens, instead of immediately thinking of blaming others with "it's your fault", be prepared to accept 100 per cent responsibility for what has happened, and for how you feel and acted.

Often the real trigger for our feelings is not known to us. It can be an unconscious "knot" from our earlier life or even a past life. Often when we are upset by something, really we are upset with ourselves.

It may be uncomfortable at first to take responsibility; a fear of punishment or rejection may show up . . . Yet you may also discover that when you do take full ownership of your own sovereign self, you actually feel better, not worse. You feel more solid, real and proud, even if you have mucked up. You may also find that you are more powerfully available to connect with other people.

For example, if you are annoyed with someone, try not to label them – even privately – as "annoying". (Certainly telling them that this is your opinion will not help the situation at all!) Try to own your personal feelings of being annoyed, frustrated, upset, impatient, sad or angry. Look to see not only what they did, but also what you did, or did not do, which led to the unsatisfying outcome.

This approach is a kind of impeccable behavioural bookkeeping, noting your own and the other's errors. Although we may fear doing it, it is actually empowering, as it makes us feel stronger if we accept full responsibility for every little mistake. Try it out on a small but frustrating situation. Experiment with fully accepting the part you played. No trying to fudge or hide. Do you feel better or worse for doing that? Actually, do you feel relieved?

Everything in life is an opportunity, a prompt to take full responsibility for our feelings and actions. In this way we own our power, we don't pretend to ourselves we are victims, and we acknowledge our own agency.

When we turn our self-responsibility into honest clear communication then we become powerful. We sense our body and take full responsibility. We say what we want and what we don't want. We keep our own power, staying "clean", without blaming others.

Nevertheless, language is a tricky thing. Admitting "I am angry" can feel to another person like a threat, while saying "you made me angry" is an actual accusation and hard for others to hear. When we phrase our response as how we are *feeling*, we are simply reporting an update in our constantly changing experience. This is much easier for others to hear, making it easier for them to respond.

191

Practise saying "*I feel . . .*", "*I don't understand . . .*", "*Please can you . . .*", "*I need . . .*" or "*I want . . .*". Because admitting to our feelings and needs is not how most of us were taught to behave by our parents or schools, it will probably take a little practice before you get into the habit of this new way of expressing yourself. It can take focus and determination to find the right words to express what you are feeling. It can also take courage and strength to perhaps run the risk of being rejected. And when you succeed, it can feel like a great relief!

Practice constant active prayer

The mistake we often make is to think we are the lords of all we survey. As we discovered in DEPTH, there is a great deal more present than just what we can see and touch. This practice is designed to help you hand over your usual sense of power to God, to a higher power or intelligence, to bigger deeper power, to true nature or the Universe of Deliciousness. Choose your vocabulary depending on your personal belief.

During the course of the day, press the pause button on yourself. Create a time and space in which you can step aside from the continuous flow of thoughts and actions and the accompanying pressure and expectation.

And then ask something bigger than yourself a question . . . Perhaps to help you with something or to make something clear so you know what to do next.

Truth doesn't race around in mental space; it is a bodily sensation and knowing at the same time. Be prepared to go through the unfamiliar discomfort of not knowing, being frustrated or bored before insight surfaces.

In that moment of open space, allow emptiness and not-knowingness, and await for something to arise. It can be a thought or feeling, an impulse, something that "makes sense" as the next thing to do. It might be as simple as "do the dishes" or it might reach you as a fully formed intuitive answer to a question you may have had. Be prepared to be surprised, expect the unexpected . . . trust . . .

By now you will be discovering that your empowerment arrives as a result of your self-discipline and practice. What will you discover and strengthen in yourself this week? Is it easeful to practice?

What?	When and where?	How long for?	Done?

Do you notice that the doing of the practices is bringing a reward? Time and space for YOU to BE.

TOWARDS THE POWER AND POTENCY OF BEING

Power is the capacity to be flexible, to be appropriate and respectful of self and others. We all have a unique route to our personal power. Most people begin in the ordinary material world, and their journey is about opening up to the subtle realms of emotion and expansion. For others already connected with the big everything, their way is down into practical manifestation.

Delicious power does not pitch us against others and is not acquired at their expense, but is about all of us being empowered, engaged and energized, vibrant together. Instinct and vulnerability allow us to lead and to be wisely led. Carl Jung said: Who looks outside dreams; who looks inside awakens.[114]

When we accept ourselves as we "really" are in the moment, this is a freedom − not in a big way for the benefit of an audience, but for and in ourselves, in integrity. What do we do with our power now that we have it? We play with each other and the world! We enjoy this wonderful wonder-filled playground of interaction, fun and creativity.

We are ready now to explore our radiant individual and collective potential, the great untapped universal energy through us. What could we become? Let's enjoy our deliciously dynamic potency.

193

7

Potency
the medicine of aliveness

"There's a song that wants to sing itself through us.
We just got to be available."[115]
Joanna Macy, environmental activist and author

"The individual human journey is to integrate the masculine and the
feminine within our soul. If we all surrender to the feminine,
we might find that the masculine is already here."[116]
Lee Lozowick, tantric spiritual guru and author

"Imagination will take you everywhere."[117]
Albert Einstein, Nobel physicist

Now that we are empowered as individuals, we are ready to explore our
deeper potential. Potential is that which we are capable of. Potency is the
ability to activate potential. When we live a potent life, our experience is
sensual, relational and dynamic, fully alive!

We humans have barely begun to explore our potential – our mysterious expansive nature. Conventional science understands the role of only
1 per cent of our DNA and is increasingly recognizing that our emotional
state affects our biology in ways that are not yet fully understood. We need
to look to ancient wisdom with an open mind to explore what might be
possible. In ancient Greece, Aristotle called the realization of potential
"entelechy".

We tend to divide our experience of the world into black and white,
good and bad, pleasure and pain. But embedded in everything is potential,
the light within the darkness. We can activate our dormant potential by
feeling, sensing into our relationship with everything. Counterintuitively,

we hold ourselves back by keeping ourselves away from the so-called bad stuff. Potency is who and what we are, once the divisions inside us and projected outside us have softened, healed and melted.

The path to potency is integration, having the full spectrum of our experience in balance inside us and in contact with the world outside. Integration is about living life in all its messy, disgusting and self-hating truthfulness and its inspiring, exciting and delightful truthfulness. We have to go through the poo in order to get to the treasure. Nothing is totally bad. Within the darkness is light. Within the blackness is the gold. If we accept the difficult stuff, rather than trying to avoid it, difficulty leads to deliciousness too.

Potential is something that we co-create together with the outside world. It is a dance woven from our interior together with our exterior. Internal resource meeting external inspiration creating manifestation. Potential is our response to the outside world, made up of positive movement in both directions, within us and around us.

So, let's begin with us.

INDIVIDUAL POTENTIAL

Potency is our active strength, our agency and life force. It is the energy available in our system – whether that system is our body, family, organization, nation or world – to fulfil our potential.

Our current potential is defined by our damaged-and-doing-our-best personality. Our vitality has become tied up, protecting us against threatening, real or imagined forces. Yet our unique soul potential wants to be fully expressed. We all know it. The gap we often feel inside is our longing to live life truly as who we are. That is, as both an expression of our unique "me" soul, and of us as one small part in the vast fabric of the universe. Whether conscious or not, we yearn to live fully both these truths. We know there is "more" to life.

We can imagine this full potential of ours as a plant. Just as seeds need the right conditions to grow to maturity, including sunshine, rain and soil, so we need the right conditions to become our fullest adult selves. A healthy plant has two parts: the flowering or leafing part above the ground, and an invisible root below. Both are equally but very differently the plant. Life is dual, and these two aspects are simply one expression of the same being, fully integrated and fully alive.

Plants might appear to be individuals, but as we have seen, a whole forest is in communication. Roots are in contact with other roots, branches and leaves connect with other leafy branches. They are communicating for the benefit of the whole forest about available nutrients and light. Just as with plants, there is a collective dimension to our human potential too.

COLLECTIVE POTENTIAL

As individuals our potential is enormous. Collectively it is awesome.

This is just as well, as we need more than our individual human minds to solve the global problem of climate crisis that we have collectively co-created. We need to acknowledge how much is unknown and, with humility, access deeper intelligence. How much more is possible that we don't yet know?

Let's imagine the arc of human history as an individual life.

Just like a young child is dependent upon its mother, ancient cultures were attuned to Mother Nature in order to survive. They worshipped the feminine, the divine goddess who created human and animal life, including the earth, crops and seasons. Life then was instinctual, sensual and unconscious, it was about vulnerability, safety and unity. Exactly as I am writing this, a baby at the next table is crawling crying over to its mother, who holds it, murmurs, and feeds it, and the baby settles, silently satisfied.

Then, as an older child naturally comes under the influence of the father, who takes them out from the safe home to explore the external world, humanity developed religion with a masculine divinity and an exploration of structure, competition, individuation and ideas. Many traditional societies have rituals at ages seven, fourteen and twenty-one, to mark and facilitate the transition between life-stages, each of which requires a different focus, skill and learning.

Today, collectively, we are perhaps teenagers moving into young adulthood. Since the 1960s there's been increasing individual empowerment and rebellion against the old structures ... Right now, government, religious and financial organizations are breaking down and new movements are beginning. Everything is shaking out and being set free.

Will we choose to grow up now? Will we become fully mature, able to live together respectfully, with responsibility, flexibility and creativity?

INTEGRATION OF MASCULINE AND FEMININE

Part of maturity is integration. Today the masculine way of being is dominant, while the feminine way is suppressed and mocked. Collectively, we are energetically out of balance. For our full individual and collective potential, we need to appreciate and synthesize both masculine and feminine qualities, values and attitudes.

Some of our masculinized behaviours have caused terrible suffering, especially to girls and women, to many people's sexuality and to the Earth, which has been mined, fracked and polluted into climate crisis. Many animal and plant species have already died and many more are at risk. There is inside the womb of a woman a sacred subtle substance[118] that creates life. In modernity we have ignored this significant invisible truth that we are all indebted to.

Throughout history, several cultural myths have described this modern state of chaotic imbalance and the next necessary synthesis of masculine and feminine . . . Consider, for example, if the biblical story about the Garden of Eden were not about a historical disaster, or just a story to blame and shame the feminine, but an allegorical prophecy of our potential collective evolution?[119] From this perspective, Eve does a spontaneously wonderful thing . . . Instead of blind obedience to Father God's fixed rules, she picks an apple from the forbidden tree of pleasure and shares it with Adam. She was inspired by her good friend the snake, who, living close to the ground, was vital and wise. The apple awakens their inner seeing. They realize they should be proud of the splendour of their sensitivity and sensuality. Eve blesses everyone forever with the gift of active engagement in the creation of their life.

An ancient Indian creation myth similarly tells a story of masculine dominance, destructive until the feminine is remembered. What if this tale were also a prophecy rather than a history? It tells of a huge black phallus rampaging, destroying mountains, forests and rivers. When people remember they have forgotten the goddess and then she appears, the phallus slips inside her and, delighted to be enjoying pleasure, no longer needs to destroy the world.

The Kogi, who have survived in isolation since the ancient times of the Inca and Aztec, talk about Aluna, an intelligence containing everything past and potentially in the future. Aluna is between humans and the universe, governing birth, growth, fertility and sexuality. The Kogi speak of the problem caused by our being disrespectfully destructive. When we plunder the physical world and dumb down our thinking, we are undermining existence.

Traditional societies talk of "the great forgetting" and the loss of their ancient "sacred way" of trusting in life.[120] Native Americans tell us that the old way is about respect, love, forgiveness and sharing. The Yanomami of Brazil and Bushmen of Kalahari still live in this feminine way.

From a healthy variety of thousands of different ancient local cultures, one masculinized version grew, to become the dominant form of life on Earth. These people did not trust in Life; instead they were takers, grabbing what they wanted, waging war on neighbours, stealing land and accumulating resources. Human numbers grew, obliterating the natural plant and animal lives already on that land. With this taking-what-we-want way of life, people became the enemy of all other life on Earth, putting our collective survival at risk. It is the way most of us now live.

Can we reintegrate these potent essential forces?

It is not too late. When masculine and feminine combine, the divine sensual becomes possible.

Yet what do we mean by divine?

UNIVERSE OF DELICIOUSNESS IS GOD

Realizing our full potential is about becoming an animal of God. Living here now in this body, in these circumstances, can be paradise; it can be living in the Universe of Deliciousness.

There are hundreds of names we can use for God, according to our cultural background and personal preference. Some say Allah, Khuda, Krishna, Yahweh, Brahmana, Kaivalya, Satnam, Akal Purakh, Ahura Mazda . . . Others say Great Spirit, Divine or Beloved . . . Or Life, Love, Source, Mystery, Ground of Being, Essence, Presence . . . all point to the same. God is not an idea. Godliness is a dynamic experience arising, unfolding, to be felt.

Yet God remains a problematic word and concept, which has been used as a stick to beat others by very many people. There are two common misconceptions. God is not an old man in a cloud as some religions suggest. Nor are you already God, as some new agers suggest. Both these approaches take us away from our internal unity. In fact, many ideas of spirituality seem to have taken us further away, abstraction upon abstraction, commentary upon commentary, away from what is real, here now, our own personal truth.

We have already discovered how, as we explore deeper and wider, higher and lower, into the immediate personal experience of the moment, pleasure opens up. Truth is not an absolute. It is not something we need to search for out there. It is something to uncover here in ourselves, changing moment by moment. The reward for uncovering it, and for our integrity, is pleasure.

My personal vision of God is as an intelligent presence enjoying delicious discovery, a little like John Travolta as an angel in the film *Michael* who delights in the sensuality of life on Earth.

Many mystics write in highly erotic language. The Song of Songs in the Old Testament is a good example; Christian mystics, especially the female saints, refer to God as the beloved; Indian mysticism and the Sufi poetry of Ibn Arabi and Rumi both talk about their experience of God as being full of desire, excitement and physical pleasure. Hindus say God is playfulness. *The Upanishads*, an ancient Vedic text, describe God as awareness and bliss.

It seems that the ancients knew that a little bit of what you like does you good. Pleasure is a signal of nourishment and growth. Pleasure stolen, however, leaves a bitter taste in the mouth, a nagging feeling of something awry. Pleasure enjoyed together, with respect and love for the other, creates more pleasure.

So, is it pleasure, not cleanliness, that is next to godliness?

Is bliss God?

DELICIOUS GOD AS AN ALMOST COMPLETE CIRCLE

Religion has attempted to guide us into the territory of the Universe of Deliciousness. But somewhere along the way, the delicious essence worth discovering got obstructed. The hints and signposts become abstracted into mental ideas, confusing many people.

Imagine an almost complete circle as a diagram of God. One end of the incomplete circular line represents the world "out there", while the other end is "me". When we imagine this, we see that the fundamental power of creation is relational. We are almost touching, just next to, whatever you want to call it – God, Allah, Great Spirit . . . We are co-creating reality all of the time. Just like being in the empty space of a synapse, a gap within the nervous system, we are the chemical and electrical impulse carrying an action potential. Anything is possible.

One end of the almost complete circle is the container – the whole, the universe. The other is the individual, the detail, what is arising in you and me right here now. Our surface identity is as an individual, while our deeper essential identity is as part of the whole. We are each like a wave on the divine ocean, all made up of the same water.

In the Universe of Deliciousness, everything is relational. It is in relationship that the circle is complete. Think of the famous image of "The Creation of Adam" by Michelangelo in the Sistine Chapel, of electricity sizzling across the gap between outstretched hands. We usually think life is linear, but it is a series of intersecting circles and spirals, affecting each other. We are all constantly affecting each other.

Others have said it before. In the Book of Revelation in the New Testament, God says, "I am the Alpha and the Omega, the First and the Last, the Beginning and the End."[121] The tantric masters say, "You are what you seek."[122] Sufi poet Rumi says, "What you seek is seeking you."[123] British poet T.S. Eliot expressed it as, "In my end is my beginning."[124]

God (or any of the many other names) is a horizontal not vertical experience. A depth of reality around, either side, behind, in front of and inside us. It is not conceptual, it is experiential.

How does our personal potential connect with this sense of experiential godliness?

LIFE IS FULL OF POTENTIAL

We are the artist, the artwork and the viewer; the composer, music and listener; choreographer, dancer and audience; perfumier, perfume and nose; chef, food and diner; the writer, poetry and reader. We are everything and nothing. We are that which is behind everything and at the same time we are a unique expression of it, in this location.

We matter and what we do matters. We are needed, in the same way that every note in a musical composition or fragrance is needed, every spice in a feast and colour in a picture. We all matter, and at the same time none of us matters more or less than any other. We are all co-creating this world, moment by moment.

201

Quantum physics shows us that every atom is always present in both wave form and particle form at the same time as a potentiality, depending on the attention of the viewer. This science matches the shamanic view of us, "dreaming our world into being".

Our world and everything in it, including the earth beneath our feet, sun and moon, plants, microbes, insects, animals and humans, are in a state of suspended potentiality. Literally anything is possible. Life is much more fluid than we usually think it is. The Universe of Deliciousness is embracing us all, with infinite possible sensual relational intelligence.

Everything is in potential. We are all turning potential into reality all of the time. Let's find out more about how we can intentionally do this . . .

THE POTENTIAL FORMULA

The clues for a deliciously good life are visible on the treasure maps of body, nature and life – all is in plain sight. Repeating patterns show us that everything is composed of equal and opposite forces that can be balanced into a central neutrality, a new creative possibility.

Within our physical body, the left and right sides mirror each other, front and back are similar, and our skull and pelvis could be swapped to the other ends of the spine and would fit well, a cosmic design joke – form is content is function.

We have two ears, eyes, nostrils, lungs, arms and legs, breasts and balls. One head with one nose, mouth, heart, gut and genital. The essential pattern of two and one repeats.

Reproduction requires both masculine and feminine. Creativity needs the faculties of both left and right brain, logical analysis and creative synthesis combined.

Within the external world of nature are many visual reflections of our internal physical world. The number of neurons in the brain at birth apparently exactly mirrors the number of constellations in the sky. The branching shapes of our internal neural network are seen outside in the branching shapes of trees. Parts of the body are echoed in the shapes of the fruits and vegetables that nourish them, like walnuts for the brain.[125]

"Jesus said to them, 'When you make the two one, when you make the inner as the outer and the outer as the inner, and the above as the below, and when you make the male and the female into a single

one so that the male will not be male and the female will not be
female, when you make eyes in the place of an eye, and a hand in
the place of a hand, and a foot in the place of a foot, and an image
in the place of an image, then shall you enter the kingdom.'"

The Gospel of Thomas 22: 4–7

I understand this quote from the Gospel of Thomas as meaning the
entrance to the Universe of Deliciousness is through the fusion of two
opposites into one, e.g.: inner/outer, above/below, male/female, until
they are fundamentally changed. This means dissolving the separateness
of these aspects of ourselves into union through lovemaking. The way is
embodiment, fully inhabiting the body, so eyes really see, hands really feel,
and imagination is imaginative.

In "Mathematics of Relationship", we saw the significance of the formula:

$$1+1 = 1$$

With the fundamental act of lovemaking, two people produce one child.
Sacred enjoyment is generated by two people combining together, the
interplay of masculine and feminine energies whatever our gender, our
being active and receptive, and imaginative.

The same pattern can also be seen in our language and symbols.
Historically, Israel was where ancient polytheistic religions slowly changed
into the modern monotheistic religions of Judaism and Christianity. In
the name Israel, "Is" could be short for Isis, the Egyptian feminine goddess, "Ra" is the Egyptian masculine god, while "El" is Divinity. That is,
Is + Ra = El: feminine plus masculine is a doorway to the Universe Of
Deliciousness.

With each breath our body and brain physiology change, we move
towards our potential. The Hebrew for God is YHVH, Yahweh, meaning,
I am that which I am, or Causing to become, or is the sound of a breath,
reminding us of the potent creativity of breathing.

The symbol of Judaism is two intersecting triangles, the Star of David.
It is a very ancient symbol representing the union of masculine and feminine; the upwards pointing triangle is masculine, the downwards pointing
triangle is feminine. The 3D version is two intersecting pyramids, expressing the harmony of equal forces balanced. This star tetrahedron shape

shows up in nature in the early cells of all living beings and is present in a cross-section of DNA.

In the New Testament, John says the only way to enter heaven is being born again of water and spirit. This is an allegorical reference to combining masculine and feminine, earth and sky, matter and consciousness.

This deceptively simple formula for potency was also recognized by the ancient cultures of Egypt, China, Mesoamerica Mayan and Indian Hinduism. They understood there are no problems, only symptoms of what is out of balance. They honoured the inner human world and the external natural world, the intelligence of astrology in the sky above and the earthly life below of plants, animals and seasons. This is visually encoded in their art and architecture.

Around the world, ancient temples[126] were built with an architectural pattern of three doors, still visible today in important old buildings, those belonging to secret societies, such as the Masons, and modern church buildings. This sacred code again represents two opposites that, when integrated, awakens the third eye in the forehead and sense of personal unity. There are many ancient symbols of the third eye, which can be represented as a dot, snake or bird between the brows. A pinecone is another symbol for it, because the pineal gland literally looks like it. A giant bronze pinecone sculpture can be found at the centre of the Vatican. The Pigna, as it is known, originally stood near the Pantheon next to the Temple of Isis. This ancient knowing is at the root of all religion.

Our two eyes look outwards at the world, while our third eye looks inwards at soul.

The third eye is the site of imagination, creativity, brilliance and discernment. It is also a gland, which when activated, causes changes in perception and a subtle aura of light.

As we can see, the pattern for potential is all around us, it is an open secret. We need to combine what appear to be opposites – imagination and body, men and women, masculine and feminine, sacred and material, darkness and light, dead and living, war and peace, pain and pleasure, inside and outside, fear and love. In the integration of apparent difference potency is found. It is forged in the intention and alchemy of creation into something new. Hot oil and water make fire. Flour and water make bread. Leaves and hot water make tea. Sunshine and rain make a rainbow.

To manifest our potential, we need to take this pattern for potency into our everyday lives.

INTEGRATING OPPOSITES

Our task is to each come into greater alignment and balance. Many of us are skewed, not just wonky in our bodies, with one shoulder higher than another, etc., but out of balance in our way of thinking, our attitudes and behaviour. It is our responsibility to even ourselves up.

There are different dimensions within which we can rebalance ourselves. We need to integrate the opposites in both our external and our internal life. It is to include, welcome home, all parts of ourselves and aspects of the world we split off and rejected.

The more balanced we are, the more we can evolve towards love, compassion and consciousness. Finding our way to harmonize differences in all aspects is our sacred human aim, a major, lifelong piece of work. It is actually our task over a series of soul lifetimes, each one offering us different experiences, possibilities and learnings. It is our sacred human work. We can heal pain into pleasure, emotional mess into radiant gold.

Can you think of any opposites in your own life that you can practise unifying?

TRUTH IS THE NEUTRAL MIDDLE PATH

When our wonky, unbalanced bits are synergized, then the radiance of neutral clarity, truth and beauty is revealed. Truthfulness is a central channel. Most of us, most of the time, do not speak the whole truth. Truth requires an effort to drill down into layers of primary feelings.

Yet truth, when spoken, has an unmistakeable effect. It is immediately recognizable as being of value. It has a specific sound (ring of truth), fragrance (sweetness) and presence (vivid). It wakes us up to hear it. It has a clarifying effect on us. When we hear sloppy half-truths we zone out. We continue colluding in the pretence. When we hear truthfulness, something in us wakes up.

We can access truth through expressing our creativity or interacting with others' art, through guided visualization or shamanic journeying, moving our body or enquiring. (Right now my heart is burning in a very particular way that tells me that this is essential. I don't know what I will write next but I do know that this is "on the spot" accurate.) We all respond to art that reveals to us a truth. We respond to being touched in just the right place and way, to being recognized by others in their feedback. Our bodies relax with truth, releasing tension and whatever we have been holding on to. It doesn't matter if the truth comes to us from outside, or is generated inside of ourselves, we respond with recognition and expansion. We realign from something superfluous to something essential, from something either too this or not enough that into focused balance.

Truth is compelling. Poise is an example of truthfulness expressed in body posture. Right now a genital pleasure response tells me, again, pleasure and truthfulness are connected. The path to the Universe of Deliciousness delights is emotional truth and physical poise.

How Can We Enter the Universe of Deliciousness?

There are seven integrative technologies that can enable us to synthesize polarities and enter the realm of potency and pleasure in the Universe of Deliciousness.

1. Imagination is the muscle of our soul

As a busy adult it is not so easy to just "imagine". Most of us are confused about the difference between thinking, fantasy and imagination. Thinking is rational and logical. Fantasy is disembodied and escapist. Imagination is a powerful capacity, rarely really used. Imagination unites minds with bodies, our potent creative capacity to dream.

Unconsciously we allow our imagination to be used by others for their agendas. It means that our potent imagination has become weaker than it could be and not used for our own potential. We have already touched upon how advertising puts us into mini altered states, capturing our imagination for commercial purposes. For a few moments we are entranced and distracted . . .

Imagination is the muscle of our soul, connecting us to deeper truths, to our soul truth. As children we entered the world of the imagination easily. After all, life is active imaginative play.

As adults, we often need some help to transition into imagination. We may need to be "charged" up with energy to be able to "consciously dream". Different cultures use different technologies and rituals that transport us from ordinary reality into the imaginal world, such as snake venom, plant medicine, tea ceremonies, drumming, dancing, clapping, stories, dreams, guided visualization and more. One of my favourites is journeying, which can begin from a guide's prompt to shut your eyes and follow an imaginative thread, noticing the sensations, imagery, stories, memories, ideas and whatever else appears is relevant and useful.

We can also create space to be receptive to imagination unfolding without our control. We can invite this by giving ourselves time to do nothing but relax and daydream. This might be through a walk in nature, a bath, lying in bed, listening to music . . . maybe we notice an image, smell or song arising within us . . . or maybe we see something outside, like a t-shirt with words that resonate with us.

Sometimes an impression arises randomly in the middle of ordinary life, like while waiting at the traffic lights or stirring a saucepan for supper. Imagery also arises in our nocturnal dreams. They contain symbols and characters from our unconscious, a message for us.

Pay attention! Notice what is happening in you and around you – and notice what you notice . . . what do you make of it? For some people, it's just jazz playing in the cafe, while for others there is an associated memory of family; there's an implicit meaning.

As part of our imaginative work, we might need to do the work of "translating" what the impressions mean to us as at that time. Decoding can be done through the tarot, enquiry, reflective conversation, poetry, synchronicity, movement, or another way of accessing our intuition.

Imagination is a bit like a projector, transmitting data between our inner invisible world and the three-dimensional "screen" of external manifest reality. Unconscious beliefs that are repeatedly thought, such as "I am lonely", "nobody likes me" or "I'm a failure", can be amplified with feelings such as "I knew it . . . ", "it's not fair" and "typical" etc., and then solidified as a tension pattern in our bodies. The "pattern" is then imprinted on our neurological pathways, physical posture and body chemistry, and also in what we see and interact with in our external reality.

The brain cannot tell the difference between what is actually happening and what is not: it processes emotions and motions in the same way, whether the source of them is real or imagined. This means that we can use our imagination actively, intentionally imagining something we would like. We can feel it, see it, smell it, hear it, taste it. In this way it becomes real to us, and we can be moved and changed. We can become the artworks we visualize. Inside us is an inner cinema screen, and its instruments are the eye, ear, nose, and mouth. The imaginative sensual experiences we have are both for the creation of artworks – such as a book, symphony, flower arrangement or new technology – and for the creation of ourselves as human artworks. We are informed and transformed by such information.

For imagination does not just take place in the head. When imagination is combined with feelings and sensations, we experience life fully. We really feel the water on our feet and the kiss on our cheek. When our imagination and everyday life combine, life feels activated, full-bodied, with 360-degree and 24-hour potential. Anything is possible . . .

In meditation and altered states, although our eyes may be closed, we can see visual imagery in the centre of our forehead. The third eye, at the pineal gland, contains light-sensitive cells – the same light-sensitive cells as those in the retina at the back of the eyes.

At the end of *The Jeweled Path*, Karen Johnson, co-founder of the Diamond Approach psycho-spiritual school, describes her experience of words written in light on her brow.[127] This occurred after many years of spiritual practice; to her total surprise she had an internal sense of shapes of light on her forehead. She drew the scribbles on paper to show her partner in spiritual work, Hameed Ali. His first language is Arabic and he immediately recognized it! She had been given a mysterious message that could be deciphered only in relationship with another. The words were:

The Capable
Te Maker of Images
The Friendly Loving One
The Alone
The Only
The Free

To me, these are beautiful names of God written by God.

2. Attention here now

Very often our attention is on the future, the past, other people or a distracting device. Maybe we are exercising without noticing our body or eating without tasting the food.

Our task is to bring attention back to our immediate internal experience and our immediate external environment. It is to notice this moment right now, whatever is here. To really listen, look and feel, with curiosity, kindness and respect. Rejecting nothing.

We sometimes hear people saying life is perfect as it is, which can seem a frustratingly untrue statement. It doesn't mean that life is perfectly complete and finished as it is. It means that together with our active attention and engagement right here, right now, life is deeply perfect. Our noticing alchemizes what is happening, transmutes it from raw happenings into a learning experience. Our attention turns any old rubbish into gold.

The wise and pleasurable Universe of Deliciousness is always bringing us what we need to experience now. It has the biggest love, context and perspective of all time, space and depth. Like the best, kindest and most containing of parents, it is constantly guiding us, to develop and live our fullest potential. It is worth paying attention to what is happening!

3. Receptivity

Today almost all of us are on alert, ready to act. We don't trust in the abundance of life and the generosity of other people; instead we tense, grab and defend ourselves.

We all need to become softer, gentler and more receptive. Being true to God or Spirit is not an idea. Practically, it is tuning in to the arising sensory data, with the whole body as a sensitive instrument, attuned to receiving information as vibration, feeling and sensation. This is to be raw, sensual, responsive, allowing . . . It requires a certain effort – but rewards that with giving us entrance to the Universe of Deliciousness, and love-making with everything.

Receiving is pleasure. Discovering how to receive is the same thing as finding out how to have more pleasure. Learning how we can let other people into our private domain of both potential and inadequacy, rather than proud isolation, is the beginning of pleasure.

Pleasure arises in our relational interactions with others, experienced in our own body and being. Power is our contact with ourselves. Potential is about opening up even more fully to that endless experience. There is a great pleasure in giving pleasure to another, but even within that, it is our willingness to receive the pleasure of giving that is pleasurable to us.

Can we become receptive? The whole of us receiving what is going on in us, around us and through us? Can we be an instrument of passive experiencing? Our whole soul-body-mind aflame and receptive like a listening ear, a tasting tongue, a smelling nose, a sensing hand, a desirous genital? Listening, attending and feeling, deeply receptive to what wants to happen, despite rarely-stopping critical judgement. When we acknowledge our essential worthiness, when we stop thinking we have to try so hard to get what we need, a beautiful sense of being breathed, lived and moved arises.

Can we be receptive to the aliveness of the universe that moves us this way or that . . .?

4. Acceptance

Somehow we think we ought to be happy all of the time. Indeed happiness is in many respects preferable. But a state of eternal happiness would mean we would miss out on the messy truth of our feeling life. Feelings of being nervous, frustrated or angry are not necessarily less good, attractive or acceptable. They are just a different kind of an experience.

We tend to be harsh on ourselves when we feel vulnerable. But actually it is the inclusion of all the different aspects in the emotional spectrum that brings us to peace and contentment.

We have all known forever, intellectually, that there is no one else for us to be but ourselves. But actually doing it, is not necessarily just that easy. Allowing ourselves to be as we are, leaving ourselves alone, takes time, practice and love. Allowing ourselves to ride the waves of the ocean of life, the ups and downs, just as we are . . .

We cannot get pleasure just by wanting pleasure; we cannot chase it and achieve it. We reach pleasure through including all of who we are, our darkness and pain. There is light within the darkness, even if it cannot be seen in this moment by our eyes. Light is behind everything, awaiting to be revealed, by embracing ourselves as we are, perfectly imperfect. When we welcome the messiness, the magical wholeness is experienced.

5. Appreciation is fuel

Most of the time, we push away who and what is here now, busy with our petty concerns. But when we do this, we are being arrogant and disrespectful to Life itself.

We open to the bounty of life when we immerse ourselves in what is going on, viscerally taking in the people we are with, the situations we find ourselves in, the colours we are seeing, and sounds we hear . . .

Let's look out of ourselves and really look at the other. Look and listen, being curious and interested in them, the details of their face and voice, not just for what we think they can do for us. Can you take in the wisdom of this interaction? Basking in what is here, deeply appreciating it, unifies our inside and outside environments. Delighting gladly activates potential!

Can you receive this other person and what they may or may not have to say or how they behave? It is to focus fully on the person you are talking to in that moment, not the next twenty-five things you need to do, or the regret you might have about what happened last Wednesday. It is to really be with that person as wholly as you possibly can, attentive, seeing, listening. This is to be holy.

Life is about relating. Personal relationships are sacred. They are nothing to do with the other person, but because they involve the other, they are everything to do with them.

6. Creative active participation

It is time to take responsibility for ourselves. Power is devolving from centralized government and corporations to local people. The era of gurus and teachers has passed.

Everyone is creative. It doesn't matter what we are creative about, it matters that we do it. An act of creativity transforms us just as much as it transforms the material we are working with. Artists know this. Therapists and healers also know this; after holding the space for a client, we are subtly changed too, not just the person who came for a treatment.

It matters that we engage, are focused, enjoying the process and are proud of our outcome. It could be gardening or basket weaving, hat design or cooking. Confidence comes from taking action, from engaging with life. Creativity is alchemical.

7. Breathing

Most of us most of the time do not pay attention to our breath. We take it for granted. In our tensed efforts to get stuff done, we live on a minimum inhalation and exhalation.

It is said we can change our lives with a single breath . . . When we breathe, we take in oxygen for our body's biological needs and we also take in a subtle spiritual substance.

We are breathing at the level of both whole organism and of individual living cells. Our breath moves from the physical two into the physical one.

Inhalation nourishes us through two nostrils and two lungs, new air moving into our single heart (which has two ventricles and two atria) and then into all our cells, nourishing and cleaning the whole body.

The less we breathe the less we feel our bodily feelings and sensations. Although we all think we want to be more alive, most of us are reluctant to actually take bigger breaths. We can breathe into our chest, our belly and also, using our imagination, into our pelvis. Actually we can have the experience of breathing happening in any part of our body, if we choose to do so.

Breathing is a fundamental component of mood. Slowing our breathing down stimulates the vagus nerve to secrete a substance that calms us down.[128] The body senses the breathing and tells the heart to slow down; we then need less oxygen and feel relaxed.[129] When we calm, the fight or flight reflex turns off, our heart rate and blood pressure reduce, and the sense of opposing polarities melts away. Breathing more slowly and fully is like giving ourselves a natural tranquilizer.

We have seen how the benefits of many contemplative practices such as yoga, prayer and meditation can be attributed to slower breathing.[130] Physical exercise stimulates breathing and eases depression. Only two minutes of deep breathing with longer exhalations improves decision-making. To increase aliveness and a sense of unity, it is good to inhale more air than we habitually do!

In these various ways, we can move forward to manifest the mystery of our potential.

The Mystery of Potential

We humans have barely begun to explore our potential, which is our mysterious expansive nature.

Conventional science disregards most of our DNA as "junk" because it is not known what it codes for.[131] About 1 per cent of it is known to code for our body's biological replication and health. What if the remaining 99 per cent is not rubbish – nature never wastes anything – but is actually responsive to our own human consciousness? Imagine if it is really a mysterious, physical gateway that can not only switch other genes on and off, but also access our collective ancestral memories and wisdom, and affect the future of our species.[132]

Remarkably, a number of different international scientists, who worked with the genome coding languages of so-called junk DNA, found nucleotide sequences similar to human language. In some places, it was almost identical to ancient Aramaic sentences from the Bible.[133] Perhaps human language did not evolve randomly, but arose from this deep biological language?

We are a biofeedback mechanism. Our state of mind affects our body, just as much as our body affects our state of mind. Our DNA is affected by our speech in prayer and by other rituals that quieten mind chatter and expand consciousness, such as chanting, meditation, sweat lodges, dancing, yoga, etc. DNA interacts with time and space, accessing timeless wisdom – phenomena we experience as instinct, intuition and insight.[134]

MANIFESTING POTENTIAL

The Universe of Deliciousness is vibrational and alchemical. As I write this, the tip of my tongue rings with deliciousness, the whole of my tongue engorged, sensate and pleasurable; pleasure spreading to my heart tells me that I am right on track! Waves of pleasure wash through me from my head to my toes, as I realize that sex is a plugging-in to this sacred subtle circuitry.

(It is ironic we use artificial vibrators, while oblivious to the vibrations of the universe!)

Vibration is the "programming" language of the universe. Sound creates form. Have you ever seen how loose sand becomes organized into shapes when the surface is vibrated by sound? The audible invocation of the creation of the universe is described in different traditions as an OM, big bang, the word of God, or lion's roar . . .

Long ago, language had an onomatopoeic quality and was an evocation in sound of the real world. Abracadabra, our "magical" word, comes from the ancient Hebrew meaning "I create as I speak". The Hebrew for bottle sounds just like liquid gurgling out, *bak-book* – try saying it! Sanskrit is another sacred language that still keeps its original connection between world and words.

Early language described a specific physical reality rather than an abstract idea, such as that rock by the big river where trout live, or the tall tree by the bottom of the big mountain, or the girl with shining red hair or boy with round brown mark on his right cheek. Early writing was pictograms, images of actual things. As writing changed into an abstracted alphabet, language became separated from what it is describing. Reading, which was once out loud and communal, is now a largely silent and isolated activity. We have forgotten the aliveness of the world and our co-creative role in relationship with it when we speak and write words.

With the arrival of individual ownership came pronouns, killing the aliveness of language. "Part" is something that is connected to the whole, but when "a" is added, "apart" is separate; and she, it, this, the all denote an inert finished object, denying the reality of everything being alive, evolving and interconnected. We saw earlier how the Hebrew name of God means "I am that, that I am", indicating constant arising and becoming, unfolding, like the universe and us, energy recycling from formlessness into form.

Our body is constantly receiving and transmitting energy. We humans are conductors and transmitters, and we can adjust our frequency – and a shiver went through me as I wrote that! We can step energy up or down, and convert energy into matter over and over again, matter into energy. We usually do it unconsciously, and we can, with attention, do it consciously.

We have seen how emotion is a vibration and how water molecules change shape when exposed to emotion. Likewise, the universe creates not from content, but from the underlying feeling state that animates whatever we say, do or don't do. Stress usually creates more stress, abuse more abuse, and love more love. It is not what we do, it is how we do it!

As we saw earlier, our DNA is affected by the vibrations and sounds of our own voice, such as humming, chanting, breathing, laughing, praying, saying a mantra and just talking. We affect ourselves all of the time, in the way that we move, breathe, act, live and love. So do we choose to affect ourselves positively, intentionally, towards balance, integrity and potential? When our body is free to naturally vibrate, to live our potential of delicious dynamic potency, anything is possible!

TOWARDS A NEW EDEN

It is time now to live the potential of a new Eden on Earth. It is for us to behave with an awareness that everything in the world is interconnected, and that our every action affects everything else. Each breath in and out, each look and touch, has an impact on others. We will bring about a new Eden by caring for our body, community and Earth.

To achieve this, there is no manifesto, strategy or rulebook. We can trust what is arising in, through and around us . . . We are vibrating and vibrated antennae of the Universe of Deliciousness, in responsive relationship with everything. It is our sensate tremoring flesh that tells us if this person, situation or choice is good for us or not. Here, now, my truth. We access creative capability, sensual pleasure and in-the-moment wisdom, through our soul-body.

Whether we speak aloud or not, our sensitive bodies communicate directly to each other in resonance or discord, and we contribute beautiful openness or ugly deception into the world. We manifest our full soul potential, our fragment of God/source/spirit, through our body and actions when we are in service, in relationship to and for the benefit of all aspects of the whole universe.

Responsibility is not a heavy obligation, but our sensitive vital ability to respond. Our sense of deliciousness or disgustingness is the language of the universe communicating with us. Let's live as intelligent sensitive sensuality, for ourselves, each other and our Earth.

Towards Deliciousness

Pleasure is the reward mechanism of the universe and our very nature. It is the calibration of "success" in becoming the truly potent Samuel, Martha, Aditi, Sefi, Carmen, Abdul, Anthony, Rebecca, Kira, Akhmed (or put your name here!) that we all really are. Iridescent shimmering potentiality awaits us in the recognition that we are living here now together.

We are not simply each living "my life" but Life as it is living through us, Life loving Life, in the Universe of Deliciousness. May you be delighted, body, heart, mind and soul.

Living Deliciousness

Life is not just something that we have, like a car,
handbag or home
Life is something much much bigger than any of us
We live within the aliveness of life
We are lived by Life

We are Life loving Life
Potent creators and enjoyers of deliciousness

Living Delicious
Let us live this life
In unconditional acceptance
Of all that is

Right now
This sensation
and this feeling
fully

Not either/or
We prefer
And/both

Let us live to the brim, dance full-tilt with life,
and know that everything is always changing –
how am I just now?

Bliss is the energy
that responds to stillness
A new consciousness
of heart

Connected
not just to me
but to all in the universe
alive

216

PRACTICES FOR POTENTIAL

We can read inspiring books and go to wonderful workshops, have insights, experiences and shifts, but what really transforms our potential into potency is having a daily practice. When you do this, you will increase your capacity to access the subtle information within and around you, and be on your way to fulfilling your potential as a valuable cell within the body of life. Potency is a quality of relaxed attention, ready to act in alignment with our senses, body and environment right here, right now.

Mythologist Joseph Campbell says, "Whenever one moves out of the transcendent, one comes into a field of opposites. The two pairs of opposites come forth as male and female from the two sides. One has eaten of the tree of the knowledge, not only of good and evil, but of male and female, of right and wrong, of this and that, and light and dark." [135]

Free your imagination

Imagining is an act of faith, co-creating our world as we go. Because we are mostly out of the habit of using our imagination, we may need to practise using it, like practising a musical instrument or meditation, or building muscles. We can use imagination actively and passively.

To use your passive imagination

Allow yourself some space to drift off, daydream and imagine. Simply look out the window, stare into space, listen to music, lie down or go for a walk . . . Do nothing for a while. Let your mind wander, shift and wonder . . . This can be a rich time as thoughts arise and synthesize. (J.K. Rowling said the idea for Harry Potter arrived while she was on a train journey.)

Notice arising images. What catches your attention? Perhaps a memory, image, smell, song, visual image or impulse. Can you be curious about what this received imagery might mean for you? Include sensations, associations or feelings . . . What do you "know"?

Can you "journey", following image after image, seeing where you are taken? This is a personal favourite of mine, and very trippy! It is a kind of surrender and easiest done within a framework such as a ten-minute timed slot or in a session with a therapist or guide.

Keep a notebook by your bed and first thing in the morning write down your dream. What do you make of it? Everything represents a part of you. Are there any symbols? Some people wake up dreaming a song, story, or picture, building or technology into existence. Others have dreams that literally come true. What are you being given?

Tarot cards are another way to tap into the big unconscious dreaming mind that is dreaming us all. What card are you drawn to? What does an image suggest to you? Be creative. Trust.

To use your active imagination
Try imagining your day in advance. There is something about this that is helpful and eases movement between people, places and activities. When the imagination sets the path, the body follows easefully.

Try imagining something you would like to happen, such as being in relationship with a partner or your business doing well. Can you see it, feel it, hear it, taste it, sense it? What does your heart desire? What would be different in your life and how would your life look and feel, if you had it?

Visionboards are a fun way to play and combine the active and passive imagination. Get a pile of old magazines, newspapers and wrapping paper. Browse through them, cutting out things that appeal to you without necessarily knowing why. Glue the images and words onto a piece of paper and observe what you have created. What have you revealed to yourself?

Co-create our world
Imagination is needed to imagine ourselves in the place of the other. It is a moral faculty. Can you imagine how your mother or father, grandfather or grandmother, boss, employee, client, son or daughter, enemy or partner might be feeling? Can you imagine, in the middle of an argument or conflict with someone, how they might be feeling? Can you imagine other people as being full of soul-beauty? Can you "see" their losses,

griefs and challenges? Or visualize their openness, lovingness, potential and joys?

Imagine something now. It almost doesn't matter what. Image it. Feel it. And let it go. Take action on images that arrive: follow the "clues" to call the person you thought of, understand the message of music in your mind, go to the place you keep seeing, or attend to what the sensation in your leg needs. Be awake to both experience and meaning.

Try imagining the world is animated, intelligent, sensual and relational. It is not just one solid, finished, fixed thing; it is constantly being created, in co-creation with us. This may at first feel awkward, but try imagining that what you usually think of as merely objects are actually imbued with a living intelligent sensuality. Try relating to objects in this way. This does not necessarily mean "talking" to them, but connecting with imagination, sensing how everything communicates in its own way. It's a shift of attention to appreciate the "subtle" aliveness of the sofa you are sitting on, the wall opposite or the plants in the corner.

Can you imagine that the space that you usually think of as empty is full of life? Full of microbes, full of unrealized potential, full of presence, full of love? How does the air feel on your body as you sit or walk? Is it trying to tell you something?

Imagine that water is a limited resource (which it is in many parts of the world): how much do you really need to drink or use to wash your plates or clothes, or use the loo? How much energy do you really need to use to light your home? Imagine energy as something that belongs to us all, to the planet, not just your home, workplace or cafe. Imagine that energy is not infinitely abundant: what can you do to conserve it right now? On behalf of us all? Can you imagine that everything you throw into the rubbish bag will become buried into the fleshy earth body of the planet and fester, like a shrapnel wound that becomes infected? There is no "away" to throw things to.

Can you imagine the world as a radiant being, in direct communication and contact with you? For you, but not only for you. As an act of generosity and co-creation, together let us dream the world into being. We can access this, we can switch it on! We can respond!

Cultivate your attention

As we've seen, cultivating attention, even for a short set period of time, develops our will, focus and peace.

Can you pay attention to that which is not usual for you? Do you always answer the phone with your right hand, always cross your left leg, clasp hands the same way? Try to do the opposite. It will be awkwardly unfamiliar at first, but persevere to rebalance yourself.

What are your strengths and weaknesses? Which qualities could be more developed? Experiment: for example, if you find it difficult to express aggression, try kick-boxing; if you think you're not creative, try life drawing; if you are naturally flowing, try something structured like a partner dance; if you're naturally structured, try a free-expression dance.

Try paying attention to two different experiences or things at the same time, such as hot and cold, hate and love, head and feet, ears and knees, contraction and expansion . . . or the left and right sides of your body, front and back, top and bottom. Or maybe itchiness and desire, overwhelm and centeredness, shyness and confidence, back pain and shoulder relaxation, rushing and slowing, collapse and action, a sensation reaching you from the outside and a sensation arising from your inside.

Can you expand your attention to notice two things at the same time? Try to attend to the whole of your sensate body and at the same time pay attention to another person or to doing a task. This is about dividing your attention. Can you sense into your body and butter bread at the same time, or type on your laptop and listen to the children, for instance?

At the back of the head is another "eye", which can sense what is behind us. Try walking backwards, a new way to develop your attention. This "eye" is the optical part of the brain and is also where God is said to look in through us and out at the world.

Attend to your choices: does doing this make me more defended? Or does it take me beyond myself, vulnerable and free, able to participate in life more fully? Might your choice lead to deliciousness?

Allow yourself to experience it all

We don't really "have" a phone, dress, car or house; what we really have is our experience of having them. Can you allow yourself to "have" your unique experience fully? Can you acknowledge what is here right now for you?

As a daily practice, allow yourself to acknowledge your discomfort as well as comfort, the yuck as well as the yum. Perhaps your left knee aches and you feel anxious without knowing why, or maybe your throat hurts or you are worried about a disagreement with a friend, or you feel disappointed or frustrated or angry at yourself for something . . . How much reality can you bear?

With support, we can transform challenging feelings such as fear, pain, anger and hatred into pleasure and delight. The key to transformation is to have enough resources in place. Enough quietness of mind to be able to sense body and breath. Enough friends to talk to, or access to a paid therapist.

If we can allow ourselves to accept ourselves and be as we are, potentiality opens up. Anything is possible. A kind of magic happens when you acknowledge what is, without pretending it is not. A surprising relaxation occurs and an opening up to a bigger sense of reality and self . . . Allowing integrates the various splits in our consciousness into one unified experience.

Can you allow your feeling body to be tremoring in response to the world around? What does your body contribute vibrationally to the sensate world? Is it discordant or harmonious music we are playing together?

Be receptive

Our body is a quivering antenna attuned to the vibration of truthfulness and integrity. We "know" when someone is telling us the truth and when someone is deceiving us. We feel it in our body. We feel when someone or something is "off" and when we are turned "on", excited and open. Our work is to tune in to the "violin" of our body-soul, to listen deeply to the music our body is revealing right now about the state of our immediate personal truth and our response to the external environment, as well as to the internal environment of ourselves.

I am constantly "interpreting" all of the sensate data arising in my body and life. Besides my truth burps, which I mentioned earlier, sometimes data takes the form for me of energetic shivers, cold, heat, pain in my heart, and more. What is the way in which God "talks" to you? How does the Universe of Deliciousness communicate with you and try to get your attention? Through which songs, imagery, sensations, smells, sounds, tastes, feelings is it reaching out to you?

All symptoms and disease are attempts by the Universe of Deliciousness to communicate with us, to get our attention, to correct our course of action. Disease often occurs after smaller symptoms (or accidents) have been repeatedly ignored.

Religion calls this form of communication the small still voice of the heart. It is about tuning in to hearing and heeding life through the unique ways in which we individually experience intuition, instinct and inspiration – which could be aural, visual, sensate, kinaesthetic, gustatory, olfactory or other. It is not necessarily an actual verbal message but a subtle, imaginal, delicate conveyance. It arises in hints and whispers, clues and hints, arising sensations and hunches, feelings and knowing . . .all of which encourage us to embrace our vulnerable and changeable humanity. Our sensitivity is our strength, and listening to it is our daily navigation system. Our body tells us what is wise action for us in this moment. What does it mean for you when your shoulders ache or your gums bleed? Learn to understand how your body communicates with you.

Be appreciative

We begin to be appreciative by suspending our judgement of others as better or worse than us. When you meet someone, let the first thing that you think be: "I wish you happiness." This is simple but can transform relationships. While it may be easy with friends and family, try it with those people you find challenging. This may be hard to do as you are tempted to judge, label and categorize them – yet you can still choose to wish them happiness . . .

We need to accept that each person is unique, and other people are different from us and from each other. Can we look across at a stranger on a train, a beggar on the street, someone in an expensive car, a person of different gender or sexuality, who has or doesn't have children, and instead of projecting our inner criticism, hatred or desire onto them, look and accept them exactly as they are?

Daniel Odier, French tantric poet and writer, says that by placing the spiritual and mystical path in the social context (we) will blossom into unprecedented creativity in the mystical, scientific, and artistic arenas in which each person regains her unity in the total acceptance of her nature.[136]

Consciously connect with someone unlike yourself. Can you acknowledge them human to human? Can you smile at someone who supports an opposing football team or whose clothes, speech and food are very different to yours? The person at work or down the street who really annoys you? Can you find something about them, even something small, that you can appreciate?

Is there a difference between me and you? Is "me" more important or less important than "you"? Is there a way in which we can balance our sense of self with sense of the other?

Remember a time when you felt really loved, appreciated, acknowledged. Perhaps by a parent, teacher, friend, lover or animal. Allow yourself to feel this in your body and heart. Do you feel more secure, relaxed and soft? Invite the sensations to grow bigger until you are encompassed in a big field of love. Then allow your feelings of warmth, openness and love to extend outwards to other people, recognizing that everyone has their burdens, which may not be obvious. Just like you, they are also doing their best . . .What creative step towards connection can you take?

Choose to see undivided wholeness, health and balance, and to stay neutral and not contribute to socially acceptable gossip, cliques and put-downs. Can we respect others, as also a part of the Big All? Can we feel the earth under our feet, trees and sky above, to also be a part of the Big All?

Moving through our day, can we consider all information present to be of real interest – from our head, heart and body, from within our own self and from the outside world?

Participate actively in the world

What is it that you would really like to see in the world? If you were to have your heart's desire, what might it look like and feel like? Can you actively participate in its ongoing unfoldment?

This is not a manifestation exercise. This is not about wish or will fulfilment. It is about acknowledging the immensity of life, within which we all live. Not just "my life" but Life itself, within which I am. Life is not just something that happens to us. It is something we co-create. It is as we think, pray, feel, understand, imagine and interact with it . . . as we accept and engage with it.

Can you honour the wild sensual freedom in others and the earth, rocks, trees, rivers, as if they could hear us, as if this reciprocity were real and essential? Can you honour everything with praise, gratitude and consideration, with singing, dancing, touching and listening? Can you relate with the aliveness of absolutely everything?

Know that we are all artists within the world. When we create in physical materials, we are artisans, craftspeople and artists, hairdressers, sculptors, cooks, writers, weavers, builders, architects and storytellers. When we create silently and invisibly inside ourselves through imagination, we are mystics, potent creators, utilizing the same power that creates the universe.

When we imagine something, when we feel it, smell it, taste it, sense it in our body, we are activating something deep, deep, deep in the universe. We are consciously dreaming something into creation. We are in the Universe of Deliciousness. We feel lit up, switched on, turned on.

Breathe

Breath connects our inner and outer environments, our biological need for oxygen and our spiritual need for refined energy. It is both a taking-in and a giving-out.

Without changing anything, notice where and how you usually breathe. Is it high in your chest, at your diaphragm or deep down in your belly?

Try to take in more breath than you think you need. How do you find that? Is it harder to do than you would have expected? Do you notice any particular thoughts about that?

Try moving your body with the breath, opening your pelvis and arms in an expansion as you inhale and closing small in a contraction with each exhalation. Play with it, explore, perhaps to music.

Try breathing into your chest, belly and pelvis, using your imagination as you inhale and exhale. Try breathing into all parts of your body. Every cell breathes. Your skin also breathes; it is like a third lung. What, if anything, do you notice?

It is recommended that each exhalation is the same length as an inhalation or longer. Try breathing in for a count of six and then out for a count of six. Repeat this a few times. Take simple, slow, rhythmic breaths for a few minutes. It is not intended that you breathe like this all of the time, but that sometimes you can make use of this breathing to calm and connect more fully with yourself. To put yourself in the zone of the athlete or the lover with increased calm and awareness.

Laughter is also great for releasing stress and increasing breath. Laughing, singing, humming, yoga, acupuncture, splashing the face with cold water or having a cold shower, like breathing slowly, all stimulate the vagus nerve, calming us down.

How will you integrate all of this into your daily life? What do you choose to bring alive now?

What?	When and where?	How long for?	Done?

I hope that you are finding your way with practising your practices – and allowing kindness for when you don't, can't or don't want to do them. Both self-discipline and self-love are necessary.

Turning Potential Into Potency

The point of regularly doing the exercises described in this chapter and this book is to prepare ourselves. They are not the end point, just a beginning, training us out of our mental chatter, into our body, and into contact with the more-that-is-possible and our deeper knowing, beyond the beyond. Our potential activates when we are in service, wanting what is best, whatever that is, for our client, child, friend, partner, or parent. We are not fixed on a result, but intending to settle upon the "best" outcome. When we prepare ourselves regularly, and intend for the best, we still ourselves, time slows, and we open up, accessing the depth of the delicious universe, which shows up as our inspired intuition . . .

When we do our practices – whether prayer, dance, chant, meditation, or whatever form they take – we change our sensitivity settings, becoming increasingly porous to information from the deep big delicious intelligent "all" that is around us. As more of us become bodily sensitized, more of us will hear the unexpected wise prompts to action. We don't need human "expertise" and "cleverness", but to listen collaboratively and act on wisdom from beyond the beyond.

While there is no ultimate goal as such, the end point of all these ideas and practices is to live well, with consideration for others. All spiritual and religious traditions teach that compassionate behaviour is what matters. Buddha said compassion brings the release of the mind. The New Testament says kindness brings the presence of God. Judaism says kind behaviour is more important than belief in God. The Dalai Lama says religion is kindness. It has also been shown biologically that being kind not only makes us feel good, but physically makes us healthier.[137]

Our potential is to live kindly, with love for ourselves and for others and for all the earth.

Karen Armstrong, a mystical Catholic writer, describes spirituality as a humbling thing. Instead of being full of ourselves, we begin to realize that the world is deeply mysterious and . . . we haven't got the tight grasp on reality that we think.[138]

In unknowingness, minds confused by lack of familiar reference points, we "know" through our heartfelt soul-body the "right" way to live with others. We act, not from fear of a doctrine, rulebook or ruler, fear of getting it wrong, but from listening to our whole body's felt response to the rightness or wrongness of this action in this moment now.

Attunement to our fertile, sensate body-knowing is our potency. We already have the key we need to the Universe of Deliciousness. We just need to use it . . .

I invite you to create your own personal practice programme, to live imbued by essential pleasure.

Rather than shut down, live in fear, think too much or disconnect, you can come back to your body, remembering and sensing your relationship with everything. You are the universe appearing as a human. It is your choice now, your practice for a week, a month or three, perhaps for the rest of your life . . .

As you bring your now embodied, true, loving, sensual, empowered, magnificent self into the world, the world is changed. You change and the world changes.

Anything is possible. The still depth of our being holds all potentiality in it – for us and for the world.

	What?	When?	Where?	Duration	Outcome
CURRENT MESS What do you want to change?					
SLOW					
BODY					
DEPTH					
PLEASURE					
POWER					
POTENCY					
MAGICAL INFINITE POSSIBILITIES What is gained?					

And So Our Story Continues

As a child I loved the line in a poem by Nina Ruth Davis Salaman: "How long the distant voices in your heart have all been silent."[139] Now finally, I am "out and proud". This book is what my heart has always known and has wanted to share; the profound, rich, delicious way of life I value and live is secret no more.

I healed the grief of beginning this life, having lost a twin brother in the womb while I continued to live – I resolved to live my life fully for both of us. I healed the trauma of being born forcibly by forceps, returning my soul into my body. I handed back to my ancestors those burdens that were not mine to carry and turned away from them towards my own life. I healed physical damage to my cells, blood and organs, and damaging emotional habits that do not serve. I transformed the huge unhappiness with which I began life into being the person I have now become, my destiny aligned. I moved from being raw, inchoate, unformed to having structure, able to communicate.

When we heal, our relationship with ourselves changes. Instead of fear, we embrace all parts of ourselves with love – changing everything in relation to everyone.

GRATITUDE

It is with great gratitude that I find myself so very well. I can sometimes hardly believe it that I feel so good in myself. Life is simple and I am confident from deep within myself, now spilling over into external relationships and expression in the outside world. I live my majesty and stillness. My life is full of rich relationships with wonderful people I am glad to know and call my friends. I feel known and loved and, with this book, even more widely known, for the truth of who I am. Ordinary, vulnerable, sensual, powerful, imperfect, unique, sacred – just like you, and yet unlike you.

TRAUMA CAN BE A BLESSING

We can view trauma as suffering and limitation, or, like everything else in the Universe of Deliciousness, we can view it as a wisdom and experience on the spectrum of pleasure and pain.

Without having known the extreme discomfort of my traumatized decades, when I felt unsafe in my own skin in society, I could not have come to appreciate the melting everyday deliciousness of my belly, heart, head and all flesh that I now live.

In the past, I could not have perceived the "wisdom" of the trauma – which I now see was protecting me, with this potent knowing, until both the world and I were grown-up enough; until the time was ripe, to express this publicly.

The ordinary is sacred.

ADMITTING MY POWER

Over the years, I've come to know without doubt that I was in a previous soul lifetime a high priestess in the ancient goddess temples. I bring into this lifetime a wisdom about fully sensual relating. This is what my heart knows and wants to share. In this lifetime, the form of wisdom I am sharing is not directly sexual. This book, the talks, workshops and sessions I offer, and my whole way of being in the world are the form of my transmission, of this important body-based way of life.

These days, there are several of us who "remember" the ancient ways and who are leading the way, feminine-style, with a gentle invitation . . . It is time for us all to respect the feminine and rebalance.

TRUST, FREEDOM AND FLOW

These days, mostly, I do not worry. I cannot go wrong, because I'm listening to the arising sensory information and "it" guides me to move. It prompts and I follow. I am obedient to it. When sometimes I'm not, in a kind of laziness, things go slightly awry. I trust deeply in the goodness of Life, of Life loving Life, Life making love with Life through me and through you, at all times, whether we rationally "get it" or not. This moment my heart is blazing warmth and love, listening to the tinny cafe music as I watch the people walking by quickly outside. I am deeply safe, as are you too.

Life reveals its meaning and purpose to us when we wake up from the slumber of laziness and our enchantment with external distractions. It happens when we are living in accord with Life and the promptings of Life, where things that happen are not always quite what they seem. My mobile phone dropped in some water when I was worrying about something, but I was not worried about damage; I knew it was an invitation from life to pause.

CONSTANT CHANGE

Nothing stays the same. My face changes, my body changes, my sense of being me changes. Each day a new fresh discovery about myself, others and the world. Always new adaptations. And as the waves of deliciousness arise and break through me, they bring with them a sense of wakefulness even if I am tired: I'm rejuvenated by this inner contact with myself.

Within the Universe of Deliciousness are many different experiences. Just now, another new one washes over me – of my chest being filled with space, the deep dark black of outer space studded with stars within me, as if a door had just been opened in my chest. It makes being alive a delicious adventure unfolding. An endless extrasensory human experience, an entertainment of discovery and delight. Always a surprise! What will I find today when I explore what is happening around and in me right now? A world without end; just being me, in constant personal evolution.

So many different dimensions and landscapes of heart I am exploring, space-time traveller indeed!

EXQUISITE SENSITIVITY

My body is very sensitive. I am a gourmet of sensation. There is no way back to numbness, disconnection and zone-out. I am immensely grateful to all my guides and teachers who helped me along the way to integrate my knowing of the sensual mystery with functioning in ordinary life.

As I write this, I can feel the pleasure of deliciousness inside my mouth. Without an external cause, nonetheless the pleasure arises and is enjoyed by me, connecting me to a sense of silence much bigger than me and an awareness of the external world. I trust in my relationship with Life.

DANCING WITH LIFE

It seems to me that the Universe of Deliciousness is always waiting for us to notice it, to notice that it is present, that it is a possibility, an option, a way of life. I have the strong sense that it wants to be known and noticed and enjoyed. That it wants to be enjoyed, is meant to be enjoyed.

Expanding, relaxing and enjoying, I melt over and over again into a thousand openings and widenings, confident in my self, in my being but one part of a much bigger whole. Of there being no separation anywhere but plenty of delightfully intricate detail in the folding and decorating of the unified fabric of the universe. It appears to want our fully sensual participation in the profound play of life in a body on Earth that we are lucky enough to be invited to. It's a game with no winners and no losers, only a vast variety of experiencers . . . and the ever-constant this moment in your body right now, in relation to this moment in mine.

And however much now I can celebrate the wonderfulness of who I have become, there are always more layers of experience and understanding to alchemize and transform further . . . There is no end to discovering the wonders of who I really am and who you really are . . . only infinite possibility.

We can transform life into a work of art by consciously living to create beauty and to enjoy the pleasure of that beauty. Life becomes something we create for us all to enjoy and not just for each separate self. We become the artist and the artworks, audience and reviewers.

Heaven on Earth is a simple matter. It is being close to our own sensual experience, receiving ourselves, into our own embrace, our own hearts, our own judgement-free minds. It is letting ourselves be – as we are, just as we are, without interfering with our experience.

What if we are exactly perfect as we are? What if you are exactly perfect just as you are? Perfectly imperfect. What if all that were needed is for you to open yourself to everything that is here right now, to experiencing the full deliciousness of this moment now, every moment now?

Join Me
in Living This

"To participate in the dance of life with senses to perceive it, lungs that breathe it, organs that draw nourishment from it – is a wonder beyond words."[140]

Joanna Macy, environmental activist

"Physical pleasure is a sensual experience no different from pure seeing or the pure sensation with which a fine fruit fills the tongue; it is a great unending experience, which is given us, a knowing of the world, the fullness and the glory of all knowing."[141]

Rainer Maria Rilke, poet and novelist

"Instinctual Intelligence stays with the body but we don't have to be imprisoned by it or oriented completely by it. Instinct has its place in the physical realm, but the delights and rewards of all things pleasurable, physical or otherwise, have their roots in the truth of Being."[142]

Karen Johnson, co-developer of the Diamond Approach

As we approach the end of the journey into the Universe of Deliciousness mapped in this book, it is time to gather in all we have explored and discovered. We will arrive again where we first began, hopefully with a new embodied experience and understanding. It is time for us to live bone-and-marrow these realizations and practices, our responsibility to ourselves, others, the Earth and divine.

We examined the MESS we are in and glimpsed the MAGIC that is possible. We travelled through seven significant practical MEDICINEs, accessing the Universe Of Deliciousness. We SLOWed right down, so that mind and body connect rather than exist as separate locations and frequencies. We sensed into the amazingly functional, sensate, feeling, physical BODY. We acknowledged the surprising true DEPTH of reality. We moved into RELATIONSHIP with everything and every being. We allowed ourselves to fully enjoy truthfulness, beauty and PLEASURE. We discovered that living with honest vulnerability in each moment in relationship is our true POWER. And we saw how harmonized opposites turn potential into POTENCY.

The Universe of Deliciousness has been here all along. With a little effort, integrity and practice, we can live our sensual spirituality, nourishing ourselves for ourselves, accessing our dynamic wisdom through subtle listening to arising sensations, signs and symbols.

LIFE IS LOVING US DELICIOUSLY

Our destiny is to live in the pleasurable, wise and dynamic Universe of Deliciousness. This universe is caring for us, for each of us, all at the same time. This is a perspective so enormous that it is hard for us small humans to think of it . . . huge in time, space and depth. Mostly we are immersed in responsive actions and caught up in distractions – got to get milk, phone the doctor, finish the spreadsheet, make my deadline and email my boss back – but we are living within, and as a part of, a much, much larger, wise and pleasurable context.

The Universe of Deliciousness is the greatest consciousness and canvas of life. It includes all of our previous lives throughout time – past and future, the depth of love that exists inside and outside of everything, and the furthest reaches of all the planets and stars, and beyond the beyond. It is a loving intelligent aliveness, capable of attending at the same time to each of us, to exactly what we need, for our individual and collective evolutions. It wisely guides us through pleasure as a signpost to the nourishment that we really need. And wisely challenges us, sometimes repeatedly, calling us to do our own inner work.

We are being invited to know that love and fear are not really far apart. They are different expressions of the same essential energy. If we really feel our fear, if we love our fear, we will after a while arrive at love. And when we love, sometimes hate arises. One turns into the other and back again. This is life in motion, in evolution, pulsating, vibrating, shaking and moving. There is no distinction, simply two locations on an energetic continuum.

The "other" is not really so very far away or so very different from us, simply a different refraction, a unique expression, of the All that is: we are both arising from the same deep energy of being. Life wants to experience itself through you and through me and through this computer, table, chair and cup of green tea, through every variation of relational experience, every shade, colour, tempo, dynamic and taste. Life is loving life through each of us, all of the time, especially right here and right now. What will we co-create?

Life leads us where we need to be . . . Not just our life, but Life within which we are living, which is living us. We are being deliciously embraced by life. Let's actively welcome it.

We are love, loving love, being guided by love, in love, and with love. We are making love with life, while life is making love with us.

ATTENTION TO REALITY

Our task is to pay attention to ourselves. Not selfishly just for the benefit of ourselves, but with curiosity in order to know ourselves better and deepen our human experience. Attention is the method for tuning our own instrument of perception, our sensitive and sensual soul-body.

As we pay attention, we notice more. We regain our appetite for life. We see the freshness of this here now, renewing our capacity to feel the world with the live wonder of a child.

The key is accepting our whole self exactly as we are without changing anything. The constant practice is being in deep contact with everything, including our embarrassing weaknesses and failings, as well as our proud achievements, creations and knowledge. It is trusting that our impulses are not to be squashed, feared as dangerous, but relished as true.

We all make mistakes all of the time. It is not what we do, but how we do it. If we are willing to be honest, to look at something with awareness and take full responsibility for ourselves, then any mistake can be transformed from darkness to light. The real mistake is to live blindly, automatically, hurting others in our clumsy attempts to find peace for ourselves.

Apparent opposites such as success and failure, spiritual and material, superior and inferior collapse, when we realize that darkness and light are states within each of us. This orientation and vigilance restores us to our natural human free will and dignity.

We tremor and vibrate with aliveness, in relationship together with the aliveness of reality. We live in harmonious response to the world around us, when we sense and trust ourselves; then our spontaneity becomes full of grace.

Sacred life is right here: we are the worshipper, we are the temple and we are the divine.

INDIVIDUAL DELICIOUSNESS

In practice, all we need to do is orientate ourselves to the aliveness of life. Pay attention to the qualities of love, joy, abundance, beauty, generosity, pleasure and celebration when they appear in your daily world, however they appear. Instead of getting caught up in thinking such as "not enough", "poor me" and "terrible them", try consciously choosing appreciation and affirmation – without words, simply in your glad reception of it all.

For example, in this moment my eye falls on a beautiful, pink pot plant; I can taste the deliciousness of the chocolate brownie I was eating still in my mouth; I feel the delight of the sunshine on my back and shoulders; I notice the lovely people around me, the uplifting sound of a woman's laughter and the sparkle of a man's eyes; the pleasurable squeak of the door as it opens, the pleasing rhythm of this person's footsteps; the flow of breath in my chest . . .

This practice of paying attention to the present moment can transform the ordinary into the extraordinary. Let your heart feel kissed a thousand times with the bounty of gorgeousness that there is all around you, all of the time . . . Let everything change into an ongoing orchestral composition for your delectation. Allow yourself to feel humbled, stilled, eased . . . soothed by the harmonious rhythms and realization that the full spectrum of various universal qualities is always present here in the world . . .

Yes, life contains challenges and terrible things are happening in the world. But when they are held in the joy and beauty of life, they are carried, and we can see them as part of the incredible dance of life, of interpenetrating darkness and light, in relational exchange and communication. Pleasure is not just a reward or a result, it is the transformational currency of life itself, of life loving life.

Supported by recognizing the joy, pleasure, beauty and generosity all around us, we can begin to soften our defences, and open up to seeing the great joke of it all, to stop taking it so personally!

This is a major shift, and it is one that is easy to make, and to turn it into our new default setting. It is as if it has been waiting in the wings for you all along, awaiting for you to notice how much goodness is here, for you to notice, respond, feel . . . This is our collective way forward: abundance is not about material objects, devices or the latest fashions; it is our receptivity to what is already here . . .the living world within which we are lucky enough to find ourselves.

This is seeing the positive, accentuating the positive, as it genuinely strikes you . . . Reality is influenced by our perception, by the filter we put onto what we see, hear, touch and say, and, in turn, reality is changed by our perception of it; quantum entanglement, as the physicists call it, in action . . .

We are not just helpless victims acted upon by external forces. We are active co-creators in life. And life is something far greater than units such as "my life" and "your life": we are *all* within Life.

If you fancy seeing life through different eyes, do give it a go! Fall in love with Life!

RELATIONAL DELICIOUSNESS

Everything is relationship and lovemaking. It is in our active looking and touching, smelling and licking, appreciating, praising and honouring the other; through interactive, interconnected play, interpenetration and mutual receptivity, darkness and light, masculine and feminine, dynamic creativity without end, that magic happens and pleasure flows, the world becoming alive to itself, including us fully alive to ourselves.

Love is so much more than we think it is.

We are love. What we want is to turn inside out. We want the big love that comes through the portal of our hearts to shine fully on the outside. To be not just something private, not just to be shared with some-one we are intimate with, but something to be shared with everyone and everything.

Turning inside out means allowing the mess, the bloody wetness of the inside of the body to show; for the truth of us to be seen, as it were, on the outside. To show our vulnerable confusion and fear. For there is no separation. No division. It is to be just like the movement of energy in our torus-shaped field, allowing that which is at our core to become visible outside.

Fierce, uncompromising, honest, free and wild. We are Love.

COLLECTIVE DELICIOUSNESS

Life itself wants to evolve through us. We sense this sometimes and we feel the possibility when we sit quietly in nature . . . We, like the ferns and trees, are yearning to be fully alive! To be lived fully! Full of passion and pleasure, humility and sensitivity – wise, dynamic and sensual deliciousness!

Who will we be when ego is not the driver, but instead is soul?

This book is a guide to a new way of being, rooted in body and relational heart, exploring how to follow the spontaneous arising of our instinctual intelligence. It is now time for listening, feeling, accepting our own wisdom, in the form of unfolding hunches and impulses, sensations, knowing and intuitions that arise within us. This way of being is a fundamental resource, helping us navigate waves of fear and anger, acknowledge changes in climate, species extinction and the possible collapse of human civilization.[143] We can celebrate our own deliciousness, our full range of personal experience, yet acknowledge the pain and challenges that will likely unfold in this process of collective planetary transformation.

Our old reaction is to be fearful amongst dwindling resources, to be aggressive, to get for self. But these challenging times are also an evolutionary opportunity to trust the inherent goodness, wisdom and deliciousness of life, to open to something new . . .

We can change our orientation, from individual advancement to collective benefit. From logic and strategy, to body sensation and feeling. From top-down external governance to bottom-up individually empowered, intuitive guidance. From taking abundance for granted to appreciation for the natural world. From pleasure in possession, to pleasure in integrity and feeling experience.

Despite a lack of external security, resources and possessions, delicious joy is still possible. There can be a freedom, a relief, from the old ways of deception and hustle, a relaxation into this here now – simple, human, local love – and a riding the waves of what is, again and again and again . . . every feeling and sensation welcomed, experienced, acknowledged . . . transformed . . .

The new global currency is compassion, consideration and cooperation. Working together with others to grow food, cook, protect ourselves when resources are scarce. Trusting our nomadic pack-animal body to sense the environment and instinctively know which action to take, and who to trust.

What will we do now? We will restore, mend, recycle, reuse and return to practical skills such as ropes, horticulture, electronics, metal and woodwork, sewing and knitting, creating what we need.

Can you be with this this grief, anger and fear about what has been destroyed and find your personal deliciousness in the experience? Can you live in the Universe of Deliciousness while the world is being torn apart? Can you hold two opposites, deliciousness and disastrous destruction?

If we don't know, how will we cope?
When our hearts break, can we be curious rather than violent?
Can we unite the oppositions within us and outside us?
Can we love what is, even when "what is" is not easy?
Can we regard change as creative?

Can we find the deliciousness within the disaster?
Can we nourish ourselves from within?
Can we trust life?
Can we coexist and co-create with life as a part of life?

GLOBAL DELICIOUSNESS

We humans are part of the planet. We are not something separate from nature. We are the Earth's consciousness, our thoughts, feelings and awareness, reflected in her health. Everything spiritual is expressed in physicality; there is no mistake: as above, so below. Material existence does not lie, it only reflects our consciousness and makes it visible, so we can act.

If we want to save the Earth, it is not just action that is needed; we need to appreciate her. When a person is ill, what heals them is not just the surgery, drugs, pills or ointments. It is our love for the flesh and the qualities of the flesh, it is self-love and self-forgiveness. Our role as protectors of the planet is not only about planting enough trees to rebalance carbon in the air and enough insect-friendly plants to maintain the ecosystem. Our task is to actively love the Earth, to thank and appreciate her for her abundance. Each insect, gust of wind, bird and spider, dandelion and elderflower, sycamore and oak, stream and rock, ray of sunshine, dung beetle and maggot has its essential place in the interconnected web of life.

Our human role is to notice the scent of the rose and the song of the blackbird, the crop of sweetcorn, apples, potatoes and tulips, to receive with gratefulness the abundance the Earth has gifted us, in the same way we receive the plenitude of pleasure our bodies give us. Our task is to receive, listen, feel, sense, smell, touch, taste, notice and appreciate the details of this earthly life with humility and gratitude.

Let us love our family and friends, neighbours and community, and let us love whatever we are doing right now – this music, this sowing, sewing, cooking and mending. Love the source of life itself, whatever we call it, without which we would not have this sensate and emotional adventure.

Our return to the Universe of Deliciousness is a return to a universal state of innocence and freshness, to sensate awareness of our vulnerable need for relationship with others, without which we would not survive. We need to remember we do all need each other.

The universe is without limitation in its creativity. May we live our wisdom and pleasure in sensual, soulful, sensitive exchange with others, with depth and the Earth. May Deliciousness flow through us, loving Deliciousness in everything and everyone else. May we co-create Heaven on Earth, even if that doesn't look anything like we thought it would! A new Eden, beginning everything again all over again . . .

May we be surprised, humbled and delighted.

Love Loving Love

Everything is being constantly created and destroyed.
When we meet another,
we see and feel
all their layers;
physical exterior of styled clothes, hair and skin,
falsified smile, eye and stilled cheek
and glistening below,
human blood and muscle unseen, and
deeper still, unique soul-essence.
Through relationship with them,
as through everything
a doorway
for us
into nothingness and everything.

They, like us, are portals
to the universal,
limitless, indescribable, constantly shifting and evolving.
Deliciousness of the universe
deep and relational,
at every level.

Life is constantly loving itself,
through us and through everything else
without pause.
The world's not static
within which we, as cardboard cut-out defined object, interact.
Life is not cause and reaction, limited time and resource.

Infinitely creative,
this aliveness, anything's possible.
Shiver through me.
We ignite ourselves, loving this now,
ignite ourselves, others and the living Earth.

The music says, 'So kiss me.'
Everything romancing us, and we romancing it,
in our every sentence, touch and task.
Not you against me, but you and me.
You and me and you and it and this and that and us all together in
a non-stop multi-relational conversation, dance, painting, song or
meal
creation without end.

Limitless creators – affecting and being affected
by everything else
all the time.

Everything containing everything
everything else containing us too,
we are never unconnected.

We matter,
as this unique iteration of life,
contributing this essential quality
into the huge
multi-dimensional
play.

Appendix

"The meaning of heart is circle because love never ends."
Ruby Hollenbery (age seven), daughter of mine

"Someday the earth will weep, she will beg for her life, she will cry with tears of blood. You will make a choice, if you will help her or let her die, and when she dies, you too will die."[144]
Hollow Horn Bear – Brule Lakota leader

"Do not be daunted by the enormity of the world's grief.
Do justly now.
Love mercy now.
Walk humbly now.[145]
You are not obligated to complete the work,
but neither are you free to abandon it."[146]
Talmud – Jewish sacred text written by many over centuries

Practice Overview

4. RELATIONSHIP – Practices for Nourishment

5. PLEASURE – Practices for Fulfilment

6. POWER – Practices for Powerfulness

7. POTENCY – Practices for Potential

Resources

Today, we are lucky enough to live in a time when lots of therapeutic, healing and spiritual paths are easily available, both in our local areas and on the internet. Please do your research carefully to find out which modality and practitioner is right for "unique you" right now.

Use discrimination, recommendation and intuition to find a therapist, healer or teacher – especially so in the area of sexual pleasure. There is today an explosion of practitioners and workshops, and some have more personal maturity and integrity than others.

See also my blog article "How To Find Your Practitioner" on my website www.universeofdeliciousness.com

Whichever form you choose, use it to release what no longer serves you. Set yourself free!

BODYWORK

Somatic tension patterns and underlying emotions can be changed via bodywork or body psychotherapy. These include Alexander technique, Feldenkrais, osteopathy, craniosacral therapy, Somatic Experiencing, Body-Mind Centering, biodynamic psychology, process oriented psychology, acupuncture, bioenergetics, Grinberg Method, Buteyko and other breathwork forms.

Physical and emotional symptoms can also be helped by remedies and supplements; look into, for example, homeopathy, ayurveda and naturopathy.

EMBODIMENT PRACTICE CLASSES

There are classes and workshops available in many kinds of practices, including martial arts, yoga, movement and dance. One methodology is not "better" than any other. Experiment to see what you personally prefer, which teacher or group you feel inspired by and comfortable with.

Movement

There are several non-choreographed practices where sensations, shapes and relationships can be explored, including ecstatic dance, 5Rhythms, contact improvisation, continuum movement, authentic movement, Non-Linear Movement, movement medicine and Amerta movement.

Martial Arts

Many traditions with roots in ancient Hinduism, Taoism and Buddhism explore defence, competition and physical, mental and spiritual development, including fencing, boxing, aikido, karate, capoeira, taekwondo, judo and jiu-jitsu.

Yoga

There are a great many modern variations on the traditional physical, mental and spiritual practices.

Shaking

These kinds of releasing practices include Osho's dynamic meditation, Wilhelm Reich's bioenergetics, David Berceli's Tension & Trauma Releasing Exercises or the chaos section of 5Rhythms dance.

Tantra

Especially in the area of sexuality, choose your therapist, healer, guide or teacher with great care.

Some programmes describe themselves as being tantra or neo-tantra (meaning new tantra) while others use the language of flirting, dating, intimacy, relationship or conscious sexuality.

Tantra is an ancient approach to life, a celebration of earthly life in all its colours, textures and complexities. It emerged in India in the first millennium BC out of Hinduism and Buddhism. Tantra literally means to weave or practise. It's a spiritual path of inclusion, of being with our experiences in daily life. Spiritual realization is shown as the union of masculine and feminine in lovemaking.

Legend says tantric practice was born out of a conversation 5,000 years ago between two lovers, Shiva and Devi. Inspired by her desire to know the mystical meaning of existence, he composed poetic instructions, to give her a direct bodily experience of how the universe came into being.

Many contemporary tantra workshops are safe, respectful, loving spaces for sexual exploration. But neo-tantra can overpromise what it delivers; rarely is anyone enlightened from this practice. There can be a danger of boundaries being overridden, of voyeurism, increased mechanization, tension, ego and addiction. A few organizations are sex-cults with abusive teachers and behaviour.

Consider what you uniquely need, not what "everyone else" says is fantastic. Trust your instincts!

Women's wisdom

The Red School teaches the cyclical wisdom of menstruation and menopause through books and workshops. There is also the Red Tent Movement, which holds regular meetings.

Notes

[1] Attributed to Albert Einstein, appears to be a fair summary of his thoughts.

[2] Peter Drucker, *Managing in Turbulent Times* (New York, NY: Routledge, 2011).

[3] Llewellyn Vaughan-Lee, *The Circle of Love* (Inverness, CA: The Golden Sufi Center, 1999), 45.

[4] Facts and Figures: "Ending Violence Against Women", *UN Women*, November, 2020, https://www.unwomen.org/en/what-we-do/ ending-violence-against-women/facts-and-figures

[5] Bonnie Bainbridge Cohen, American movement artist, therapist and educator, founder of MindBodyCentering®. Much of her teaching is spoken, books include *Sensing, Feeling and Action: The Experiential Anatomy of Body-Mind Centering* (Berkeley, CA: North Atlantic Books, 1994).

[6] British YouGov survey 2019. Connor Ibbetson, "Young Britons are The Most Lonely", YouGov (October 2019).

[7] Y. Kelly, A. Zilanawala, C. Booker and A. Sacker, January 4 2019 "Social Media Use and Adolescent Mental Health: Findings from the UK Millennium Cohort Study." www.thelancet.com/journals/eclinm/ article/PIIS2589-5370(18)30060-9/fulltext

[8] "Special Report: Global Warming of 1.5°C, Summary for Policymakers", IPCC (2018), https://www.ipcc.ch/sr15/chapter/spm (2018).

[9] Damien Carrington, "Humanity has wiped out 60% of animal populations since 1970, report finds. The huge loss is a tragedy in itself but also threatens the survival of civilisation, say the world's leading

scientists." The *Guardian*, October 30 2018. https://www.theguardian.com/environment/2018/oct/30/humanity-wiped-out-animals-since-1970-major-report-finds. Damian Carrington, "Humans just 0.01% of all life but have destroyed 83% of wild mammals – stud", the *Guardian*, May 21 2018, https://www.theguardian.com/environment/2018/may/21/human-race-just-001-of-all-life-but-has-destroyed-over-80-of-wild-mammals-study. Katie Pavid, "40% of plants are threatened with extinction", Natural History Museum, September 30 2020, https://www.nhm.ac.uk/discover/news/2020/september/two-in-five-plants-are-threatened-with-extinction.html

[10] Oliver Milman, "Earth has lost a third of arable land in past 40 years, scientists say." *Guardian*, December 2 2015, https://www.theguardian.com/environmnet/2015/dec/02/arable-land-soilfood-security-shortage. Speaking at the 21st Conference of the Parties in Paris, experts from Grantham Centre revealed almost 33% of the world's arable land has been lost to erosion or pollution: "Soil Loss: an unfolding global disaster", Grantham Centre for Sustainable Futures, December 2 2015, http://grantham.sheffield.ac.uk/soil-loss-an-unfolding-global-disaster

[11] Migration Data Porta: "The bigger picture", July 8 2020, https://migrationdataportal.org/themes/forced-migration-or-displacement

[12] William Butler Yeats, *The Countess Cathleen* (Overland Park, KS: Digireads, 2011).

[13] William Blake, *The Marriage of Heaven and Hell* (Oxford, UK: Oxford University Press, 1975).

[14] Daniel Pinchbeck, "The universe only pretends to be made of matter. Secretly, it is made of love." Twitter comment, February 24 2012, https://twitter.com/DanielPinchbeck/status/172950055752445952?s=20

[15] Margaret Heffernan, *Beyond Measure: The Big Impact of Small Changes* (New York, NY: Simon & Schuster, 2015).

[16] J.M. Barrie, *Peter Pan* (London, UK: Puffin Classics, Penguin Random House, 2008).

[17] Ali Sundermier, "Science Alert" in *Business Insider* (September 2016).

[18] Peter Wohlleben, *The Hidden Life of Trees* (New York, NY: William Collins, 2017).

[19] Meeri Kim, "Can plants hear? In a study, vibrations prompt some to boost their defences." *Washington Post*, July 6 2014.

[20] John Martineau, *A Little Book of Coincidence in The Solar System* (Glastonbury, UK: Wooden Books, 2018), 24.

[21] "In the first years of life more than 1 million new neural connections form every second. After this period of rapid proliferation, connections are reduced through a process called pruning, which allows brain circuits to become more efficient." Center of the Developing Child, Harvard University, Key Concepts, Brain Architecture, https://developingchild. harvard.edu/science/key-concepts/brain-architecture

[22] Dr Hannah Critchlow, *Consciousness: A Ladybird Expert Guide* (London, UK: Penguin, 2018).

[23] Richard Rudd, *The Gene Keys: Unlocking the Higher Purpose Hidden In Your DNA* (London, UK: Watkins, 2015), 25th Gene Key, 278.

[24] J.K. Rowling, *Harry Potter and the Deathly Hallows* (London, NY: Bloomsbury, 2007).

[25] "Differential role of CBT skills, DBT skills and psychological flexibility in predicting depressive versus anxiety symptom improvement", *Behaviour Research and Therapy*, Vol 81, June 2016, 12–20. https://www.sciencedirect.com/science/article/abs/pii/S0005796716300420

[26] Robert Rosenthal and Lenore Jacobson, *Pygmalion in the Classroom: Teacher expectation and pupils' intellectual development*, (Holt, Rinehart & Winston, 1968).

[27] David Eagleman, *Incognito: The Secret Lives of The Brain* (Edinburgh, UK: Canongate, 2011).

[28] Joseph Campbell, spoken, cited by Czech psychiatrist Stanislav Grof, *Psychology of the Future: Lessons from Modern Consciousness Research*, (Albany, NY: State University of New York Press, 2000), 136.

[29] Llewellyn Vaughan-Lee, *The Return of the Feminine and the World Soul* (The Golden Sufi Center, Point Reyes, 2009).

[30] Julia Cameron, *The Artist's Way* (New York, NY: Tarcher/Penguin Putnam, 1992) 53. Week 2: Recovering A Sense of Identity.

[31] Bert Hellinger, well-known quote without a written source, perhaps spoken while working.

[32] Alfred Mercier, doctor in Lousiana, USA, in the 1800s; this quote is appparently one of his well-known musings.

[33] Mae West, American actress, spoken.

[34] Ralph Waldo Emerson, *The Complete Works*, 1904, Vol X. *Lectures and Biographical Sketches*, www.bartleby.com/90/1005.html

[35] Roger Housden, spiritual author of many books, gave his permission to use this quote.

[36] Research from University of Illinois/Draugiem Group cited by Holly Pevzner, "Building the Perfect Day", *Psychology Today* (January 2015).

[37] Naomi Stadlen, *What Mothers Do: Especially when it looks like nothing* (London, UK: Penguin, 2007).

[38] Naomi Judd, country and western singer, spoken words, apparently her personal mission statement.

[39] Llewellyn Vaughan-Lee, *The Circle of Love* (Inverness, CA: The Golden Sufi Center, 1999), 20.

[40] Attributed to Joanna Macy, but although this quote sounds like her it may not be by her.

[41] Inspired by Non-Linear Movement ™ that I teach, developed by Michaela Boehm, Kashmir Shaivism tantra lineage holder.

[42] Gabrielle Roth, founder of of 5Rhythms Dance, a phrase she often spoke when teaching. Robert Ansell gave me permission and the correct wording for this.

[43] Kalu Rinpoche, Tibetan Buddhist meditation master and author, 1905–1989.

[44] Rumi, probably translated by Coleman Barks. Rumi poems were not originally titled.

[45] Stanley Keleman, American therapist, founder of formative psychology. He wrote several books about anatomy, posture and life experience, including *Your Body Speaks Its Mind* (1975), *Emotional Anatomy* (1985) and *Embodying Experience* (1987).

[46] Dr Peter A. Levine, wrote several books about trauma including *Waking the Tiger: Healing Trauma; In an Unspoken Voice: How the Body Releases Trauma and Restores Goodness and Healing Trauma: A Pioneering Program for Restoring the Wisdom of Your Body.*

[47] *MIT Technology Review*, 2019.

[48] Nicolas Handoll, *Anatomy of Potency* (Hereford, UK: Osteopathic Supplies, 2000).

[49] Rudolf Steiner, nineteenth-century Austrian philosopher and educator; his ideas explored further by Albert Soesman, *Our Twelve Senses: How Healthy Senses Refresh the Soul* (Stroud, UK: Hawthorn Press, Anthroposophy series, 1990).

[50] Anna Pitts, "Only 7 Seconds To Make A First Impression", *Business Insider*, (April 8 2013).

[51] Daniel Kahneman, *Thinking, Fast and Slow* (New York, NY: Farrar, Straus and Giroux, 2011).

[52] Modern science shows a robust body of research into the roles of cognition, emotion and intuition in decision making. G. Soosalu, "Head, Heart and Gut in Decision Making: Development of a Multiple Brain Preference Questionnaire", March 18 2019 journals.sagepub.com

[53] Dr Masaru Emoto, Japanese scientist; his books include *Messages From Water, Vol 1* (Japan: Hado Kyoiku Sha Co, 2003), *The Hidden Messages in Water* (New York City, NY: Atria Books, 2005) and *The Miracle of Water* (New York City, NY: Atria Books, 2007).

[54] David R. Hamilton Ph.D.; his books include *The Little Book of Kindness: Connect with others, be happier* (London, UK: Gaia Books, 2019); *The Five Side Effects of Kindness: This Book Will Make You Feel Better, Be Happier & Live Longer* (UK: Hay House, 2017); *Why Kindness is Good For You* (London, UK: Hay House, 2010).

[55] David Abram, *Becoming Animal: An Earthly Cosmology* (New York, NY: Vintage Books/Random House, 2010).

[56] I learnt this in a London Gurdjieff Spiritual Group with James Moore. Since then I've learnt variations in other spiritual contexts.

[57] I first learnt this as a client and student of the Grinberg Method of Bodywork in Tel Aviv, Israel.

[58] Hilary Hart gave her permission to use this quote. Her books include *The Unknown She: Eight Faces of an Emerging Consciousness* (Inverness, CA: Golden Sufi Center Publishing, 2003) and *Body of Wisdom: Women's Spiritual Power and How it Serves* (Winchester, UK: O-Books, 2012).

[59] William Butler Yeats. It is not certain where this quote comes from, a poem, letter or essay.

[60] Lee Lozowick, *The Alchemy of Love and Sex* (Prescott, AZ: Hohm Press, 1996).

[61] Ali Sundermeir, "99.9999999 of your body is empty space", *Business Insider* (September 23 2016).

[62] Viscount Ilya Prigogine, Chemistry Nobel Laureate, described as the "poet of thermodynamics". His books include *Order Out of Chaos, The End of Certainty* and *Being and Becoming.*

[63] New Testament, John 10:10.

[64] The meaning of my name appears similar in different languages. Energy rippled through me when at the Osho Ashram in Pune I received my Sanyas name, Ma Deeva Veechi, also meaning Divine Wave. Julia in Latin is feminine, another way to say the same thing. We are all who we are.

[65] Margery Williams Bianco, *The Velveteen Rabbit, or, How Toys Become Real,* (New York City, NY; HarperCollins, 2004).

[66] Tiokasin Ghosthorse, a Cheyenne River Sioux Tribal member, musician, radio host and international speaker on peace, indigenous beliefs and Mother Earth. He said this at an event at St Ethelburga's Centre for Reconciliation and Peace, London, UK.

[67] New Testament, Psalm 139.

[68] Al-Ansari, quoted by Llewellyn Vaughan-Lee, *Travelling the Path of Love: Sayings of Sufi Masters* (Inverness, CA: The Golden Sufi Center, 1995).

[69] Rumi, translated by Andrew Harvey, quoted by Llewellyn Vaughan-Lee, *Prayer of the Heart in Christian and Sufi Mysticism* (Inverness, CA: The Golden Sufi Center, 2012).

[70] Inspired by Llewellyn Vaughan-Lee and Hilary Hart, *Spiritual Ecology: The Cry of the Earth* (The Golden Sufi Center, 2013).

[71] Translated by Robert Bly, *The Kabir Book: Forty-Four of the Ecstatic Poems of Kabir* (Boston, MA: Beacon Press, 1993).

[72] Brené Brown, *Daring Greatly: How the Courage to be Vulnerable Transforms the Way We Live, Parent, and Lead* (London, UK: Penguin, 2015).

[73] Virginia Satir, pioneering American psychotherapist, was known for saying this.

[74] Martin Buber, *I and Thou* (London, UK: Bloomsbury, 2013) quoting Rabbi Akiva from the Babylonian Talmud, 17a.

[75] Fritjof Capra, *The Tao of Physics: An Exploration of the Parallels Between Modern Physics and Eastern Mysticism* (Boulder, CA: Shambhala Publications, 2010) and Danah Zohar, *The Quantum Self: Human Nature and Consciousness Defined by the New Physics* (London, UK: Bloomsbury Publishing, 1990).

[76] Sara Reardon, "Son's DNA found inside mother's brain", *New Scientist* (September 27 2012); Laura Sanders, "Children's cells live on in mothers", *Science News* (May 10 2015) and Viviane Callier, "Baby's Cells Can Manipulate Mom's Body for Decades", *Smithsonian* (September 2 2015).

[77] Psychometry was first described by Joseph Rodes Buchanan, *Manual of Psychometry: the Dawn of a New Civilisation* (1885).

[78] Geologist William Denton, *The Soul of Things*, first published 1871 by William Denton; published 2018 by CreateSpace Independent Publishing, print on demand imprint of support.creativemedia.io.

[79] The term "meme" was first used in Richard Dawkins' *The Selfish Gene* (Oxford University Press, 1976).

[80] See note 84 about Rupert Sheldrake.

[81] Fractal mathematics was pioneered in the 1980s by Benoit Mandelbrot; he ran computer simulations of the patterns in nature.

[82] The earliest reference to Indra's Net is found in *Atharva Veda*, a Hindu text developed by the Mahayana School in the third century and later by the Huayan school between the sixth and eighth centuries.

[83] New Testament, Corinthians 1.

[84] Rupert Sheldrake Ph.D.'s books include *Morphic Resonance: The Nature of Formative Causation* (Rochester, VT: Park Street Press, 2009) and *The Presence of the Past: Morphic Resonance and the Memory of Nature* (Rochester, VT: Park Street Press, 2012).

[85] John Bowlby, British psychologist, psychiatrist and psychoanalyst, founder of attachment theory. His books include *A Secure Base* (New York, NY: Basic Books, 1988); *The Making and Breaking of Affectional Bonds* (Abingdon, UK: Routledge, 1979) and *Attachment and Loss: Separation: anxiety and anger* (New York, NY: Basic Books, 1972).

[86] Carl Jung, Swiss psychologist and psychiatrist, founder of analytical psychology. In his theory of the collective unconscious, animus is the unconscious masculine side of a woman, and anima is the unconscious feminine side of a man. His books include *Memories, Dreams, Reflections; Modern Man in Search of a Soul, The Undiscovered Self* and *On the Nature of the Psyche.*

[87] Bert Hellinger, German therapist, synthesised family systems work in the 1980s, from the practices of indigenous Zulus and Native Americans, Jacob Moreno's psychodrama, Virginia Satir's family sculpture and Boszromeni-Nagy's intergenerational work. Moreno's psychodrama is guided drama to examine problems. Satir's family sculpture is a way of seeing the whole system, with rules that help or hinder to improve communication – people in a group physically "sculpt" each other to represent now and future.

[88] Aristotle, Classical Greek philosopher and polymath, a fair reading of his comments in Topics VI.13.

[89] Inspired by a fragment of unattributed poetry glimpsed on the internet.

[90] Anais Nin, *The Diary of Anais Nin* (San Diego, CA: Harcourt Brace, 1969).

[91] Gary Chapman, *The Five Love Languages: The Secret of Love That Lasts* (Chicago, IL: Northfield Publishing, 2015).

[92] Virginia Satir, pioneering American psychotherapist, developed the daily temperature reading in the 1970s. It is described in *The Satir Model* (Palo Alto, CA: Science and Behavior Books, 1991), 309.

[93] This is a way of being I know naturally. It was a great pleasure to find this in my contact with teachers of the Diamond Approach. This practice was later taught as dialectic inquiry. It is centuries old; Rumi, the great thirteenth-century Persian poet, and his teacher and lover Shamz spent hours looking into each other's eyes noticing what arose in them as individuals, both together in relationship.

[94] Inspired by the practice of mutual awakening by Patricia Albere.

[95] Esther Perel, *Mating in Captivity: Unlocking Erotic Intelligence* (New York, NY: HarperCollins, 2017).

[96] Christiane Northrup, M.D., *Women's Bodies, Women's Wisdom: Creating Physical and Emotional Health and Healing* (New York, NY: Bantam Books, 2010) p.231. Chapter 8: "Reclaiming the Erotic", We Are Sexual Beings.

[97] John Keats, "Ode on a Grecian Urn", first published in *Annals of the Fine Arts for 1819*.

[98] Roger Housden, *Soul and Sensuality: Returning the Erotic to Everyday Life* (London, UK: Rider, 1993) p.17.

[99] Howard E. Gardner, *Multiple Intelligences: New Horizons in Theory and Practice* (New York, NY: Basic Books, 2006).

[100] This ancient ritual practice enacts the sacred marriage between a goddess and a god, based on the agriculture fertility stories of Demeter

and Iasion, or Inanna and Dumuzi. In this way, the valuable potency of the mother goddess is shared.

[101] William J. Cromie, January 31 2002. "Pleasure, pain activate same part of brain." https://news.harvard.edu/gazette/story/2002/01/pleasure-pain-activate-same-part-of-brain

[102] Lee Lozowick, American tantra teacher, author and singer, founder of Western Baul communities in America and Europe, student of Yogi Ramsuratkumar, influenced by Chögyam Trungpa and Gurdjieff. Lee Lozowick, *The Alchemy of Love and Sex* (Prescott, AZ, Hohm Press, 1996) p.155.

[103] Inspired by Dr Emily Nagoski, *Come As You Are* (London, UK: Simon & Schuster, 2015).

[104] Jean Liedloff, *The Continuum Concept: In Search of Happiness Lost*, (London, UK: Penguin, 1989).

[105] Hsi Lai, *The Sexual Teachings of the White Tigress: Secrets of the Female Taoist Masters* (Destiny Books, 2001), Opening Page. Quoting the *White Tigress Manual*.

[106] Marianne Williamson, *A Return To Love: Reflections on the Principles of A Course in Miracles* (New York, NY: HarperCollins, 1992) p.190. Chapter 7, Section 3.

[107] Scilla Ellworthy, *Power and Sex* (Rockport, MA: Element, 1997), 6.

[108] Thomas Hobbes, English political philosopher, wrote the influential book *Leviathan* in 1651.

[109] G.I. Gurdjieff, nineteenth-century Russian philosopher, spiritual teacher and author, founder of the Fourth Way school. My Gurdjieff group teachers spoke about "false consideration" and it is written about by Gurdjieff's student, P.D. Ouspensky: *In Search of the Miraculous: Fragments of an Unknown Teaching* (Abingdon, UK: Routledge, 1950).

[110] Psychiatrist, Holocaust survivor, founder of logotherapy humanistic psychotherapy, healing through meaning. Viktor E. Frankl, *Man's Search for Meaning* (London, UK: Penguin, 2004).

[111] David Hamilton Ph.D., *Why Kindness is Good For You* (Hay House, 2010); *The Five Side Effects of Kindness* (London, UK: Hay House, 2017).

[112] Amy Cuddy, *Presence: Bringing Your Boldest Self to Your Biggest Challenges* (London, UK: Orion, 2016). TED Talk, "Your body language may shape who you are", October 1 2012, http://www.ted.com/speakers/amy_cuddy; "Power Posing: Brief Nonverbal Displays Affect Neuroendocrine Levels and Risk Tolerance", Dana R. Carney, Amy J. C. Cuddy, Andy J. Yap, 2010, https://journals.sagepub.com/doi/full/10.1177/0956797610383437

[113] Zero-point fields of consciousness have been written about by German scientist Karl Popp, Hungarian philosopher of science Ervin László, British scientist Rupert Sheldrake and later American spiritual change agent Lynne McTaggart, in *The Field*. One could argue that all essential states and centres are zero-point fields.

[114] Carl G Jung, *Letters Vol 1 1906–50* (Abingdon: Routledge, 1973). Letter to Miss Fanny Bowditch.

[115] Joanna Macy, "A Wild Love for the World", interview by Krista Tippet, *On Being*, September 16 2010. https://onbeing.org/programs/joanna-macy-a-wild-love-for-the-world/#transcript

[116] Lee Lozowick, *The Alchemy of Love and Sex* (Prescott, AZ: Hohm Press, 1996).

[117] Albert Einstein, attributed by BBC; there is some confusion but this quote is considered to be a fair summary of his ideas.

[118] Aleut elder Larry Merculieff has spoken about this: https://www.sacredfire.foundation/elder/larry-merculieff

[119] Inspired by Roger Housden, *Soul and Sensuality: Returning the Erotic to Everyday Life* (London, UK: Rider and Co, 1993).

[120] Daniel Quinn, *Ishmael* (London, UK: Bantam Press, 1995) and *The Story of B*, (London, UK: Bantam Press, 1997). See also his article (an excerpt from The Story of B) "Have you heard of the Great Forgetting?" https://www.filmsforaction.org/articles/the-great-forgetting

[121] Rev. 22:13.

[122] Referenced by Swiss spiritual author Daniel Odier: *Desire: The Tantric Path to Awakening* (Rochester, VT: Inner Traditions, 2001) p.23. Chapter 5: We are what we seek.

[123] Sufi poet Mawlana Jalal-al-Din Rumi, probably translated by Coleman Barks.

[124] British poet T.S. Eliot, *Four Quartets* (London, UK: Faber, 1941) East Coker, last line.

[125] https://www.womansday.com/health-fitness/nutrition/g2503/foods-that-look-like-body-parts-theyre-good-for

[126] From the work of Richard Cassaro, author and filmmaker: https://www.richardcassaro.com

[127] Karen Johnson, *The Jeweled Path: The Biography of The Diamond Approach to Inner Realization* (Boulder, CO: Shambhala, 2018) p.300. Chapter 29, Through the Jeweled Portal.

[128] Christopher Bergland, "The Athlete's Way" in *Psychology Today*, May 2019.

[129] Edith Zimmerman, "I Now Suspect the Vagus Nerve is the Key to Well-being" in *The Cut*, May 2019.

[130] Christopher Bergland, *The Athlete's Way: Sweat and the Biology of Bliss* (Manhattan, New York City, NY: St Martin's Press, 2007).

[131] The website for the American Indian Council: www.manataka.org

[132] Brendan D. Murphy, *The Grand Illusion, A Synthesis of Science and Spirituality* (Indiana, CA: Balboa Press, 2012).

[133] Brendan D. Murphy, "Junk DNA: Your Hyperdimensional Doorway to Transformation (Part 1) Global Freedom Movement": https://globalfreedommovement.org/junk-dna-your-hyperdimensional-doorway-to-transformation-part-1

[134] Bruce H. Lipton, Ph.D., *Biology of Belief* (Carlsbad, CA: Hay House, 2011) says that all the cells in the body are affected by our thoughts and consciousness. Also, author David R. Hamilton's article, "Harvard Study finds that Meditation Impacts DNA", https://drdavidhamilton.com/harvard-study-finds-that-meditation-impacts-dna, discusses a Harvard University study published in 2008 that found compelling evidence from studying blood samples that the relaxation response – the physiological response to meditation, yoga, tai chi, qi gong or repetitive prayer – affects our genes (April 2011), in which he cites Jeffery A. Dusek, Hasan H. Otu, Ann L. Wohlhueter, Manoj Bhasin, Luiz F. Zerbini, Marie G. Joseph, Herbert Benson, Towia A. Libermann, "Genomic Counter-Stress Changes Induced by the Relaxation Response, Plos One" (July 2008) https://journals.plos.org/plosone/article?id=10.1371/journal.pone.0002576. See also Keys of Enoch at https://keysofenoch.org/dna-and-the-divine-names

[135] Joseph Campbell, "Message of Myth", interview by Bill Moyers, on the 1988 TV series *The Power of Myth*. https://billmoyers.com/content/ep-2-joseph-campbell-and-the-power-of-myth-the-message-of-the-myth

[136] Daniel Odier, *Desire: The Tantric Path to Awakening* (Rochester, VT: Inner Traditions, 2001) p.10.

[137] David Hamilton, Ph.D., *The Five Side Effects of Kindness: This Book Will Make You Feel Better, Be Happier & Love Longer* (London, UK: Hay House, 2017).

138 Karen Armstrong, "To Go Beyond Thought", An interview with Karen Armstrong, Parabola Magazine, Vol 31: No 3, Fall 2006: "*Thinking*", https://parabolaorg-4jzhg7c.stackpathdns.com/wp-content/uploads/2019/01/Parabola-Index-1976-2019.pdf

139 Nina Ruth Davis Salaman, *Songs of Many Days* (London: Elkin Mathews, 1923) Lost Songs.

140 Joanna Macy, *World As Lover, World As Self* (Berkeley, CA: Parallax Press, 2007).

141 Rainer Maria Rilke, *Letters to a Young Poet* (London: Penguin Classics, 2014).

142 Karen Johnson, *The Jeweled Path: Biography of the Diamond Approach to Inner Realization* (Boulder, CO: Shambhala, 2018).

143 Professor Jem Bendell, "Deep Adaptation: A Map for Navigating Climate Change", Institute of Leadership and Sustainability, IFLAS Occasional Paper 2, July 27 2018 (2nd ed. July 2020), www.iflas.info, https://www.lifeworth.com/deepadaptation.pdf

144 Jn Hollow Horn, spoken word, 1932, attributed by James Wilson, *The Earth Shall Weep: A History of Native America* (New York City, NY: Grove Press, 2000).

145 The Talmud, Micha, 6:8.

146 The Talmud, Ethics of the Fathers, B16 Rabbi Tarfon.

Further Reading

As a child, books were my saving grace, a silent secret route to that which made sense. Over the years I read a lot, initially finding that which was resonant in lyrical literature and later finding it in mind-body-spirit books.

These books listed below are some of those in my personal library, kind of like old friends that I love.

You might also find them useful guides, taking you deeper into some of the subjects discussed here. In my experience, people often begin their personal journey by reading a number of inspiring, motivating and educational books, and then they move on to exploring and embodying the ideas more fully. Enjoy!

Abram, David. *The Spell of the Sensuous: Perception and Language in a More-Than-Human World.* New York, NY: Vintage, 1997.

Abram, David. *Becoming Animal: An Earthly Cosmology.* New York, NY: Penguin Random House USA, 2011.

Almaas, A.H., and Johnson, Karen. *The Power of Divine Eros: The Illuminating Force of Love in Everyday Life.* Boulder, CO: Shambhala, 2013.

Anand, Margot. *The Art of Sexual Ecstasy: The Path of Sacred Sexuality for Western Lovers.* New York, NY: Tarcher, 1991.

Barks, Coleman. *Soul of Rumi: A New Collection of Ecstatic Poems.* New York: HarperOne, 2002.

Blake, William. *The Complete Illuminated Books.* London, UK: Thames & Hudson, 2000.

Boehm, Michaela. *The Wild Woman's Way: Unlock Your Full Potential for Pleasure, Power and Fulfillment.* Miami, FL: Atria, 2018.

Bowlby, John. *The Making and Breaking of Affectional Bonds*. Abingdon, UK: Routledge, 2005.

Capra, Fritjof. *The Web of Life: A New Scientific Understanding of Living Systems*. London, UK: Flamingo, 1997.

Capra, Fritjof. *The Tao of Physics: An Exploration of the Parallels Between Modern Physics and Eastern Mysticism*. Boulder, CO: Shambala, 2010.

Capra, Fritjof. *The Turning Point: Science, Society and the Rising Culture*. London, UK: Harper, 2011.

Damasio, Antonio. *The Feeling of What Happens: Body, Emotion and the Making of Consciousness*. New York, NY: Harcourt Brace, 1999.

Davies, Paul. *The Mind of God: Science and the Search for Ultimate Meaning*. London, UK: Penguin, 1993.

Eliot, T.S. *Four Quartets*. London, UK: Faber & Faber, 2001.

Ellworthy, Scilla. *Power and Sex*. London, UK: Vega Books, 2002.

Emoto, Dr Masaru. *Messages From Water*. New York, NY: Pocket Books, 2005.

Ezrahi, O.P. *Kedesha*. Scotts Valley, CA: CreateSpace Independent Publishing Platform, 2018.

Gendlin, Eugene T. *Focusing*. London, UK: Rider, 2003.

Gibran, Khalil. *The Prophet*. Charlotte, NP: Information Age Publishing, 2020.

Goleman, Daniel. *Emotional Intelligence: Why It Can Matter More Than IQ*. London, UK: Bantam, 2012.

Hafiz; Ladinsky, Daniel. *The Gift – Poems by Hafiz the Great Sufi Master*. London, UK: Penguin, 1999.

Hart, Hilary. *Body of Wisdom: Women's Spiritual Power and How it Serves.* Winchester, UK: O-Books, 2013.

Hellinger, Bert; Weber, Gunthard; and Beaumont, Hunter. *Love's Hidden Symmetry: What Makes Love Work in Relationships.* Phoenix, AZ: Zeig, Tucker and Theisen, 1998.

Hellinger, Bert. *Acknowledging What Is: Conversations with Bert Hellinger.* Phoenix, AZ: Zeig, Tucker & Theisen, 1999.

Housden, Roger. *Soul and Sensuality: Returning the Erotic to Everyday Life.* London, UK: Rider, 1993.

Johnson, Karen. *The Jeweled Path: The Biography of the Diamond Approach to Inner Realization.* Boulder, CO: Shambhala, 2018.

Juhan, Deane. *Job's Body: A Handbook for Bodywork.* Barrytown, NY: Station Hill, 2003.

Keleman, Stanley. *Your Body Speaks Its Mind.* Berkeley, CA: Center Press, 1981.

Keleman, Stanley. *Emotional Anatomy: The Structure of Experience.* Berkeley, CA: Center Press, 1989.

Kinstler, Clysta. *Mary Magdalene, Beloved Disciple.* London, UK: Cygnus Books, 2005.

Lai, Hsi. *The Sexual Teachings of the White Tigress: Secrets of the Female Taoist Master.* Rochester, VT: Destiny Books, 2001.

Lawrence, D.H. *Lady Chatterley's Lover.* London: Penguin, 2006.

Levine, Peter A. *Waking The Tiger: Healing Trauma.* Berkeley, CA: North Atlantic Books, 1997.

Levine, Peter A. *In an Unspoken Voice: How the Body Releases Trauma and Restores Goodness.* Berkeley, CA: North Atlantic Books, 2010.

Liedloff, Jean. *The Continuum Concept: In Search of Happiness Lost.* London, UK: Penguin, 1989.

Lozowick, Lee. *The Alchemy of Love and Sex.* Prescott, AZ: Hohm Press, 1996.

Lozowick, Lee. *In The Fire.* Prescott, AZ: Hohm Press, 1978.

Macy, Joanna. *World As Lover, World As Self. Courage for Global Justice and Ecological Renewal.* Berkeley, CA: Parallax Press, 2007.

Miller, Alice. *The Drama of Being a Child: The Search for the True Self.* New York, NY: Basic Books, 2008.

Nagoski, Emily. *Come As You Are: The Surprising New Science that Will Transform Your Sex Life.* London, UK: Simon & Schuster, 2015.

Nuland, Sherwin B. *How We Live: The Wisdom of The Body.* New York, NY: Vintage, 1998.

Odent, Michel. *The Scientification of Love.* London, UK: Free Association Books, 2014.

Odier, Daniel. *Desire: The Tantric Path to Awakening.* Rochester, VT: Inner Traditions, 2001.

Ouspensky, P.D. *In Search of The Miraculous: Fragments of an Unknown Teaching.* New York, NY: Mariner Books, 2001.

Pert, Candace B., Ph.D. *Molecules of Emotion: Why You Feel The Way You Feel.* New York, NY: Scribner, 2010.

Phillips, Adam, *Monogamy.* New York, NY: Vintage, 1999.

Phillips, Adam. *Going Sane.* New York, NY: HarperPerennial, 2007.

Qualls-Corbett, Nancy. *The Sacred Prostitute: Eternal Aspect of the Feminine.* Toronto, ON: Inner City Books, 1988.

Quinn, Daniel. *Ishmael: A Novel.* New York, NY: Bantam, 1995.

Quinn, Daniel. *The Story of B: An Adventure of the Mind and Spirit.* New York, NY: Bantam, 1997.

Roche, Lorin Ph.D. *The Radiance Sutras: 112 Gateways to the Yoga of Wonder & Delight.* Louisville, CO: Sounds True, 2014.

Rosenberg, Marshall B. *Nonviolent Communication: A Language of Life.* Encinitas, CA: PuddleDancer Press, 2015.

Roth, Gabrielle. *Sweat Your Prayers: Movement as Spiritual Practice.* Dublin, IE: Gill, 1999.

Roth, Gabrielle. *Maps to Ecstasy: A Healing Journey for the Untamed Spirit.* London, UK: Thorsons, 1999.

Rothschild, Babette. *The Body Remembers: The Psychophysiology of Trauma and Trauma Treatment.* New York, NY: W.W. Norton & Co, 2000.

Somé, Sobonfu. *Welcoming Spirit Home: Ancient African Teachings to Welcome Children and Community.* San Francisco, CA: New World Library, 1999.

Somé, Sobonfu. *The Spirit of Intimacy: Ancient African Teachings in the Ways of Relationships.* New York, NY: William Morrow, 2000.

Vaughan-Lee, Llewellyn. *Alchemy of Light: Working with the Primal Energies of Life.* Point Reyes, CA: The Golden Sufi Centre, 2019.

Vaughan-Lee, Llewellyn. *The Return of the Feminine and the World Soul.* Point Reyes, CA: The Golden Sufi Centre, 2017.

Vaughan-Lee, Llewellyn (ed.) *Spiritual Ecology: The Cry of the Earth.* Point Reyes, CA: The Golden Sufi Centre, 2016.

Watts, Alan. *The Wisdom of Insecurity: A Message for an Age of Anxiety.* New York, NY: Vintage, 2011.

White, Andy. *Going Mad to Stay Sane: The Psychology of Self-Destructive Behaviour*. London, UK: Duckworth, 2007.

Williamson, Marianne. *A Return to Love: Reflections on the Principles of a Course in Miracles*. New York, NY: Harper, 2015.

Wilmot, John. Earl of Rochester. *The Debt to Pleasure*. Abingdon, UK: Routledge, 2002.

Zeldin, Theodore. *An Intimate History of Humanity*. New York, NY: Vintage, 1998.

Zohar, Danah. *The Quantum Self: Human Nature and Consciousness Defined by the New Physics*. London: Flamingo, 1991.

Zohar, Danah and Marshall, Ian. *The Quantum Society: Mind Physics and a New Social Vision*. London, UK: Flamingo, 1995.

Index

Acknowledgments

With Thanks to My Family

My parents Susan and Martin Hollenbery for their good values, love and wisdom, their practical support that enabled me to make this healing journey, and to them and my uncle Michael Banes, whose support gave me space to write. As a little girl, I always "knew" I would write a book . . . I was amazed that without my telling him, my brother Neal "knew" this too, telling me he would be interviewed on the radio about the book I would one day write. My sister Adele who helped me through the difficult times. My sister Claire for her love. Gratitude, thank you all.

My daughter Ruby for her unique spirit and her loving patience while I was writing.

With thanks to all those who sometime upset or frustrated me, my feelings were motive fuel to complete the circle.

With Thanks to All My Teachers

So very many healing journeys within the one, I cannot remember everyone's names, but I remember and appreciate your love, witness and kindness, as I walked through the long dark night of the soul. A deep bow to George, homeopath, Robert Lever, osteopath and my kind counsellor at university; Sefi Sarid, the first person I felt "saw" me, who said I had absolutely no idea what would come out of me in the future, who with Rachel Putter and other practitioners taught the Grinberg Method of Bodywork; Osho and all the teachers at the Puna Ashram in India: although I knew it was not my spiritual home, I was grateful for the doors it opened for me; psychotherapists Poppy Niv Sharon, Jochen Encke and Maggie McKenzie; James Moore, who called me the find of the century, John Hunter and all my Gurdjieff Group teachers in the lineage of Madame Lannes, pupil of G.I. Gurdjieff; Ma Ananda Sarita and Swami Anand Geho, and also Shakti Malan who taught tantra, Batty Gold and Rose Fink who taught Quodoshka Sacred Sexuality, Michaela Boehm and Steve James who taught Kashmiri tantra; Shaman Judith Seelig and her teachings; Gabrielle Roth, founder of, and Yaacov Darling Khan and Sue Rickards who taught 5Rhythms Dance; Shaman Chris Luttichau; Franklyn Sills,

Clare Dolby and Karuna Institute team who taught biodynamic cranio-osacral therapy, Hugh Milne who taught Visionary Craniosacral Work; Bert Hellinger, founder, Judith Hemming, Richard Wallstein, Jutta Ten Herkel and others who taught a systemic approach; Ed Rowland for systemic coaching; acupuncturists including Dr Yan Li; Philippa Lubbock for Life Alignment; Sacha Kriese and Baba Ram Dass for the Tantric Ayurvedic tradition; Naqshbandiyya-Mujaddidyya Sufi Sheik, Llewellyn Vaughan-Lee with whom I sat many times; Tantric guru Lee Lozowick for his energy; spiritual teachers Amma and Mother Meera; Mirabai Devi, a new paradigm spiritual teacher; Hameed Ali and Karen Johnson, co-founders, Tejo Jourdan, Joyce Lyke, Candace Harris and all my Diamond Approach teachers; John Oakley for Gnostic Kabbalah; Candice Marro and Sylvie Leboulanger for osteopathic conversations; Teresa Evans for pranic healing; Virginia Dutton for naturopathy. Gratitude for all your supports, enabling me to turn my inside sense of who I am, over decades, into reality. Thank You.

With Thanks to My Friends

Ingrid Velleine who supported me writing the first emotional part of this book twenty-five years ago, I "knew" the second part would be written when I was healed and "evolved". Nigel Anthony for his recognition, belief and support for the work he knew I had to do. Justine Huxley, Sarah Rozenthuler, Charlotte Koelliker and Kathryn Ariel, spiritual adventurers themselves, who helped me birth this book. For all the conversations that helped this book to fruition, including with Jackie Crovetto, Irida Hysenbelli, Sandra Distelli, Nikki Slade, and Jonathan Shine. And Grae Sutherland who has become a partner in living many kinds of deliciousness with me.

With Thanks to the Writing Professionals

Alison Jones who helped me to find structure and shape for my raw passionate poetry; Sue Belfrage who edited; and Sabine Weeke, Findhorn Press editorial director; we had an immediate fun spark. Nick Williams who understood and wrote the book foreword.

It has felt as if together with me, in a glorious five-dimensional process, this book has been co-created by Life itself.

About Julia

Photo by Richard Munn

I've been a professional bodyworker, therapist, and healer for more than twenty-five years, holding space for people in individual sessions and group workshops. I'm a practitioner of the Grinberg Method of Bodywork, biodynamic craniosacral therapy, systemic constellations, and Kashmiri tantra.

But my healing work began long before that. . . . Even as a small child I loved to "help" my mother, a physiotherapist working from home. With her clients' permission, I was given an arm or leg to hold while the client lay clothed on the table. My mum thought I was playing, but even back then, I "knew" what I was doing and was focused and serious.

Now, I enjoy the depth of life in a delicious relationship, love dancing wildly, and celebrate being near oceans and forests. I am delighted to share with you the sensually rich way of life that I love. I hope you will find the guidance in *The Healing Power of Pleasure* to be inspiring, practical, and useful, as have the numerous clients I have worked with. May you feel yourself to be Life loving Life!

For courses, sessions, resources, and more information
about my work visit my website
www.universeofdeliciousness.com

*"Her complex simplicity
breeds a kind of radiance,
that only the truly living can appreciate.*

*She is alive with the sense
of not wanting to waste
one precious moment,
and moments with her are precious.*

There will be a room full of strangers I know (to say hello to)

And there will be Julia . . ."

1990 Clair Barlow

Also of Interest

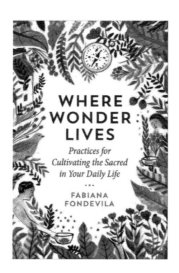

WHERE WONDER LIVES
Practices for Cultivating the Sacred in Your Daily Life
by Fabiana Fondevila

Where Wonder Lives invites you on a journey through your own inner landscape to reawaken the mystery of life. Readers are led through a rich set of contemporary and time-honored practices–from mindfulness and dreamwork to working with plants–that help rebuild a life of vitality, connection, and enchantment.

ISBN 978-1-64411-174-1

Also of Interest

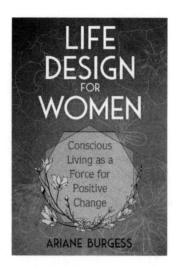

LIFE DESIGN FOR WOMEN

Conscious Living as a Force for Positive Change

by Ariane Burgess

This hands-on guide engages you in a simple visioning process to help you consciously redesign your life to be more satisfying, meaningful, and aligned with your goals. Drawing on the regenerative principles of sustainability, *Life Design for Women* provides exercises and tools to find your authentic self and bring positive change to the world around you.

ISBN 978-1-62055-915-4

Also of Interest

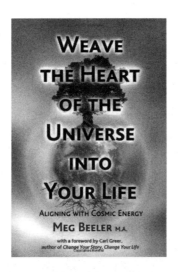

WEAVE THE HEART OF THE UNIVERSE INTO YOUR LIFE

Aligning with Cosmic Energy

by Meg Beeler

Medicine for spirit and soul, this transformational guide offers simple, effective, potent ways to connect with the energy, mystery, and power of nature and the universe. Imbued with indigenous wisdom and shamanic insight, *Weave the Heart of the Universe into Your Life* offers 84 experiential practices to change your story, let go of the old and reconnect with the web of life.

ISBN 978-1-84409-739-5

FINDHORN PRESS

Life-Changing Books

Learn more about us and our books at
www.findhornpress.com

For information on the Findhorn Foundation:
www.findhorn.org